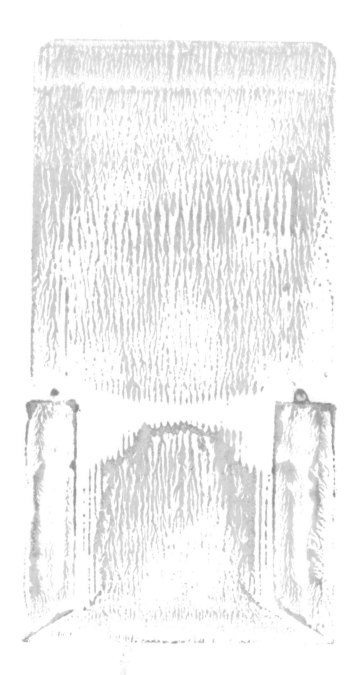

Cambridge Studies in Social Anthropology

NO. 4

THE ROPE OF MOKA

Cambridge Studies in Social Anthropology

General Editors

M. FORTES, J. R. GOODY, E. R. LEACH

THE ROPE OF MOKA

*Big-men and
Ceremonial Exchange in
Mount Hagen
New Guinea*

ANDREW STRATHERN

*Research Fellow
Australian National University*

CAMBRIDGE
AT THE UNIVERSITY PRESS
1971

Published by the Syndics of the Cambridge University Press
Bentley House, 200 Euston Road, London N.W.1
American Branch: 32 East 57th Street, New York, N.Y.10022

Library of Congress Catalogue Card Number: 73–130911

ISBN: 0 521 07987 X

Printed in Great Britain
at the Aberdeen University Press

72-6333

To
MY FATHER AND MOTHER

CONTENTS

TABLES

Tables

ILLUSTRATIONS

FIGURES

MAPS

Plates

xi

PREFACE

Accounts by New Guinea Highlanders of their reactions to the first arrival of Europeans show both their initial shock at meeting complete strangers and the means whereby the shock was overcome: the exchange of valued goods. It was fortunate indeed that explorers in the Central Highlands carried, besides steel tools, shell valuables which were prized as wealth tokens throughout the area. Hageners' feelings about the explorers are typified by the words of an old man, who told me how, when he was a boy, Kiap Taylor (i.e. J. L. Taylor, an Australian Administration Officer) first passed through the territory of a tribe allied to his. When they saw Taylor's white skin, they thought he must be one of the pale-skinned cannibals who figure in Hagen folktales, but 'then he gave us shell valuables in return for pigs, and we decided he was human'.

Shells in the Highlands are valued as prestige symbols, an integral part of elaborate, competitive ceremonial exchange systems which are manipulated largely by 'big-men'. Europeans in the 1930s and 1940s brought these shells into Hagen in great numbers, until eventually their value was deflated, but the Hagen exchange system has survived: in 1969 one young man told me that soon he and his people might discard shells as a currency, but they would continue to exchange pigs, which have retained high economic value and ceremonial significance.

In this book I have attempted to analyse the Hagen ceremonial exchange system – the *moka* – both as an institution linking groups together in alliances and as a means whereby men try to maximise their social status. Both a 'substantive' account of group structure and processes of payment and a 'formal' account of economising in inter-individual and inter-group competition are required for an understanding of the *moka*, although I have not managed to carry the formal account beyond the point of displaying empirical processes of competition. In the early chapters of the book, I set out background material; in the later ones I take up the analysis of actual prestations and of big-men's activities in them.

The book is based mainly on two periods of fieldwork, from January 1964 to February 1965 and between August and November 1965. I spent most time at Buk, some 30 miles by road out from Mount Hagen township, within the Melpa-speaking area. At first I relied on Melanesian Pidgin as a medium of communication. Some of the younger Hageners speak this, and I found interpreters among them. After nine months I became

Preface

reasonably fluent in Melpa and used it in most conversations, although I still needed an interpreter to obtain translations of rapid or stylised speech and of unfamiliar words.

During these first two periods in the field I was supported by grants from the Emslie Horniman Anthropological Scholarship Fund and from the Smuts Memorial Fund in the University of Cambridge, as well as by a William Wyse Studentship from Trinity College, Cambridge, and a supplementary grant from the Mount Everest Fund. Trinity College also supported me, as a Research Fellow, on a shorter trip to Mount Hagen in 1968; and in 1969 I have made another short trip of 2½ months, supported by a Research Fellowship from the Research School of Pacific Studies in the Australian National University. To all of these institutions I am more than grateful for enabling me not only to undertake the initial fieldwork but to make return trips subsequently. For pre-field and post-field advice and discussions I should like to thank Professors Meyer Fortes, Paula Brown (my Ph.D. supervisor), Ralph Bulmer, John Barnes, and Mervyn Meggitt; Dr Jack Goody, who has given me constant help and encouragement since I was an undergraduate; Professors A. L. Epstein and Ann Chowning, Dr Marie Reay and Mr Nigel Oram in Canberra and New Guinea; Dr Nancy Bowers of Duke University; and Father E. Brandewie, who was working among the Western Melpa Kumndi in 1964 and 1968. For botanical identifications I am indebted to Mrs Jocelyn Powell of the Biogeography Department at Canberra. To my research student age-mates in Cambridge I am grateful for numerous discussions of anthropological problems and field experiences.

Most of my periods in the field have been shared with my wife, Marilyn, while she has been following her own research work; and she also read patiently through and commented on drafts of my dissertation, of which this book is a revised version. I cannot thank her enough.

For help with typing the manuscript of the book for publication I am grateful to Mrs Pamela Fox and Mrs Dorothy Aunela of the Department of Anthropology at Canberra.

Turning to New Guinea itself, I wish to thank many Administration Officers for their assistance: Mr T. Ellis, Mr S. M. Foley, Mr R. Hearne, and Mr M. Belfield; and, most recently, Mr R. Gleeson, Mr R. Allen, and Mr and Mrs M. Morris. Many kindnesses have also been shown us by Mr J. F. Broomhead of Baglaga plantation and by the staff of the Lutheran Mission Stations at Kotna and Ogelbeng.

Finally, my thanks to the people of all the groups with which I have worked, for their friendship and their humour. I think particularly of

Preface

people of the Kawelka and Tipuka tribes and of Minembi Yelipi clan;
and, among these, of my main sponsors in 1964–5, Kawelka Ndamba and
Ongka; of my chief companion and instructor, Ru; of Ndamba's son,
Nykint; of Rokla, Ndoa, and Nøring, friends on whose land I lived among
the Tipuka in 1968 and 1969; and of many other friends and helpers:
Kont, Puklum, Pim, Kum, Køi, and Moka among the Kawelka; Minembi
Yelipi Rongnda; Oke, Yakomb, and Møit among the Elti; and Ambra,
Rumb, and Namb among the Ulka. In Melpa: *enem kumb-køm nanga
kongon təp rapndorong omba tin rup rop øndərəmon e-nga akop na-nt enem
noman ngop angke nimb nint.*

ANDREW STRATHERN

Canberra 1969

BIBLIOGRAPHICAL ADDENDA

Berndt, R. M. (1962). *Excess and restraint: social control among a New Guinea
mountain people*, Chicago: University of Chicago Press.
Bowers, N. (1965). 'Permanent Bachelorhood in the Upper Kaugel Valley of
Highland New Guinea', *Oceania* XXXVI, pp. 27–37.
Bus, G. A. M. (1951). 'The Te festival or gift exchange in Enga (Central high-
lands of New Guinea)', *Anthropos*, 46: 813–24.
Harding, T. G. (1967). *Voyagers of the Vitiaz Strait; a study of a New Guinea
trade system*, The American Ethnological Society of New York, Monograph
No. 44, Seattle: University of Washington Press, x.

ABBREVIATIONS AND ORTHOGRAPHY

Some tribe and clan names which appear frequently are occasionally abbreviated, thus:

T.	Tipuka	Kund.	Kundmbo
M. or Min.	Minembi	Okl.	Oklembo
K. or Kaw.	Kawelka	Kit.	Kitepi
Yel.	Yelipimbo	Elt.	Eltimbo
Me.	Membo	Nggl.	Ngglammbo
Mand.	Mandembo	Kur.	Kurupmbo

Kinship abbreviations are used in some tables as follows:

B	brother	M	mother
D	daughter	S	son
F	father	Z	sister
H	husband		

The special symbols I employ are:

$\imath$ = a high, open, front, unrounded vowel
∂ = a mid, close, central, unrounded vowel (the schwa)
$\emptyset$ = a mid, open, front, rounded vowel
y = a high, close, front, rounded vowel

Examples: $\imath$ as in Eng. 'bit';
∂ as the first vowel in Eng. 'banana';
$\emptyset$ as in German 'hören';
y as in French 'mûr'.

'When we want to make a prestation to our allies, we go to another group and make a gift to them, asking them to return a larger gift to us later. Later, when the time for our main prestation comes closer, we send messages telling them that they are holding the rope of moka. Then they give to us, and we are able to dance and make the payments to our allies.'

1

INTRODUCTION

'Moka is like a card game. Now it comes to us and we win. Later it passes
to someone else; and so it goes round.'

Kont, a big-man of the Kawelka Membo clan

THEORETICAL CONSIDERATIONS

In this book I discuss the *moka* ceremonial exchange system of the Mount
Hagen area in the Western Highlands District of Australian New Guinea.
In particular I relate the exchange system to activities of 'big-men', or
self-made political leaders, who are so prominent throughout the Highlands.
Big-men are important in many of the Highlands societies as manipulators
of wealth and accumulators of prestige. It is not surprising, then, that they
have been eager, since pacification, to take up new channels for obtaining
wealth offered by the Australians' introduction of cash-crops into their
economy (Finney 1969). However, other workers in Hagen have studied
cash-cropping in more detail than I myself have;[1] my work has been
concentrated on the *moka* exchanges, which are the traditional channel for
obtaining the status of big-man (*wuə nyim*) in Hagen.

To understand New Guinea Highlands societies we must focus on
competitive processes. In Hagen it is the moka system which provides an
explicit arena for recurrent bouts of competition between individuals and
groups. As R. F. Salisbury (1968) has put it: 'Analyses of the actual working
of societies widely labelled as "reciprocative" ... have shown that inter-
individual transactions are always unbalanced and involve a continual
struggle to obtain as much advantage over an opponent as possible.'
Salisbury's statement here may be too strongly phrased, but it cogently
draws attention to the phenomenon of latent competition in systems of
ceremonial reciprocity such as the moka.

Any analysis of exchange activities in terms of competition must be able
to state what the competition is for, who is engaged in it, what are the rules
governing it, and how the competition is played out against a variety of

---

[1] Professor W. Rowe of the New Guinea Research Unit, Australian National University,
now at Minnesota University, U.S.A.; Mr W. Straatmans of the Department of Economics,
Research School of Pacific Studies, at A.N.U.; and Dr D. P. Sinha of the Department of
Anthropology, A.N.U., now at the Indian Institute of Management, Calcutta.

constraints. For Hagen one can answer these questions briefly as follows: the competition is for prestige or status-ranking; it is waged both by whole groups and by individual big-men; it is governed by the exchange rates and categories of the moka system; and it is played out against a background of certain limitations in technological, ecological and human resources which set problems for the big-men who are struggling for success.

In addition to clothing this bare scheme of analysis with the material description of moka exchanges in Hagen, I shall take up a pair of specific hypotheses about the control which men exercise in New Guinea societies. The first is the argument of Sahlins (1963) that a limitation of the big-man's position is his segmentary enclavement within a particular group. The big-man relies on the members of this group as his close supporters. Yet his activities constantly involve the distribution of property to the population at large outside his own group, and this is the only means he has of increasing his own status in the society. A major danger for the big-man, therefore, is that he may extract too much from his supporters in favour of the population at large in order to increase his renown. If he does so, his supporters may eventually deny him the help he requires for his transactions and the basis of his position is cut away.

Sahlins's hypothesis applies well enough to at least one case, that of the Siuai of Bougainville (see Oliver 1955), but it does not meet all the conditions of New Guinea Highlands exchange systems. Meggitt (1967: 22) has made the point that the more successful a big-man becomes, the more chance there is that his group of supporters will benefit from the goods which flow back to him in return for those which he gives out. This is certainly a possibility, and to the extent that a big-man has the *same* kind of exchange relations with his supporters as with his external partners it must hold good. The situation is complicated, however, by the further point that a big-man does not necessarily depend on his own group-members as the sole underpinning agents for his exchanges. Far from it: instead he maintains an extensive network of exchange-partnerships outside his own group and uses these to finance many of his transactions. To that extent he can free himself from his 'segmentary enclavement' and can also avoid taxing his group-mates too heavily. By the same token, he need not always channel gifts he receives from outside partners back to the members of his own group, although he is likely to do this to some extent. As we shall see, Hagen big-men act partly in concert with, partly independently of, their clan-mates, and it is this interplay between independent and concerted action which I shall examine.

Introduction

Sahlins's picture of the 'over-extractive' phase of a big-man's career is reminiscent of the second hypothesis which I shall take up. Salisbury (1964: 225) has suggested that in some New Guinea societies before the time of European contact, 'although the indigenous ideology was one of democratic equality and competition, the empirical situation ... was one of serial despotism by powerful leaders.' Salisbury also argues that whereas analysts have in the past concentrated on subordinate leaders, they have failed to study the actions of the really powerful big-men, who control these lesser subordinates and prevent them from reaching 'the top'. As I have mentioned elsewhere (1966), Salisbury's hypothesis raises a number of empirical questions as to how leaders gain control and how they hold sway over subordinates and personal rivals. Putting his hypothesis along with that which Sahlins proposes, one could suggest that perhaps the 'real big-man' is likely to be overthrown when the extent of his extraction – in whatever terms – from his supporters too grossly exceeds the value of the advantages which he can bring them.[1] In such a case, his defeat would most probably result from the revolt of his supporters.

While there is no doubt that the position of big-men in Hagen is not entirely secure, predictions about their rise and fall which rely either on a theory that real big-men can directly control others, or on the assumption that the danger to their security comes from their followers only, are likely to prove inaccurate. Even if one posited that big-men were dependent on their own segmentary group for support, one could argue that the greatest likelihood of danger for them comes from the possibility that their supporters might transfer their allegiance, either by shifting their group affiliation or less drastically by simply shifting the focus of their economic activities to a rival big-man. A further possibility is that where a rival springs up in the big-man's own group, the struggle between the two may become factional and the group may split, thus resolving the conflict by separating the two leaders' support-groups. Where, as in Hagen, it is an explicit rule of the exchange system that big-men can recruit supporters from outside their own formal group-membership, the possibilities for competitive activities between rivals are greatly increased: big-men, both of the same clan and different clans can compete for prestige by operating a number of complex networks of partnerships which are partly separate from and partly conflict with each other. The real strength of the big-men thus rests on their organisation of these financial networks. They do not directly control other big-men, nor do they have a complete command of the services of their lesser group-mates; hence neither Salisbury's nor

[1] Meggitt 1967: 21–2 also quotes the discussion of Hogbin (1958: 158–9) on this point.

Sahlins's analysis can apply directly. Instead, we have to show how big-men – and indeed whole groups of men – manage their networks of ex-change partnerships in the drive for status.

In order to approach this competitive process and to understand the workings of the moka system, it is necessary to know some of the features of group-structure, alliances between groups for warfare, and patterns of revenge-taking and compensation between groups in the recent past. In Chapters 1–4 of the book, then, I discuss these topics; in Chapter 5 I describe the mechanics of moka and media of exchange; and in the later chapters I analyse the system in action, when the competitive behaviour of big-men is openly displayed.

PLACE AND PEOPLE

Hagen Sub-District takes its name from the solid heights of the mountain which stands near to its western limits. The mountain's indigenous name is Mul, 'that which stays'; its European name of Mount Hagen derives either from that of the General Director of the Neu Guinea Kompagnie, Kurt von Hagen, who was killed in 1897, or from Bernhard Hagen, a medical doctor and anthropologist, initiator of the Museum für Völker-kunde in Frankfurt; and this name was subsequently given to the Mul mountain by the first explorers of the Central Highlands, the Leahy brothers, J. L. Taylor and K. Spinks, during their expedition of 1933.[1]

South-east and north of the present-day township of Mount Hagen live some 60,000 speakers of *Melpa*,[2] represented by S. A. Wurm as the Hagen language (Wurm 1964: 79). Wurm lists a second language, *Gawigl*,[3] as closely related to Melpa, and spoken by some 30,000 persons living south of Hagen in the Nebilyer Valley and westwards to Tambul (cf. Map 1).[4]

[1] Cf. Spinks 1936: 225. Vicedom and Tischner 1943–8 [hereafter referred to as Vice-dom 1943–8], vol. 1: 2–5 discuss the naming of Mount Hagen. I am most grateful to Professor Vicedom for correspondence on this problem and for obtaining further informa-tion from a German Geographical Institute on my behalf.

[2] = Metlpa, Medlpa. The term is taken from a native geographical term, referring to the North Wahgi areas and eastwards from these.

[3] There is a multitude of variant spellings of this word, all relating roughly to the same language area, and resulting from research workers taking the word down in different dialect forms and transcriptions. Thus: Kâwudl, Køwul, Kaugel, Kawil, Gauil, Kauil, Kakoli.

[4] Wurm also lists as a separate language *Aua*, which he locates on his map as spoken within the Kambia area, and to which he assigns only 439 speakers. There is some difficulty with this assignment, resulting partly from Wurm's choice of a name for this tiny language group. Hageners themselves use the name Aua for the whole area south of the Kaugel river as far as the Government station at Ialibu. In this area live perhaps 15,000 speakers of *Imbonggu*, which is either a dialect of the Gawigl language or a separate language within the Hagen sub-family of languages.

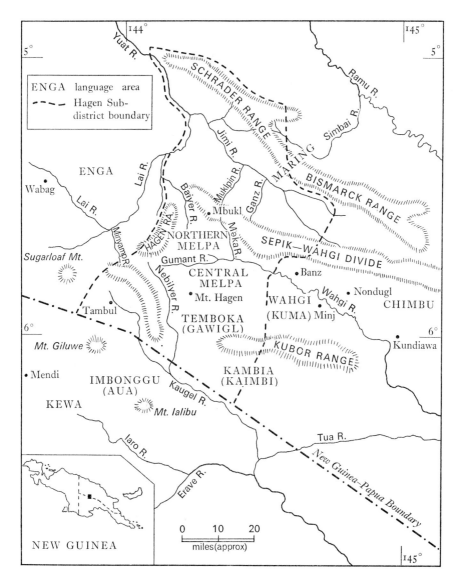

Map 1   Mt. Hagen and surrounding areas

The map is adapted from the Australian Geographical Series (1 : 1,000,000) sheets for
Lae and the Fly River, Division of National Mapping, Canberra.

5

Hageners themselves make a number of distinctions within, and partly cross-cutting, this linguistic classification. They divide themselves into speakers of *Melpa, Temboka* and *Køwul*. '*Temboka talk*', with a number of named sub-dialects, is spoken in the Nebilyer Valley and by persons who belong to groups which have migrated northwards from the Nebilyer. '*Køwul talk*' belongs to certain groups along the slopes of Mount Hagen, stretching across to Tambul. '*Melpa talk*' is co-extensive with Wurm's Hagen language. Around Hagen township people are often bilingual in Melpa and Temboka, and if they understand the latter they can follow 'Køwul-talk' (and Imbonggu) also. Within this category of Melpa, which they are more likely to refer to as *mbo-ık*, = 'plant talk' or 'native talk', the people distinguish further between *Kuma (or Koma)-ık* and *Kopon-ık*. The high plains rolling down from Mount Hagen out to the Wahgi Valley (= the Ogelbeng Plain in the usage of CSIRO 1958) are the *Koma* or 'cold' region, where a dialect or sub-dialect which is closer to Temboka-talk is spoken. Over the range of hills which bounds this region on its north side, is the area spoken of as *Kopon*, 'bush country', and thought of as hot and heavily forested; although the people in this area themselves reserve the term *Kopon* for the much more low-lying Jimi Valley and refer to their own area as '*Korka*-place'. It was at Buk,[1] within this northern part of the Melpa-speaking area, that most of my work was done. I distinguish the Koma and Kopon areas as the Central and Northern Melpa respectively.

Diacritical features, besides linguistic differences, which men pick on in distinguishing particular groups and areas from each other are: ornaments and clothing, mourning custom, bridewealth exchange rates and categories of payment, and rules of ceremonial exchange. In particular, they emphasise the cultural similarities between all those groups, from the Northern Melpa to the Tambul area, whose men wear the *omak* or *koa mak* pendant.[2] This is a set of bamboo tally-sticks, worn suspended from the neck over the chest. Each tally indicates that either eight or ten shell valuables have been given away by the wearer in a *moka* transaction, in response to an initiatory gift of two valuables and a pig. To have given away valuables in such a transaction is to have gained prestige, and the *omak* is thus a direct reckoning of a man's moka achievements and it functions as a status-symbol. People remark that the omak is worn by both Melpa and Gawigl speakers, except in the outer parts of Kambia and Aua.

---

[1] This is Administration spelling. Elsewhere in the book I use the spelling Mbukl. Other variants are Bugl, Bugal, Bukul, and Marabugul (the last in Spinks 1934: 414).

[2] The criterion here is similar to the Kuma (Wahgi Valley) criterion of all those who share the use of a certain leaf (*beg*) for cooking food (Reay 1959: 1). *Omak* appears as *aumak* in Ross 1936.

Introduction

For these informants, then, the wearing of the omak defines a supposed area of broad cultural unity (although in fact the situation is more complicated); for example, in the southern Nebilyer area within a part known as 'Kulir-place' men pointed to their omak tallies and announced to me that they were the 'last people who follow the law of Hagen and make moka exchanges', while those to their south (Aua groups) were different. The omak thus stands for an adherence to moka exchange customs.

Possibly this degree of awareness of shared customs between Nebilyer and Hagen men (whom I classify roughly together as 'Hageners') is a result of European influence and the marked growth of Hagen township in recent years. The Leahy brothers entered the Highlands as gold prospectors in the early 1930s. Together with Taylor, the representative of the Australian Administration, they built airstrips in the territory of the Mokei people beside what is now Hagen township, and at Kelua in an area belonging to the Ndika group. Shortly after this, in 1934, Catholic missionaries came to the Mokei area – conspicuously Father W. Ross,[1] who is still at Hagen – and Lutheran missionaries opened a station among the Ndika at Ogelbeng.[2] An Administration post was set up near the Mokei airstrip. Pacification and patrolling were interrupted by the events of the Second World War[3] and the Japanese invasion of New Guinea, but were renewed after 1945 and extended to the south and north of the Administration post. Economic development came much later, from 1960 onwards, when coffee-trees were introduced by Agricultural Officers, but has since proceeded apace: Hageners now regularly take foodstuffs to market for cash, sell their coffee to a number of buying companies, and travel in trucks purchased by entrepreneurs or whole groups, build trade stores and also buy from European-owned stores in the township. European plantations and mission stations are dotted over the countryside. There are three Local Government Councils, all begun since 1960. The drive for economic change accelerates, as these Councils require more money in taxes in order to develop schools, aid-posts and hospitals, and as Hageners learn more about the rest of New Guinea through their representatives in the national House of Assembly which was established in 1964.

Yet, despite these changes, basic patterns of settlement and many traditional activities remain. Flying over the Wahgi Valley towards Mount

---

[1] See Ross 1936; 1969.

[2] Vicedom and Strauss, to whom we owe major studies of Hagen society: Vicedom 1943–8, and Strauss and Tischner 1962 [hereafter referred to as Strauss 1962].

[3] For a part of this time American air-force men were stationed at Hagen. Among these was A. L. Gitlow, who subsequently (1947) published a study of Hagen economics, based largely on Fr. Ross's material.

7

Hagen as Michael Leahy originally did, one can see settlement patterns much the same as those he described in his book, *The Land that Time Forgot* (Leahy 1937: 150): 'Below us', he wrote, 'were evidences of a fertile soil and a teeming population: a continuous patchwork of gardens laid off in neat squares like checkerboards, with oblong, grass-thatched houses, in groups of four or five, dotted thickly over the landscape.'

The unit of local settlement is a homestead,[1] as Leahy described it. Homesteads are scattered over territories belonging to clan groups (cf. Chapter 2). Settlement is at altitudes between 4,000 and 8,000 feet above sea level, and on terrain ranging from flat, grassland-covered valleys to partly forested mountain slopes. Within each homestead there are tradition-ally separate houses for men and women, since men consider that women, especially when menstruating, can pollute and weaken them by too close and regular contact. Each house has a fireplace where most of the daily cooking is done. Men's houses are round, with sleeping compartments at the back; women's are long and equipped with two doorways, one for women and children, leading to a central living room with sleeping-rooms at one side, and the other for pigs, which forage in bush and fallow areas during the day but return to the homestead at night to be fed with sweet potatoes harvested by the women who are in charge of them. A wife cares for her husband's pigs in this way, as well as for her children by him. Girls continue to sleep in these women's houses till they are married, when they are expected to move to their husband's homestead: most girls experience this change of status before they are twenty years old. Boys join the men in men's houses after about the age of ten, although no formal initiation marks this or other stages of their progress towards adulthood, and there are no rigid sanctions employed to make them switch to the men's house at a certain point in time.

Homesteads may be close to a ceremonial ground or park, and if the homestead owner is a big-man he may well have a ceremonial ground associated largely with himself. These grounds are expanses of cleared, smooth, grassy areas, flanked by casuarina trees, flowers, and cordyline shrubs, and often headed by a ceremonial men's house, where discussions on important exchanges are held. The grounds may back onto a cemetery belonging to a particular group, or onto a cult-place where sacred stones are buried. The term for the ceremonial ground is *moka pena*, 'open space for making moka', and it is indeed at these that ceremonial dances and

---

[1] Nowadays, there are also many 'house-lines', i.e. expanded settlement areas where persons converted to the Lutheran mission live. These usually centre on a church. The largest are those near to Hagen township.

8

displays of wealth are held, and wealth-objects – mainly live pigs, cooked pig-meat, and pearl shells – are handed over to recipients. It is men who are the formal participants and speech-makers on these occasions; but they rely on their wives for most of the labour in pig-production, and on their affinal ties, established through marriages, for their most valuable exchange-partnerships. It is also men who most often decorate themselves elaborately and dance on moka occasions.[1] Like most of the Highlands societies, Hagen appears to be male-dominated; but women are not entirely without redress against male dominance (Strathern A. M. 1968a). This prominence of men in ceremonial activities is undoubtedly facilitated by the ecology of the area and by the social division of labour. Thus, subsistence is by sweet-potato horticulture, supplemented by cultivation of bananas, sugarcane, taro, yams, maize and cassava,[2] and a wide variety of green vegetables. Gardens are cut either from fallow areas of grassland or secondary regrowth woodland, or, less often, from long-standing forest. Men do the initial work of clearing, and also fence and ditch gardens with the drainage channels which reminded Leahy of checkerboards. Sweet potatoes are harvestable within 6–9 months of planting, and continue bearing for many months. Part of the reason for this is that throughout the year temperatures and rainfall are fairly constant (temperature varies from about 45° F at night to 90° F at noon around 6,000 ft a.s.l.; although there is usually more rain from October to March and less from April to September, there are few periods of drought: total rainfall amounts to about 100 in. per annum).[3] Other crops are more seasonal and are consumed more quickly: there is usually a flush of greens and maize corn in the middle of the wet season from gardens planted towards the end of the dry period; whereas in the middle of the dry season there is likely to be a month or so when both sweet potatoes and other vegetables are scarce.

The continuous harvestability of sweet potatoes, their high yield, and the short duration of the hungry period, are all factors which enable ceremonial activities to take place at any time in the year. Moreover, all the regular harvesting work is left to women, who also cook the food, tend the pigs, and rear the young children. Some gardens are likely to be near the homesteads; but others, perhaps those where crops other than the staple sweet potato are planted, may be an hour's walk away from home

---

[1] Strathern, A. J. and A. M. 1971. We have described Hagen dances in some detail in this book, so I do not give an extensive account here.

[2] Both crops introduced recently by Europeans.

[3] Awkward periods of dry weather do occur, when people are waiting to plant green vegetables and corn in their gardens. For seasonal variations throughout the Highlands, cf. Brookfield 1964.

or more. Clearly, women's daily work activities are more onerous than those of the men, and this leaves the men relatively free to pursue the game of prestige-seeking through moka; the more so since warfare has been stopped by the Administration, and steel tools have replaced the wooden spades and polished stone axes which were important in their technology prior to the 1930s.[1]

MOKA AS A GAME

Considered in formal, abstract terms the Hagen moka system is based on a small number of rules specifying categories of exchange transactions and the rates of exchange appropriate to these. Participants can enumerate these rules readily, if asked to do so. We may call these the 'ground rules' of moka.

In Chapter 5 I shall describe these ground rules in more detail. Here I want to give only the most abstract summary of them.

A basic principle of moka is that the person who is 'making moka' on a given occasion is the one who gives more to his partner than he himself has received in the form of an initiatory gift.

Since the work of Mauss and Malinowski, anthropologists have been aware of the complex social and political functions of the gift. A leading idea has been the suggestion that a unilateral gift creates or demonstrates superiority: the giver is superior to the receiver. Whether this superiority implies political control over the recipient or whether it merely indicates a gain in prestige on the part of the giver are matters in which individual systems vary; and in analysing the political implications of gift-giving it is most important for us to consider what kind of superiority, if any, the giver obtains.

In Hagen, this notion, that the giver is in some way superior, is explicit. To attain superiority he must give *more* than he received from his partner at the last bout of exchanges, as we have noted. It is the increment, strictly, which can be referred to as 'moka'; the rest is there simply to meet 'debt'.

But if we consider the ground rules further, we see that there is provision for the reversal of superiority–inferiority relations. Moka must be returned, *otherwise* the recipient certainly does lose prestige. We can present the situation schematically:

---

[1] I regret that I have not included in this book a fuller account of the ecology of settlement and, in particular, of pig-keeping, which is obviously an important basis of the moka system. I hope partly to make good this omission in a separate publication.

Introduction

Sequence 1	Initiatory gift	$A \rightarrow B$	x goods
	Main gift	$B \rightarrow A$	$x+y$ goods
Sequence 2	Initiatory gift	$B \rightarrow A$	x goods
	Main gift	$A \rightarrow B$	*at least* $x+y$ goods

If, in sequence 2, A's main gift consists only of $x+y$ goods, it can be seen that in economic terms the partners are now equal. If they wish to continue the relationship on a competitive basis, A can give more than $x+y$, say $x+y+z$. When B makes returns, he must then return at least as much as $x+y+z$; and so the competition continues. Should the giver's gift at any time fall below the level of the gift it is compared with, he loses prestige.

From this scheme it can be seen that in the first sequence the main gift must exceed the initiatory gift; in the second sequence, it must at least equal the first main gift and if it does so it will satisfy moka rules, for it will at the same time exceed the second initiatory gift.

The ground rules of moka, then, provide for the superiority of the main giver in any given sequence, together with an alternation of incumbency of the position of main giver through sets of sequences. Since such alternation allows the partners to be superior to each other in turn, one could label such a situation 'alternating disequilibrium'. Alternatively, since, within two sequences, the partners may be at quits with each other, one could say that the rules are conducive to long-term equilibrium or equality.

In practice, this situation of clear equilibrium does not exist. One can see that the ground rules allow for a number of possibilities beyond that of simple alternating disequilibrium issuing in equilibrium. For example, in my scheme individual or group B in sequence 2 could give more than x goods as an initiatory gift, thus compelling group A to raise its main gift to a higher level. A might fail to do this, in which case A would lose prestige.

If now we ask what kind of 'game' is being played in the scheme which I have outlined, we can give two alternative answers. The first answer is that it is a two-person zero-sum game. The ground rules provide for a situation in which the gains and losses of A and B cancel out with the completion of two sequences. But if A or B follow certain strategies they may be able to bring the situation to a different conclusion in the same number of moves. The only complication in this outcome is that the game is not necessarily over in two sequences. Indeed, if there is an imbalance at this time, the game is continued, ostensibly with the aim of wiping the imbalance out. Moka exchanges theoretically continue indefinitely over the years and no final reckoning is made. Nevertheless, there can be a definite outcome of what we may regard as the equivalent of a 'match', and we can regard such an outcome as zero-sum if the winner's gains (in prestige) are equal to the loser's losses.

The task for analysing such outcomes would then be to discover the strategies and conditions which enable a person or group to win any set of sequences.

Although this answer certainly corresponds to one set of aims in the moka system, it can be argued that it is not comprehensive enough. It misses out conditions which are important in the actual operation of the system. First, the recipient of the main gift may accept a temporarily inferior position or, *per contra*, he may assert that the gift, although exceeding the initiatory gift is really much smaller than he expected. Second, the recipient in any case *gains* the main gift, which enables him, if invested correctly, to make adequate returns later. Third, he may use the main gift himself to make moka to a third party, in which case he now assumes a role of superiority to a recipient, even before he makes returns to his first partner. The Hageners do not look on this situation as creating a stable hierarchy of relations in the form of: A is superior to B who is superior to C who is superior to D etc. This is because of the rule we have already stipulated, that relations of superiority can be reversed.

The superiority which the moka-giver establishes over his partner is thus highly limited. In fact, it is doubtful whether the moka-maker's prestige is really thought to be equivalent to prestige lost by the recipient, since the participants know that the game will go on. Yet prestige certainly *is* gained. It is gained not simply in relation to the recipient, but in relation to other men or other groups who are making prestations at the same time or have done so in the past. In other words, the donor's rivals include his own clansmen and men of other clans around, as well as the recipient.

Moreover, the conditions of competition between the donor and these rivals are different from those between donor and recipient. The recipient at least gains moka gifts. The rival is attempting to emulate his co-clansman in making gifts. Here, then, we can adopt a different scheme:

Sequence 1 A successfully gives $10x$ goods in moka
             B gives $8x$ goods in moka
Sequence 2   The situation *may* be altered, but the ground rules do not provide for a reversal of the situation in sequence 1.

If A thus gives away $2x$ extra goods we may say that he gains prestige over B. If direct comparisons are made between A and B, A's gain can be said to be B's loss, and hence we are dealing again with a zero-sum situation. If A cumulatively gains over the years, he will become a big-man, whereas B will not. We see how inequalities of status arise within the clan.

Here, however, another point emerges. It is important to notice that the rivals are not directly giving to each other. We have not even specified that they are directly competing for supporters, although they may also be doing this. If this were a system in which the rivals shamed each other, say, by making direct gifts, it is possible that a stable hierarchy of dominance and subordination could emerge between them. Even given the ground rules of moka, that relations of superiority *should* be reversed over time, it *could* happen that one man gave a crushingly large gift which the other could not emulate. In some systems of ceremonial exchange, competition of this kind actually occurs, notably in the Kwakiutl 'rivalry' potlatch; and it is noticeable that in this kind of potlatch property is sometimes actually destroyed by the donors: that is, they do not give the 'recipients' the opportunity to use property to finance a successful return gift. It is noticeable also that the principle of rank is highly developed among the Kwakiutl. In directly defeating his rival a Kwakiutl contender may vindicate his right to succeed to a ranked title within the potlatch system.[1]

In moka such harsh, direct combats do not take place. A big-man outshines his rivals, but he does not necessarily (although, again, he may) humiliate them. The gift is not used as a direct instrument of political coercion. A big-man who has lost in a particular prestation does not move up or down in a definite, established dominance hierarchy. It may be that the successful big-man can directly dominate his rivals in other ways: for example, by speech-making in court disputes. But he does not do so by moka; what he gains by moka is prestige – 'his name goes on high'. This in turn does have a feedback effect on his relations with supporters and other big-men in his clan. But it does not automatically result in any greater political control for him, nor does it make his recipients or his rivals into his permanent subordinates.

Another factor involved here is the nature of a big-man's support-groups. This has been mentioned already and it may be repeated here briefly that big-men can rely on an external network of exchange-partners outside their clan, with the result that direct competition for supporters within the clan can be minimised. Here again, then, we see that the big-men of a clan can operate independently of each other in the pursuit of prestige. One does not control the other by dominating him in direct exchanges (although they may make direct exchanges without attempting to dominate each other by them); nor do they necessarily have to compete for supporters. Nevertheless, I argue that the big-men of a clan may be in

[1] See P. Drucker and R. F. Heizer, *To Make My Name Good*, Berkeley, University of California Press 1967, pp. 98–124.

implicit competition with each other, and that their competitiveness is often shown over the issue of the *timing* of prestations. This step in the argument, however, takes us far forward into the book, and we must now go back to consider various features of Hagen social structure which form an important background to the activities of big-men. I have, for example, used the term 'clan' in this chapter. In the next chapter I shall explain what I mean by this and other terms for groups in Hagen society.

2

GROUPS

But, tell me, what are your origins, where are you from? You did not spring from the fabled oak, or from a rock.

Homer, Odyssey 19. 163

At Hagen the fieldworker rapidly becomes aware of the high-level, named groups in his area, for a person's group-membership is regularly indicated in conversation by prefixing it to his (or her) personal name.[1]

The most regularly mentioned high-level groups are those which I call tribes. These are the groups one is likely to hear mentioned most often: the Ndika, Mokei, Kumndi, Nengka, and so on near to Mount Hagen township, the Tipuka, Kombukla, Minembi, Kawelka and others in the area north of the township where most of my work was done.

Despite the frequency with which one meets such tribal names, defining a tribe in general terms is no simple matter. One reason for this is that these major groups vary greatly in size and segmentation pattern, and correspondingly in the functions carried out by segments at various levels. In this chapter I shall discuss this problem of variation in the size of tribes first; second I shall attempt to establish a set of working definitions for different group-levels; and finally I shall describe the idioms in terms of which Hageners themselves refer to their groups and how these relate to actual processes of individual affiliation to groups.

VARIATION IN GROUP SIZE

The largest tribes are those living on the Ogelbeng Plain, or just south of it, and on the slopes of Mount Hagen. The smallest may be found associated with or partially incorporated into the larger ones throughout the Hagen area, but there is a concentration of small groups in the south-west part of the Nebilyer Valley. The basic pattern is that while certain groups have expanded through success in warfare, others have shrunk and have either

[1] The level of group chosen as the prefix depends on the 'segmentary' context of discussion; and the prefixing occurs usually in reference to the person, not while one is addressing him, unless some special request is being made, when the group name is used by a co-member of the group as an equivalent of the kinship-term *ang-wuə*, or 'brother'; or else to mark out the natal origins of a wife married into one's group.

become linked to larger groups as their protectors or have occupied areas peripheral to the territories of the stronger groups.

For most of my population data on tribes I rely on Administration figures. There are difficulties with these. Sometimes they place together as one unit a pair of separate small tribes, which are closely allied to each other. Again, they may include immigrant segments of a tribe with a host tribe. In my calculations, I have separated allied groups and noted where a tribe is host to immigrants of another tribe. Unfortunately, I cannot include the Nebilyer groups, as I do not have figures for these.

The figures include: men, unmarried children, and other persons co-resident with the men and considered to be affiliated to the tribe; and also in-married wives. The inclusion of the wives requires explanation. Residence at marriage is usually patrivirilocal, but wives do not lose membership of their natal tribe nor adopt membership of their marital one. The inclusion of wives in figures on tribal population can be supposed roughly to balance the number of sisters who have married out, but this is only roughly so, because in many tribes intermarriage between tribe-segments is possible, and hence a proportion of the sisters do not marry out of their tribe. With this proviso we may consider the figures shown in Table 1.

TABLE I *Size of tribes*

| Population | Areas and nos. of groups of particular population sizes | | | |
	South Wahgi	Central Melpa	Western Melpa	Northern Melpa
6–7,000	—	2	—	—
5–6,000	—	—	1	—
4–5,000	—	—	—	—
3–4,000	—	—	1	—
2–3,000	1	1	—	2
1–2,000	—	1	2	4
0–1,000	11	9	8	13
	12	13	12	19

The actual figures on which the table is based are given in Appendix 1. From these figures we can compute that the average size of tribes or tribe-fragments in the four areas is: South Wahgi 670, Central Melpa 1,590, Western Melpa 1,115, Northern Melpa 820. Overall, the average is about 1,059. (Had I included the tribe-fragments with the larger groups they are associated with, or had included the fragments with the main sections of their tribes, the average sizes would have been higher.) This overall average figure is much lower than that which Meggitt (1965: 6) gives for Mae-Enga phratries (high-level groups, equivalent in order to the Hagen tribe). Of 14 Mae phratries, Meggitt found that the mean population was 2,290, and the range 920–5,400. The range is also much greater for the Hagen tribes: 26–6,749. Even omitting the tribe-fragments, as one strictly should, the lower end of the range is 68 persons. This suggests that the vagaries of expansion and decline have been greater in the case of Hagen groups than among the Mae-Enga. If, however, fringe Enga groups were to be included, this contrast might be considerably lessened.

From Table 1 it can be seen that the Central and Western Melpa areas are each dominated by a pair of tribes, in the Central Ndika and Mokei, in the Western Kumndi and Nengka. In the Northern Melpa area there are no such dominant tribes. The largest tribes, however, often could not retain their unity in the past, and the pattern of warfare among them tended to break down to population levels at which it operated elsewhere in the Hagen area. For example there are major enmities between different sections within both the Ndika and the Mokei. Yet the possibility of segmentary combination up to the level of the tribe remained, if only because the largest tribes could be ranged against each other in warfare; and there is no doubt that, overall, large tribes have been successful and small ones vulnerable and unsuccessful in warfare in the past.

There seem to be no clearly established ecological correlates of this distribution of tribes within the Hagen area. One can point out, however, that the largest tribes live in the central parts of the area occupied by speakers of the Hagen language, and that in these parts population density is also highest. In other words, the largest tribes are probably occupying areas which are ecologically favoured, and can support a higher population density than is found elsewhere. Given their initial occupation of a favoured area, one could expect them to expand more rapidly than other groups, and possibly also to force other groups away from their own territories.

Whatever the causes of it may be, this variation in tribe-size produces difficulties for group-terminology. The Hageners themselves are able conceptually to equate tribes of greatly different size, since they are all 'big names' (*mbi ou*). But they recognise that some groups expand while others contract, that some have been partially incorporated into others as refugees, and that as groups change in size there are gradual changes in rules of exogamy and in degrees of opposition between segments.[1]

---

[1] The fact that there can only be rough matching of segment-levels in different tribes is actually an aid to flexibility in the operation of marriage rules rather than any kind of obstacle to their 'perfect' application.

c

It is this fact of diachronic change which makes for terminological difficulties.

Usually terms for group structure are based on correlations between
particular group functions and particular segmentary levels, such that we
are able to say that a clan, for example, is the exogamous, territorial, war-
making unit, and so on. Difficulty arises when there is variability between
different units. Although it is possible to see that the variability results
from differences in processes of segmentation, the terminological difficulty
remains. One possible solution is simply to number the levels in each group
in a standard way. But this in itself would produce only apparent com-
parability. We would have to specify that whereas in one group level 1 was
the exogamous unit, in another it was level 2, and so on. The terms level
1, level 2, etc. would refer to minimal structural criteria only; functional
attributes of the levels in each segmentary group would have to be stated
separately.

The opposite solution to the problem would be to decide by functional
criteria only. For example, we could call any maximal exogamous group a
'clan', whether it contained 100 or 1,000 persons. In this case, the inter-
correlation of criteria would produce difficulties. All 'clans' so defined would
be exogamous, but not all would necessarily be independent war-making
units. The smallest would try consistently to combine with others for
warfare and would not experience internal warfare, while the largest might
be more independent of other groups and at the same time more subject
to internal fighting as segmentary opposition increased within them.

It is clear that the difficulties in both of these solutions result from
complexities in segmentation processes, which in turn result from the
expansion of certain tribes and the contraction of others. The great
differences in the size of tribes could have led us to predict that this
would be so. Other analysts of New Guinea Highlands societies have also
found that diachronic processes must be taken into account in a description
of group structure (e.g. Reay 1959, Rappaport 1967, Meggitt 1965, and
Vayda and Cook 1964). Vayda and Cook, for example, argue that there are
'lags' in processes of group change: if a clan, say, is in process of splitting
into two clans, the two incipient clans are named separately and their
members live separately before their garden claims are separated. At a
later stage, the two groups no longer co-operate closely for festivals; and
finally they begin to intermarry.[1] Thus, whether a set of definitional criteria,

[1] In this paper, Vayda and Cook also adduce factors which precipitate changes in segmentary groups – for example, quarrels, sorcery accusations, and shortage of land. But
they do not fully work out models for *inter-relating* these factors.

or only a single criterion, would be true of a particular clan would depend on its internal state of change.

A concomitant of these processes is that many more levels of segmentation are found in some tribes than in others. To cope with this, we can establish a hierarchy of terms, realising that in some groups certain levels are present which are missing in others. Some tribes, for example, are divided into major sections, while others consist of clans not aggregated further into sections. This approach is adequate for purposes of formal description; but it has to be remembered that tribes which are now small may show a segmentary skeleton at certain levels which is the same as that of much larger tribes – but with a different allocation of functions to the levels. In adopting this approach, then, we must at least specify differences between small and large tribes; although the statement of differences cannot be made more precise without a detailed examination of the total structure of a number of tribes, which falls outside the main themes of this book.

TERMINOLOGY FOR DIFFERENT LEVELS OF GROUP-STRUCTURE

I present the account here schematically, from the highest levels downwards:

1. *Great-tribe.*[1] This level is rarely found. A great-tribe is a loose linkage of a number of separate tribes in terms of a myth of common origins or original association. The tribes so linked often share a single mystical divination object, and the myth of their origins tells how this came to be associated with them.[2] By no means all of the members of the tribes linked in this way know the myth which associates them, although they are likely to know *of* it. Their linkage may carry no implications at all of contemporary alliance. The great-tribe should thus be distinguished from local alliances between tribes and from the incorporation of tribe-fragments into a larger, dominant tribe.

2. *Tribe-pair.* Most, but not all, tribes are linked with a pair-tribe. Sometimes the linkage is supported by an origin myth associating the first ancestors of the two tribes, but this need not be so. One reason for the absence of a myth of this kind is that a tribe whose members migrate to a new area is likely to lose its original pairing and to develop another with one of its new neighbours. The new pairing may not be supported by a myth.

The functions of pairing at this level are also variable. Some pairs are staunch allies, others have little to do with each other. Small tribes are likely to have strong pairings, if only because these were important for survival in the past.

[1] I would use the term 'phratry' for this level, were it not that phratry is used by other writers on the Highlands (e.g. Reay 1959, Meggitt 1965) for a level of group which is more similar to the Hagen 'tribe'.
[2] Cf. Strauss 1962, for an elaborate discussion of the importance of the divination object (*mi*) in social control within Hagen tribes.

The Rope of Moka

Brookfield and Brown (1963), discussing the Chimbu, distinguish between alliance-tribes and phratry-tribes. The former are political blocs which emerge from the close intermarriage and military alliance of two major origin-groups (phratries). Phratry-tribes are similar blocs formed by military alliance between the segments of a single origin-group. In other cases phratries are scattered, and their segments belong to different alliance-tribes. In Hagen, some of the tribe-pairs are closely allied and are therefore comparable to the Chimbu alliance-tribe; but as this is not invariably so I have retained the term tribe-pair.

3. *Tribe.* What I call the tribe corresponds to the Chimbu phratry-tribe, except that it may have incorporated within it a number of small groups unconnected to it by origin-myths. We cannot call such a composite group an alliance-tribe, for its situation is different from that of tribes composed of phratry pairs among the Chimbu. Moreover, it is only the larger tribes which have incorporated or partially incorporated whole segments of other tribes in this way.

The precise degree to which such outsider groups are incorporated by their hosts varies considerably. Sometimes the incomers are not segments but whole tribes, in which case they and their hosts become solidary allies but retain their separate existence. In the Nebilyer Valley there is one such powerful alliance set, which in the past was highly successful in warfare.[1] When a large tribe took in refugee sections from other tribes, the incomers would usually be related to them through marriage, and they would be obliged to help their hosts in subsequent warfare. A particular clan in a large tribe could play host to the whole of a small refugee tribe, which is afterwards likely to make constant ceremonial exchanges with its hosts.[2]

I shall discuss the functions of the tribe in warfare later. Here we may note that tribesmen combined for warfare against major, traditional enemies. Nowadays the segments of a tribe occasionally combine for large ceremonial exchange or cult occasions. The tribe is sometimes a single exogamous unit, but not usually so.

4. *Major section of tribe.* Many tribes are divided in this way, whether they are large or small, as can be seen from Table 2.[3] Thus, the existence of major sections does not depend simply on the current size of the tribe.

It can be seen from Table 2 that there is wide variation in the size of group which is exogamous. At the upper end of the table Ndika Maepanggil section, which contains as many as 3,409 persons, still forms a single exogamous unit; while at the lower end a section of the tiny Klamakae tribe is not exogamous.

---

[1] The Ulka–Ronye–Waepka–Kamilika set. Here, the large Ulka tribe is host to the other three. The alliance set was swelled by the addition of the Okopuka, pair-tribe of the Ulka.

[2] An example is the Elti tribe, given refuge by Ndika Opramb clan. The Elti and the Opramb intermarry constantly, and as recently as May 1969 the Elti gave some 400 pigs in moka to the Opramb.

[3] Closer examination would probably show that few tribes with over 1,000 members are not divided in this way. Those with less than 1,000 may have been expanding or shrinking in the recent past; in the former case, they are unlikely yet to have developed sections; in the latter they may have section names as a kind of survival from a time when they were much larger.

Groups

TABLE 2 *Major sections in twelve tribes*

Population of tribe	Name	Names of sections	Sections exogamous or not	Warfare within sections	Warfare between sections
6,749	Ndika	Maepanggil	yes	no	yes
		Andapønt	no	yes	
		—a			
6,199	Mokei	Kwipi	no	yes	yes
		Ndepi			
		Nambakae			
5,414	Kumndi	Komonkae	yes	no	yes
		Akelkae or Oklaka	yes	no	
		—a			
3,677	Nengka	Komonkae[b]	yes	no	yes[c]
		Akelkae[b]	no	yes	
		—a			
2–3,000	Ulka	Pingga	no	yes	yes
		Kundulka[d]	no		
2,813	Minembi	Andaoukam	no	yes	yes
		Andakelkam	no		
2,419	Tipuka	Anmbilika	no	yes	yes
		Akelkae	yes (recently)	no	
		Kengeke-Kendike[e]	no	yes	
1,542	Kombukla	Andaoukam	no	yes	no[f]
		Andakelkam	yes	no	
		(very small)			
1,196	Kendipi	Komonke	no	yes	yes
		Akelke			
		Krangembo			
678	Penambe	Andaoukam	no	no	yes
		Andakelkam	no		
364	Nølka	Andakomone	yes	no	no[g]
		Andakel	yes[g]		
241	Klamakae	Komonke	no	no	no
		Marake	yes		

a Plus an isolated clan, in case of the Ndika, Mukaka clan; the Nengka, Piamb; the Kumndi, Witke.

b Note these and variants (Andaoukam/Andakomone, etc.), = 'elder and younger grandfather'.

c Not as direct enemies, but as allies of groups which were enemies.

d Plus four small allied tribes.

e A pair of allied clans.

f The two sections are spatially separated by clans of other tribes.

g Whole tribe is exogamous unit. No internal warfare within recent past.

Special reasons explain these two extreme cases. Maepanggil section was opposed to Andapønt in major warfare, and its clans may have held together as a single unit in order to ensure their success in warfare. In the Klamakae case there was no such opposition between the major sections. Moreover, the non-exogamous section comes to be so only because a segment from the other section has joined it but can still technically provide wives for it. The other segments of the section cannot intermarry.

One generalization which also emerges from the table is that exogamy and a prohibition on internal warfare are closely related. Major sections which remain a single exogamous unit do not apparently experience warfare between their constituent segments. This suggests strongly that the decision as to whether a group should remain an exogamous unit or not is, or at least was in the past, a political matter. The size of the exogamous unit thus seems to be a function both of the size of the total tribe and of the degree of political cohesion within the tribe. We may suggest, in fact, that the members of a shrunken tribe may attempt to weld themselves into an exogamous unit if they are faced with more powerful groups around them and are not under the direct protection of one of these. Here exogamy is maintained for purposes of survival, not so much, as in the classical argument of Tylor, in order to forge external alliances, but in order to maintain internal cohesion. Somewhat differently, larger groups may maintain themselves as exogamous units in order to retain a position of political dominance.[1]

In the tribes which have a population of over 1,000 persons this relationship between exogamy and warfare holds quite clearly. In the three which are below this size, the situation changes: while sections are not invariably exogamous units, warfare within sections is less likely to occur. Thus, in the case of the Penambe, neither of the tribe's two major sections is a single exogamous unit, but the intermarrying clans within each of its sections apparently did not make warfare against each other. In the very small tribes there is no warfare *between* major sections either.

My table is not drawn from a random sample of tribes in the Hagen area. However, it does cover a range of different tribe-sizes, and it gives a reasonably comprehensive picture, at least for tribes which are divided into major sections. It should be noted that some tribes lack this sectioning: the Kawelka tribe, for example, with which most of my work was done, consists simply of three inter-marrying clans, two paired together in opposition to the third.

In many tribes there is a single large ceremonial ground, perhaps with smaller ones running off from it, at which large-scale prestations and dances are held. Clans, sub-clans, and sub-sub-clans (see below) may also have ceremonial grounds of their own. This association between groups and dancing grounds I shall examine in more detail later.

The major sections of a tribe may be described as descended from the sons of a single tribal ancestor; similarly, separate clans within a section are referred to as 'brothers', sons of the major section's founder. I deal with these idioms for levels of group structure in a separate part of this chapter.

5. *Clan-pairs.* The pairing of clans carries considerable political importance.

---

[1] In Appendix 2 I discuss the size of exogamous units further, in relation to population density in different parts of the Hagen area.

Paired clans may be closely linked by an origin myth or simply be spoken of as 'a pair'; and they may maintain bonds of exogamy or *per contra* be closely intermarried. Ideally they should not fight against each other with spear, axe, or bow and arrow. I shall examine the degree of their effective alliance for war-making and moka exchanges in subsequent chapters.

6. *Clan.* This is a level of central importance in political action.[1] It is within the clan that men most regularly refer to and address each other as 'brothers'. Clansmen have a special responsibility for taking blood-revenge and paying compensation for killings inflicted in warfare. They organise moka exchanges together. They possess, and are settled on, a single territory, except in cases where segments of the clan have migrated, to colonise a new territory or to return to a previous one.

Clans vary in the completeness of their genealogical frameworks. Such a situation of micro-variation in the depth and span of genealogies offers a possibility of testing Salisbury's assertion (Salisbury 1956) that depth of genealogy is related to residential instability and migrations, while shallow genealogies are related to stability of residence.[2] Salisbury offered this as a hypothesis to account for differences between group-structure among the Siane and in Hagen, basing his picture of Hagen society on the material given by Vicedom (Vicedom 1943–8: vol. 2), so it may be apposite to consider it briefly here. My most accurate knowledge of genealogies was obtained from men of the Kawelka tribe, living near to Mbukl. In one clan of this (Membo clan) leading men can provide a complete agnatic lineage skeleton for all the clan's small segments, proceeding down to the level of certain living old men. The other two clans of the tribe lack such a consistent and overarching framework. Yet they do not seem to have had a markedly less or more stable residence history than the Membo. What does seem likely is that Membo clan has had a higher rate of population growth and of territorial expansion than the other two clans. It is possible, then, that this example can be fitted into Salisbury's scheme, but the 'fit' is only partial. The difficulty lies in the use of the term 'instability' to cover a number of different kinds of change: expansion or decline of population, expansion or dwindling of territory, shifts of persons from group to group, and so on. Salisbury maintains that long genealogies mask instability of settlement and give an appearance of stability; but this begs the question of why groups should wish to see themselves as entirely stable in terms of all the criteria I have mentioned. Territorial expansion from a core area is a matter of pride for the Membo clan, and hence the Membo genealogies are not likely to be a *post hoc* attempt to give the clan an

---

[1] The importance of the clan was recognised by the Australian Administration when it first set up Local Government Councils in Hagen. Each clan had its own Councillor, unless it was very small, when an attempt was made to combine it with an allied group. Nowadays paired clans are often amalgamated together under a single Councillor. For clan territories around Mbukl see Map 2.

[2] Reay (1959: 34) has already pointed out that this hypothesis is untenable for the Kuma, among whom shallow and incomplete genealogical frames are a result, not of stability, but of its opposite: 'a continuous shedding and re-forming of groups that are continually changing their structure.'

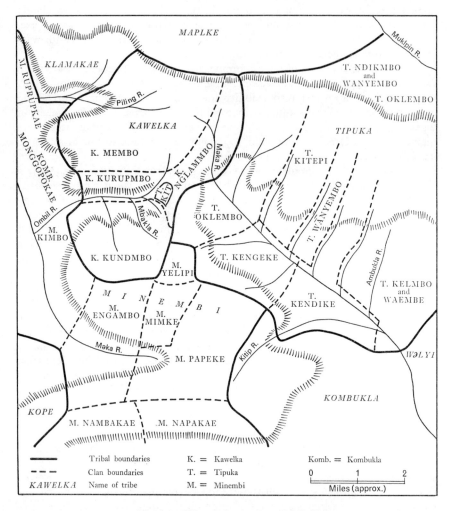

Map. 2   Clan territories around Mbukl

Boundaries are shown *only approximately, and some complications are not represented.* For example, the position of the Tipuka Kitepi enclave settlement in Kawelka territory is shown partly, but other enclaves are not shown. The boundary between Kombukla and Wəlyi tribes is not indicated. Kombukla Monggopokae are a small clan living in association with Minembi groups, so I do not draw a boundary round their territory.

appearance of stability. In short, direct correlates of the kind which Salisbury suggests are difficult to demonstrate.[1]

7. *Clan sections.* Not all clans are divided into sections. Those that are, seem to be in process of fission, that is, the sections appear to be incipiently taking on the status of clans. If fission is completed, the section-names become clan-names, and the original clan name may disappear or may move to the level of a major-section name.

Sections of clans are recognisable by the greater social distance between them than between sub-clans in clans not sectioned in this way.

For example, sections are likely to have discernibly separate territories (although individual men can garden on the land of friends in a section other than their own). In the past sections also sometimes became separately involved in warfare. The mate-section would be expected automatically to come to the help of the one which had initially become involved in fighting, but if it then lost a man the latter should pay reparations for this. In Melpa terms, the section which started the fight is *el pukl wuə*, 'war root man', while the other is *kui wuə*, 'dead man', and the death must be paid for.[2] Ideally there should be no lethal fighting within the clan, but a *kui wuə* section would at least resort to stick-fighting against its mate if reparations for a death were not made. In practice, further deaths sometimes occurred in those stick encounters, and had to be met by direct compensation in pigs, or even transfers of men, between the sections. In one case, men of the guilty section tacitly allowed the aggrieved section to steal a large number of pigs from them without retaliating.[3]

In general, there is a degree of mutual disparagement and rivalry between sections which is not found between their constituent sub-clans. Such disparagement can be fostered by the rivalry of big-men. Clans are supposed to unite for moka activity, but big-men of opposite sections may attempt to establish different schedules for the completion of a prestation. The death of a big-man can affect the situation also, for his section mates will be in mourning for his death and unwilling to make moka. After a few years of this, men of the opposite section begin to accuse them of sloth and of a fondness for eating their pigs (in sacrifices to the dead big-man's spirit) instead of improving clan prestige by giving them in ceremonial exchange.

Finally, the degree of separation between sections is shown in marriage rules. Widows are supposed to be inherited within the clan of their husband,[4] and the

---

[1] The residential history of the Kawelka clans is discussed at greater length in Strathern A. J. 1965.

[2] For a parallel distinction among the Maring, cf. Rappaport 1967: 117–18. Rappaport also reports that 'principal combatants are responsible for casualties sustained by their allies' (p. 118). The significance of the relationship with allies was first elucidated by Glasse on the Huli (Glasse 1959a).

[3] The phenomenon here is analogous to *el kaep* behaviour, which I shall describe later.

[4] The inheritor is most likely to be of the same small group (sub-sub-clan) as the deceased. Occasionally he belongs to a different small group, but he is likely at least to be of the same clan-section. The pigs which the inheritor pays are called 'widow bridge pigs' (*amb wøyə pol kng*), that is, they effect the transfer of sexual rights over the widow from one man to another.

clan-section is the widest group within which the one or two pigs which the inheritor pays as a sacrifice to the dead husband may be shared. Again, men of opposite sections within a clan may marry the immediate daughters of each other's sisters, whereas men of the same section may not.

All these points are probably indices of developing fission within the clan.

8. *Sub-clan.* A sub-clan is not held separately responsible for initiating warfare as a whole clan-section may be.

Sub-clans of two different clans can conduct mutual exchanges independently of the other sub-groups within their clans. Only influential big-men within the two sub-clans are likely to organise exchanges of this kind. Between sub-clans of the same clan there can be a further category of exchanges of cooked pig-meat, which are based upon reciprocal payments for mourning services.

Sub-clans are often paired in the same way as are clans.

In warfare sub-clans of a clan were expected automatically to aid each other against outside attackers. Internally, fist fighting is expected within them from time to time, since, as Hageners say, 'brothers are jealous', but it is disapproved of. Sub-clans may on occasion corporately attack each other with sticks, but they usually avoid causing deaths in these mêlées. Fighting within the clan with shield and spear in the fashion of warfare would be greeted with horror by clansmen not immediately involved, as it sometimes was in the past between men of paired clans. Individual sub-clan mates who begin a fight are separated by their fellows, and lengthy discussions on the dispute follow. Big-men are again likely to be prominent in this process.

From these remarks it can be seen that a good deal of animosity can arise within sub-clans, but it is not regularly allowed to develop into dangerous physical action.

9. *Sub-sub-clans.* This level of group may not be present in all clans, and it may or may not be co-terminous with the lowest level, which I call the lineage. Sub-sub-clans are the lowest-level groups which have a name that is separate from the name of a putative founder. Men of another clan are likely to say that they do not know the sub-sub-clan names within a particular clan in any detail, since these are divisions internal to the groups themselves. As an informant put it: 'those are names which men give to themselves when they are sharing out gifts of cooked pig-meat and vegetables internally. We give to the big names [= larger named groups] and they divide it out among their own little names.'

There is some fluidity at this level: slightly different divisions and names may be created from time to time. Either the named divisions are changed, or the names are left as they are and individuals change their affiliation from one division to another. The latter is spoken of as 'going inside' a new sub-sub-clan.

Men say that they create these small subdivisions in order to give the impression to outsiders that their group has many men and to obtain separate shares in ceremonial gifts for each little segment. Privately they admit that sub-sub-clans may be very small. As one big-man put it: 'We really had only five men here and ten men there, not many at all, but we decided to adopt different names for them for purposes of ceremonial exchange.' Big-men

sometimes invent new sub-sub-clan names for segments within their own clan;
and in one case a big-man of a different clan is supposed to have inventively
called out new names at a distribution of pig-meat, and so to have given a clan
its current small segment names.

10. *Lineage.* Unlike writers on African segmenting systems, New Guinea
Highlands anthropologists have been reluctant to identify group segments as
'lineages'. An exception is Meggitt, who has described the Mae-Enga, west of
Hagen, as having an elaborate lineage system. Even Meggitt does not use lineage-
based terminology for all the levels of structure which he describes. There are
two questions at issue here: first, are groups asserted to be the descendants of
apical ancestors who are related to each other as brothers, etc., in the classical
'nesting' fashion of segmentary lineage systems? Second, is there a stress on each
member of a group being able to trace a relationship, by unilineal descent, to
one of these apical ancestors, as should formally be true of a lineage system?
In Hagen, while the answer to the first question is yes, the answer to the second
is no. Moreover, precise genealogies of the relationships between named apical
ancestors are not made a prominent focus of assertions about segment inter-
relations either. This is why I have not used the term lineage so far in my account
at all. Nevertheless, I prefer to use it for this low level of group structure rather
than some other term, because the smallest group segments are specifically called
'the sons of' a named ancestor and they have no other name at all. Moreover,
genealogical relationships between all their members are known, at least to older
men, and in great part to younger men as well; or at any rate the genealogical links
and breaks are known, for lineages do not always have a neat genealogical structure.

The named ancestor of a lineage is usually not more than two generations away
from living adult men, so that the span of relationships within it among those
who are linked genealogically is not great. As is implied above, by no means all
of the accepted members of a lineage are patrilineal descendants of the founding
ancestor. Indeed there is no firm rule that they should be. Yet each lineage as a
whole is known as 'the sons of' its supposed ancestor.[1]

Bulmer (1966), in commenting on Meggitt's account of the Mae patrilineage,
has remarked that in other Highlands societies this level of grouping is somewhat
shadowy and does not appear in all clans. This is true of Hagen, but, as in the
case of the sub-sub-clan level, we have to distinguish between the views and
knowledge of outsiders to a given clan and the knowledge of clansmen themselves. To outsiders the lineage is likely to appear shadowy, since its functions
are largely internal to the clan; whereas to clansmen the existence of small
lineages within their clan is well-known. The lineage acquires a large size and
a degree of permanence, however, only in clans which are expanding in population. Otherwise it is a fluid and potentially short-lived group.[2]

[1] I have discussed these points in more detail in *Descent and Group-Structure among the
Mbowamb* (1965). There are discussions of some of the points at issue in, e.g., Barnes
1962, 1967; Langness 1964; Kelly 1968; Strathern A. J. 1969a.
[2] Waddell (1968) has pointed out that, in the Raiapu Enga groups with which he
worked, solidary patrilineages emerged only in clan-segments which were becoming
short of land. These segments may well have been ones which were expanding in population also.

Although over periods of time lineages may thus prove labile, at any given time lineage mates are likely to live close to each other and to co-operate closely in garden work. This is related to the fact that if a male member of a lineage dies without sons, his lineage mates are the first to have a claim on his garden lands. On the other hand, there is no formal head of a lineage who is regarded as the steward of its lands, as among the Siane of the Eastern Highlands (Salisbury 1962).

Lineage members also co-operate in raising bridewealth payments. A man who goes to live with men of another lineage within his clan will no longer aid his original lineage in this way. But he cannot entirely ignore his original affiliation, because he must continue to share in marriage prohibitions resulting from it.

The pairing principle may come into play at the level of the lineage also, for the group may be said to descend from a pair of ancestors who were brothers rather than from a single 'father'. It may be admitted that the father of the two brothers is not known, or that in fact the two were of different fathers but came to live together and so founded a single group. The pairing can sometimes be retrospective: a *de facto* alignment of men is represented by linking together two of their ancestors as brothers.

From this schematic account of the levels of grouping in Hagen tribes it appears that tribes are elaborate assemblages of segments, the various levels being differentiated in terms of a range of functions. From the level of the clans downwards, at least, it is also clear that big-men and the ceremonial exchange system are important in establishing segments and maintaining their inter-relations. Thus, big-men sometimes create new sub-clan or sub-sub-clan names; and by their rivalry they tend to draw sub-clans, or more prominently clan-sections, into opposition to each other. These activities of big-men complicate processes of group segmentation and fission and make it unlikely that these are solely dependent upon group size, as Meggitt has argued for the Mae-Enga. In summary, big-men sometimes create new group-segments, and the functions of these segments are at least partly defined in terms of the ceremonial exchange activities and responsibilities which are appropriate to them.

IDIOMS IN TERMS OF WHICH GROUPS ARE NAMED AND
DESCRIBED

Tribe-names occasionally refer to the tribal divination objects. Strauss (1962: 17–48) has posed the question of the significance of tribal names in Hagen and discussed it thoroughly, so I need not deal with it here. Again, I have already given examples of major section names. Often these relate directly to a myth of origin in which the ancestor of the tribe is represented as having two sons, the elder of whom founds one section, the younger the other; and the two are thus known as *Komonkae/Akelkae*, or *Andaoukam /Andakelkam*, i.e. 'elder/younger sections'.[1] There are variants, as can be seen from Table 2. For example, among the Mokei, the two main sections are named Kwipi and Ndepi, i.e. Grassland-dwelling and Forest-dwelling, and this is related to a part of the Mokei origin myth, which I shall give here briefly to illustrate the form of these myths.[2]

Kewa Mo lived on the slopes of Mount Hagen. He came down to the place Maep, where he found an omen-spot. Here he saw the shoots of the *kwang*, *pulya*, *kraep*, and *waema* trees[3] and of all other kinds of plants and trees growing in a single spot, while all around the rest of the countryside was grassland razed in parts by fire. 'This is my *kona wingndi* (creation-place)', he said. He decided to stay there, and he planted large gardens about the place.

The Enga woman Pila descended from the Kubor hills (south-east of Hagen), wearing her long reed apron. She had seen fires burning at Maep, and had decided to see what they were. On her arrival Mo questioned her: had she heard a dog bark or a pig squeal that she had come to see? But she replied that she came simply to see what the fires were.

The two married, and Mo fathered two sons, Ndepi and Kwipi, by her. He equipped each son with an axe, a boar pig, and bows and arrows, and sent the two to hunt in different areas. But one day the two quarrelled over the right to strip a tree of its edible leaves and its bark. Kwipi took all the produce in secret, and when he and Ndepi fought over this, he struck Ndepi with an arrow made of the pulya tree. Ndepi went away in anger, taking his boar pig and a dog. He came to the place Roklmukl, and planted there new sprigs of the kwang and pulya trees.

For a time he lived there by hunting marsupials and eating wild greens, sheltering in a rough hut. But he had no fire and was cold at night when it rained. One day he saw a fire burning, and found an old woman and her daughter washing the dirt from harvested sweet potatoes beside the river Koklma. He told them that he was Mokei Ndepi, chased away from home by his brother Kwipi; and he planted a garden for them in the woods. As they had a sow he put his boar to it, and when it farrowed the old woman gave him the piglets. She asked him also if he would like a pearl shell, an axe,

---

[1] This idiom is employed simply to differentiate the sections, not to provide a charter for any ranking relationship between them.

[2] This is a version which I have collated from the accounts of two Ndepi men and one of Kwipi. The 'Ndepi bias' in the story shows clearly in the emphasis on the actions of Ndepi rather than Kwipi in the myth. The major informant was Yaep, a young big-man of Ndepi.

[3] I am grateful to Mrs Jocelyn Powell of the Australian National University for identifying the *kraep* as *Nothofagus* spp (Southern Beech), *kwang* as *Castanopsis acuminatissima* (Oak), and *waema* as *Araucaria cunninghamii* (Hoop-pine). The *pulya* has not been identified.

or an apron. He said no, he would take only her daughter, and to this the old woman agreed. He gave bridewealth by returning the piglets and the old woman then gave him a pack of salt, a sow, and a work-axe, as well as her daughter.

Ndepi's first child was called Komonkae (the elder) and the second Akelkae (the younger). These founded the groups named after them. The Nambakae section joined Mokei afterwards as incomers. Kwipi stayed at Maep and founded the Kwipi section of the tribe.

Two kinds of theme run through this myth. The first is the familiar one, that the actions or situation of the mythical protagonists are in some way different from those of ordinary men. For example, the two founders of the Mokei tribe, which is 'native' to Mount Hagen, are both 'foreigners'. The two brothers born of the marriage of these foreigners quarrel and separate, whereas brothers should stay together and co-operate. Ndepi, once driven out, lives without the comforts of civilisation, eating forest-foods, living in a hut, lacking fire and a wife to look after him. The myth describes his switch from this savage mode of existence to civilisation, effected through complementary exchanges, by means of which he eventually obtains a wife and founds a section of his tribe. The initial mating of his boar and the old woman's sow produces the piglets which are subsequently exchanged to enable himself and the old woman's daughter to mate. The gift of material objects by the prospective mother-in-law is again the reverse of what actually obtains in ordinary bridewealth payments, when the groom's side must make the initial prestation. Ndepi, however, is the opposite of an ordinary man: he is a man alone, without resources, and so must be initially financed by his in-laws to be.

The second kind of theme is the mention of specific cultural ideas which are important in the definition of tribes and tribe-sections in Hagen. The tribal ancestor discovers shoots of the trees which are mystically associated with his tribe, and one of these is usually the one which can be used in divination ordeals by members of the tribe. The place where he finds them is also a central cult-place for the tribe. When one of his sons, Ndepi, quarrels with the other and leaves the original cult-place, he plants new sprigs from these important trees as a mark that he will found a new section of the tribe. The myth clearly reflects the extent of separation and enmity which actually exists between these two sections of the Mokei tribe, and this is the message which the quarrel of the two brothers conveys. It also explains their names. Kwipi is the grassland-dweller, who stays at Maep; Ndepi is the forest-dweller who is driven from Maep and founds a new home for himself in the wilds.

Groups

The naming of groups from the clan downwards may follow the same logic as that for major sections, although the group names at these levels are not usually 'explained' in the tribe's origin-myth. The names distinguish groups either (1) by means of analogies drawn from the natural world,[1] or (2) by reference to their actual geographical situation, or (3) by reference to their putative maternal origins.

In the first two cases names are often used to make a binary distinction between groups that are in a relationship of paired alliance. For example, such pairs may be called *Kund-mbo/Pøndi-mbo* = Red-root/Black-root, or *Rok-mbo/Kønya-mbo* = Long-root/Short-root. Examples of geographical terms are *Nuwurung/Numering* = Up from the river/Down from the river, and *Rondung/Mandung* = High up in the hills/Low down in the valley. The suffix -mbo added to the first category of names indicates that the segment is thought of as a 'root' or 'stock' related to other such stocks in a single large root or tribe; and it is used in the third category of names also, in which a series of different tribe-names+-mbo appears, thus: Ndikambo, Mokeimbo, Eltimbo. The rationale for this usage is that the original ancestor of a tribe, or major section, or clan took wives from a number of different tribes, and separate segments grew from the families of sons produced by these marriages. These segments are thus spoken of as 'roots' of disparate large groups within their own large group, a usage which effectively represents their separate identities.[2] The use of bound contrastive pairs as names for allied groups is similarly neat. It corresponds to the fact that the groups are separate and different but nevertheless closely linked. The same may be said of the descent charters which underpin the differentiation of group-segments down to the level of the sub-clan. These, and other terms describing groups at different levels, I shall now consider in more detail.

Great-tribes: there may be a myth known to a few leading men which links the component tribes of a great-tribe as the sons of a common father and mother. Such a myth is not likely to possess much significance in ordinary affairs. More important may be the possession of a common name which can be invoked or of a common divination object. I have not worked closely with a set of tribes

---

[1] Cf. Lévi-Strauss's discussion of the logic involved in group-names, which he undertakes in *Le totémisme aujourd'hui* (1962).

[2] The idiom employed here, of differentiation by maternal origins, is one which is familiar to anthropologists from African examples. For example, Fortes (1945: 200) writes: 'Matrilateral origin works as a factor of cleavage only within a patrilineal group.' However, I am not here arguing for Hagen that this is literally how segmentation occurs, but only that the idea of separate maternal origins is taken as an idiom (or model) in terms of which group differentiation is described by the Hageners themselves.

linked in this way, however, and cannot say whether these idioms of linkage are used in political contexts or not.

Tribe-pairs may similarly lack a common origin-myth (although many are associated in this way, e.g. the Kombukla–Minembi pair whose myth is given by Strauss 1962: 35–6); but they are always said to be 'helping names to each other'. This is a favourite concept, expressed by holding up the two index fingers on either hand and pressing their tips together, to show how the two groups meet closely, yet are separate. The action sums up the notion of alliance which is so important in Hagen society.

While tribe-pairs are most often spoken of as 'helping names', single tribes are described as 'of one big-name only' (*mbi ou tenda mint*). If an appeal is made to the different segments of the whole tribe at a meeting it is most likely that the call for solidarity will be made in terms of this single shared name. The tribe can also be described as *wamb mbo tenda* = people of one root, or *unt tepam tenda* = (descendants of) a single original father. For some tribes this putative ancestor is not even named in a myth, yet the segments of the tribe are still asserted to be 'of one father'. In cases where the founder is named, he may also be assigned a wife in the origin myth, but in the cases known to me this is not cited as a charter for an alliance relationship between the founder's and his wife's tribes. In myths it is the association of the divination objects of a pair of tribes that stands for their alliance. For example, the Minembi tribe's origin-myth links it with the Kombukla, since their primal ancestors found their divination-objects in the same place; and Kombukla–Minembi do form an actual alliance-pair. The Minembi ancestor also courts and marries a woman of the Tipuka tribe in the same myth; but Tipuka and Minembi are in fact major enemies of each other.[1]

In tribes which have a named founder and contain major sections, the sections are spoken of as descendants of the founder's sons, and the clans are in turn regarded as the descendants of the sons of the section founders. At this level the ancestors involved are likely simply to be eponyms of the groups they are alleged to have founded.[2] This kind of model which the Hageners use to describe segment interrelations within the tribe is often impeccably patrilineal in form; but, as I have pointed out, it is difficult to characterise the whole system as 'patrilineal', since there is no norm that each current member of a tribe-segment must be able to link himself patrilineally to one of these high-level ancestors. Instead of maintaining this, what one can say is that a patrilineal model is employed to conceptualise relations between the segments as whole units. The focus is on ancestors as representing segments rather than on the links between living individuals and the ancestors.

---

[1] This does not directly represent Hagen marriage patterns either, since, although a few marriages are contracted with major enemies, most take place between minor enemies and allies. I shall take up this theme in more detail in the next chapter.

[2] At the next level down in group-structure, paired clans sometimes are linked by a genealogical pedigree in which their named ancestors are regarded as brothers; and the ancestors in this case are not simply eponymous to the two clans. Such linkages, however, are known to few men of the clans involved. For most men, the statement of pairing is sufficient.

Groups

It is in agreement with this point that there may be a gap in genealogies between a sub-clan or small lineage-founder and the clan founder, or a lack of correspondence between the assertion that the clan ancestor had many wives who founded the sub-clans and genealogies obtained by actually working up from living men. In one case[1] two sub-clans of a clan are named after the wives of named ancestors, but these ancestors are not in fact apical to all the small lineages within their sub-clans. The sub-clans are thus not even represented as having literally descended from the women whose tribal affiliations have been used to give the sub-clans their names.

The clan is spoken of emphatically as *tepam tenda* = '(founded by a) single father', and this dogma is referred to as the basis for rules of exogamy, and co-operation in warfare and ceremonial exchange. Clans within a single tribe are sometimes linked as the descendants of two sisters or of a brother–sister pair. This is an assertion of a special alliance between them. It does not prevent the two clans from intermarrying. Clearly the idiom here is similar to that employed by the Kuma, among whom clans which frequently intermarry are described as 'like brothers' (Reay 1959: 58).

There are other terms which can also be used to describe the clan: *anda kangəm* = 'old father and sons' (in shortened form *andakam*, also used for different *kinds* of creatures and plants in the natural world), and *pana ru* = 'garden ditch'. The first of these is similar in idiom to the dogma that the clan is 'of a single father'. The second compares the clan either to a ditch between gardens or to shallower divisions between different plots in a garden, thus aptly symbolising the fact that the tribe is segmented into a number of clans.

There are no special terms for the level of the clan-section. It is simply referred to as the sum of its component sub-clans. It is at the level of the sub-clan that an idiom distinct from that used for the clan appears. Whether the sub-clans of a clan are held to be descended from a polygynist's wives or not, the regular term for them is *rapa tenda*, 'one men's house group'. This does not imply that the sub-clansmen in fact live in a single clubhouse, but rather that they are likely to have a single men's house in which they meet to discuss ceremonial exchange plans. The men's house in question is often one belonging to a prominent big-man of the group, and it may also be located at the head of a small ceremonial ground belonging to the sub-clan.

Sub-clansmen sometimes claim to be descendants of a single ancestor or of a number of men who originally shared a men's house; but this is not a prominent dogma. In practice, even if this assertion is made, it is rarely possible to fit all members of a sub-clan together on a genealogical frame. Most often, small lineages within a sub-clan can be traced upwards for a few generations, when the genealogies come to a halt, and the last ancestor mentioned is described as having 'joined' the sub-clan. The top-linkages *between* sub-clans are provided by the dogma of a polygynist clan-ancestor and his separate wives; and these linkages do not often exactly mesh in with the lower-level lineage genealogies.

Sub-sub-clans are more likely to have a complete genealogical frame. They are

---

[1] Yelipi clan of the Minembi tribe.

D

spoken of as *manga rapa kel* = 'small men's houses', sometimes as *rapa ru kel kel* = 'very small men's house divisions'.

At the lowest level, the lineage, as I have noted, the 'men's house' idiom is no longer employed, and we return to a kinship model. Lineages are spoken of as 'father-son groups' (*tepam-kangəmal*), and each one is referred to as 'the sons of so and so', the founder's name being supplied. A more strikingly physio-logical idiom is also often used: lineage mates are *noimb tenda* = 'one penis', or *ndating tenda* = 'one semen'.

This completes the schematic description of terms used for groups at different segmentary levels within the tribe. It can be seen that at the highest and the lowest levels a kinship model is used to conceptualise groups and their inter-relations, while in between, at the level of the clan and sub-clan, there is additional stress on territorial and residential idioms: the clan is a 'field ditch', sub-clans and sub-sub-clans are 'men's house groups'. The terminology here reflects the importance of territoriality and residence in political relations between, and in affiliation to, groups at this level; and it is the clan and the sub-clan which are also the major co-operating groups in *moka* exchanges.

A further point which must be made is that the same terms *can* be used for a number of different levels of grouping. We cannot simply say that the clan level is unambiguously identified by a certain idiom, and so on.[1]

Thus *mbi tenda*, 'one name', is a phrase which can be applied from the level of the tribe at least down to the clan. More inclusive segments are *mbi ou tenda*, 'one big name', smaller ones are *mbi kel*, 'small names'. Again, the term *reklaep* = 'row' (i.e. a row of dancing men, a row of houses, etc.) can be used for groups at any level. *Tepam tenda*, 'one father', can similarly apply to the whole tribe, the clan, or to a small lineage.

There are alternate terms for the same level also, as we have seen in the case of the clan, which can be described as *pana ru*, *anda kangəm*, or *tepam tenda*. Such alternate terms may bridge notions of both agnatic and cognatic kinship. Thus, while the lineage is at times described as a 'one semen group', it is *also* described as *mema tenda* = 'one blood group'.[2] In other contexts *mema tenda* relationships are those held to exist between men related by cognatic ties. To call the lineage by this term seems to indicate a recognition of the importance of cognatic links within it. But

---

[1] In Appendix 3 I discuss the terminologies adopted by Strauss and by Vicedom, making the point that they tend to link particular terms too closely with particular group-levels.

[2] Cf. the Chimbu term *boromai suara* for sub-clan sections (Brown 1967: 41). The Chimbu also use the 'men's house' idiom for clan segments.

what is perhaps important in these idioms is not their precise patrilineal or cognatic reference, but their rhetorical appeal as charters for group unity, based on the assertion of sharing something fundamental, whether this be common semen or common blood.

This last idiom, with its alternate stress on ties of semen and ties of blood, certainly fits with the actual processes of affiliation to lineages. Lineages show a considerable degree of incorporation of persons other than the sons of agnates, and the most frequently incorporated are sisters' sons of the lineage, who are either brought as children by divorced, separated, widowed, or refugee mothers and subsequently stay, or else they are men who themselves switch affiliation from their father's to their mother's group, perhaps owing to quarrels or to a lack of close kin in their father's lineage. Sisters' sons are usually welcomed as recruits to a settlement and to the clan group, especially if they join a big-man, who is keen to gather supporters around him. As one big-man among the Northern Melpa[1] put it: ' ground is nothing, it is men who are strong.'[2]

It is in accordance with this set of facts that the formal dogmas relating to recruitment of persons to groups are filiative rather than based on descent criteria. Men whose fathers were accepted as group members are spoken of as *wuə-nt-mei* = 'born of the man', while those who have been incorporated through their mothers are *amb-nt-mei*, 'born of the woman'. The sons of such *amb-nt-mei* male members are called *wuə-nt-mei* and are not formally distinguished from other patrifiliative members who are also agnates. Husbands who reside uxorilocally are accepted also, but are likely to be criticised both by their natal clansmen and their affines. They are spoken of as *wuə eta* or *elta*, 'incomers', by contrast with sister's sons, who are referred to honorifically as *məi pukl wuə*, 'owners of the ground', i.e. persons who have a right to come and live at the place of their maternal kin provided they join the mother's brother's clan group.[3]

Actual affiliation patterns depend on a number of factors: the incidence of divorce, the ability of a mother to remove her children from her estranged

---

[1] Roltinga, of Kawelka Kundmbo clan, whose moka partnerships are described in a later chapter. Roltinga has two divorced sisters and their children living at his settlement-place.

[2] Such an evaluation is no doubt partly dependent on the sufficiency of land resources among the Northern Melpa, and partly also on the limited opportunities men have of exploiting their ground in order to obtain a cash income. But it expresses succinctly the viewpoint of the big-man, who can increase his moka activities only with the help of other men. Roltinga is not saying that ground is worthless, but that good supporters are scarcer than good land.

[3] Meggitt (1965), Ryan (1961), and Bulmer (1960*b*) have all argued that non-agnates in the societies they studied are *de facto* less successful than agnates in gaining high social status. I discuss this topic later (Chapter 9).

or deceased husband's group, and, in the past, patterns of warfare. Non-agnates may come to form a considerable proportion of the current members of a clan group. In the Kawelka tribe the percentage of current male members in the different clan groups who are non-agnates varies from 18 per cent in one clan to 51 per cent in Membo clan.[1]

If this argument is correct, it seems reasonable to suggest that in comparing Highlands societies we must bear in mind the distinction between dogma applied as a calculus of intergroup relations and dogmas applied to processes of affiliation to groups. It is for this reason that it is inadequate to state that 'the area as a whole appears to be characterised by cumulative patrifiliation rather than patrilineal descent' (Barnes 1962: 6), or that we can rank Highlands societies along a continuum, 'one pole of which is cumulative patrifiliation and the other agnatic descent' (Meggitt 1965: 280).[2]

In the next chapter I shall consider group-segmentation further, in order to bring out the importance of big-men as founders and 'managers' of ceremonial grounds with which group-segments are associated.

---

[1] Thus, the clan which has the most comprehensive agnatic genealogical framework representing relations between its segments *also* has the highest proportion of individual non-agnatic members.

In my calculations here I count as agnates those whose father's father was accepted as a clan group member. If one insisted on only those with pure agnatic pedigrees being accepted as agnates, then the figures for agnates would become very low. Such an insistence would have little point, for beyond the level of grandfathers of living men there is either a hiatus in genealogies or genealogical rearrangement sets in.

[2] Cf. Glasse 1959a, Sahlins 1965a, Scheffler 1965, Strathern A. J. 1965, 1969a, for more lengthy examinations of this theme.

3

CEREMONIAL GROUNDS

In the Mount Hagen area were beautiful park-like enclosures of ornamental trees and shrubs, surrounding well-kept lawns of fine grass.

E. W. P. Chinnery, *Central Ranges*
of the Mandated Territory, 1934, p. 409

DESCRIPTION

The term which I translate as ceremonial ground is *moka pena*, 'open flat area used for making moka'. There is at least one ceremonial ground in each clan territory, laid out in a flat space or along a sloping hill ridge. New ones are constructed from time to time. It is men's work to clear the ground, plant shrubs and trees along its edges, and maintain it in good order.

Individual men plant casuarina trees and bamboos beside the pena, and the planter has the right to use these subsequently.[1] Rows of cordylines are also planted, but individual men do not have exclusive rights over these; clansmen may use the fresh leaves to replenish their rear-coverings occasionally, but the cordylines should not be cut down. Particular types of cordyline are the divination-stuff of numbers of the Hagen tribes, and for other tribes also cordylines are closely associated with ancestral ghosts; so that to cut them down would be an offence against the ghosts. When a small pena is not to be used for a year or so it may be converted into a garden in the meantime; but its cordyline boundary-markers are left standing.[2]

In former times, according to Vicedom (1943–8, vol. 1: 150) a new pena was sown with a special grass; and most established pena are in fact

---

[1] If he does not, the trees in time become 'ancestral', and men say they would not think of cutting these down. Leahy (1936: 243), Chinnery (1934: 409, cf. caption to this chapter), and Vicedom (1943–8 vol. 1: 148) were all impressed by the trim and colourful appearance of Hagen ceremonial grounds.

[2] Rappaport (1967: 132–3) remarks that the Maring plant a type of cordyline in an enclosure near to their men's houses when they go out to battle. The cordylines hold the *min*, life-stuff, of the warriors while they are away fighting. Red cordylines figure similarly as 'external souls' (Frazer 1922: 667) in two Hagen folk-tales (Vicedom 1943–8 vol. 3: nos. 60 and 71). Barrau (1965: 338–9) quotes references from other parts of New Guinea and Oceania, which reveal a similar set of ritual ideas to those of the Maring and Hageners. Cf. also Williams 1940–.

pleasantly grassy. Flowers may be planted in bare patches to prevent weeds from taking root.

The ritual focus of a moka pena is the special men's house at its head and a set of trees and shrubs planted in an enclosure of stakes surrounding a mound of earth, which stands in line with the door of the men's house. The men's house is the *manga puklum*; the trees form a *poklambo*, 'leaf-root place'.

The *manga puklum* is sometimes occupied by a big-man; otherwise it is used only for occasional discussions on moka plans and to accommodate visitors. When a new ceremonial men's house is built, a ritual expert plants a piece of pearl shell and a foetus from a pregnant sow in the hole made for the central house post; and he recites spells to 'draw in' valuables to the house from distant places. In the Nebilyer Valley these spells include the names of places along the traditional trade-routes by which pearl shells entered Hagen in the past: the expert speaks of the shells as leaping from hill-top to hill-top, attracted by the gleam of shells already placed in the men's house. He asserts that shells will slip away from other men's houses, but come and 'stick' (*rømb ni*) to this one. He also leads a song-performance which is in effect a communally-spoken spell, calling on plants, birds, and trees which are associated with the acquisition of wealth.[1]

A sacrificial cooking of pork for ancestors of the men who use the pena follows this ritual. Visiting female kin, in-laws, and exchange partners are given portions of the leg and stomach, while the clansmen themselves take the heads and tail-pieces of pigs, cook them in a sacrificial hut at the back of the men's house,[2] and consume them privately. Prayers to the ancestors, to favour the ceremonial ground and ensure that its owners will be wealthy, are made at the same time.

The planting of trees and shrubs on the *poklambo* is also a ritual act. In the Northern Melpa area a poklambo is established only when a new ceremonial ground is made or when a new moka is planned. Beside it are buried magical stones (often prehistoric mortars of the kind which also appear as ritual objects in Hagen spirit cults), to attract wealth, and in its trees clan ancestors are supposed to come and lodge themselves. In the Nebilyer Valley, a whole series of poklambo may be planted down the centre of a ceremonial ground, and a greater variety of trees chosen:

[1] Cf. Appendix 4. Rituals of this kind are opposed by Christian missions, and are not often performed nowadays.

[2] Or nowadays simply in a separate oven. The special huts have in many cases been allowed to decay, in order not to attract the notice of mission evangelists.

besides the casuarina, cordyline, and Araucaria pine which one finds in the Melpa area, Nebilyer men plant red-flowering trees credited with the power of attracting wealth again.[1]

To cut a poklambo tree places a man in severe ritual danger, for the *mi* (divination-stuff) of his group will kill him for his assault on the group's ancestors. The act is done only as an extreme form of protest during a dispute with a co-clansman, and is regarded as similar to suicide.

At one ceremonial ground in the Central Melpa area[2] I was told that the part nearest to the poklambo is the head (*rapa am*) of the ground, while the other end is its tail (*øi*). At the head big-men are supposed to stand and make speeches and to cook their pigs close to the poklambo, so that it is their pork which ancestors smell when a sacrifice is made, and it is they who consequently receive most help from the ancestors in their affairs. Unimportant men cook pigs and listen to speeches at the 'tail' end of the pena. This piece of ideology was not repeated to me elsewhere; but it fits with the importance of the poklambo as a ritual focus of the ceremonial ground.

At the back of a clan ceremonial ground there may be a clan cemetery-place,[3] and, if the group is one of those which has performed one of the spirit cults which circulate around Hagen, a further grove in which spirit-stones are buried. When a cult-performance is held, celebrants break out from behind a high fence and dance on to the ceremonial ground.

A similar constellation of men's house–burial-ground–poklambo is traditionally constructed at smaller ceremonial grounds which are closely associated with a particular big-man. In the Nebilyer Valley, at the settlement of an eminent big-man, Ulka Ukl, there was in 1965 a small, lineage burial-ground at the back of Ukl's men's house, and in a part of the ground Ukl had built a 'spirit-house' (*kor manga rapa*) for his dead father, in which he cooked pieces of pork and made prayers. Not far off Ukl had built a separate sacrificial house for his mother's ghost also. Combining piety with magic, he had planted cinnamon, a potent love-charm, beside the

---

[1] Vicedom (1943–8 vol. 1: 149) was puzzled by this point. He notes that people told him that the number of poklambo at a pena indicated the number of moka ceremonies celebrated there; but in fact he found as many at new ceremonial grounds as at old ones, The solution lies partly in the planting of new *trees* at a previously established poklambo. and partly in differences between Nebilyer and Melpa custom. On the meaning of poklambo, cf. also *ibid.*, vol. 2: 444.

[2] At Kelua. The ground belongs to the Elti Andakomone and Weimb groups.

[3] When the site of an old ceremonial ground is cleared again after its abandonment, a pig is cooked as a sacrifice to the ghosts of its previous users, and the pig's jawbone is hung on a pair of bent cordylines (*køya palimb*) as a mark to the ghosts that their descendants understand they may be upset by the disturbance of their old pena but have cooked the pig to appease them and dissuade them from sending sickness.

house of one of his wives, and near to the poklambo in front of his men's
house he had laid out a patch of short red cordylines with hook-like leaves
(*pokla mak*): the hooks are considered to 'trap' valuables and draw them
to the place. Ukl told me proudly that he was a traditionalist and had
preserved the old forms of ancestor worship, and that this explained his
success and high status.

Mission preaching has elsewhere driven out many of the overt signs of
magic and ritual associated with moka. Perhaps we may also suggest that
in the past, when shells were notably scarcer (cf. Chapter 5), there was a
more urgent 'need' to employ magic in order to obtain shell valuables for a
moka. One young big-man himself advanced this theory to me: 'In the
past we had few pearl shells, and so we had to make them come to us by
spells.' But the theory is inadequate, for the task of obtaining shells in time
for a specific moka can be very risky even nowadays, and one might have
expected magical action to continue in these circumstances; and indeed
traditionalists such as Ukl in 1965 *were* maintaining magical practices.
Other men had suspended their performance as an adjustment to the
presence of evangelists; while a few had formally renounced them on
becoming baptised as Christians.

DISTRIBUTION

In the previous section I have mentioned 'clan' ceremonial grounds and
also grounds which big-men lay out for their personal use. There is in fact
a range of associations between groups or big-men and particular ceremonial grounds: while the grounds may be spoken of as belonging to a
single group, others may use it as well. In addition, possession of a ceremonial ground is a matter of pride for group-segments and individual men.
In fact, ceremonial grounds are closely connected with the fact of group-
segmentation itself, as Vicedom notes (1943–8, vol. 1: 147–8) in an interesting passage:

> The centre of the settlement is the dancing ground. Each settlement has at
> least one of these, on which the men's house of the leader is built. Settle-
> ments without a dancing ground are branches from a main settlement,
> indicating that the greater part of the clan has remained with its leader on
> the dancing ground, whereas the other part with a less influential leader
> has built a new settlement. Rivalry between influential men, not land
> shortage, leads to these divisions.

Vicedom thus explicitly associates the building of new ceremonial
grounds with rivalry between big-men. Clearly, it is only a short step from

40

this argument to suggest that segmentation within the clan actually takes place through the creation of new moka pena by leaders.

Some of Vicedom's statements here may apply better to settlements among the Central Melpa Ndika clans, with whom much of his work was

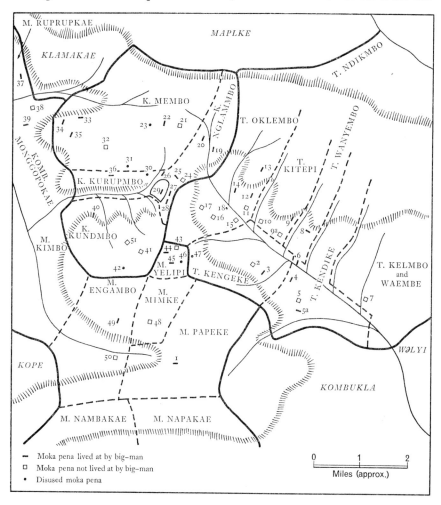

Map 3   Distribution of ceremonial grounds around Mbukl

The grounds are numbered 1–51, including 5a and 9a, and are marked as they were in 1964–5. By 1969 there were changes: for example, no. 15 had been converted into a garden and house site.

done, than to the Northern Melpa area. Among the Northern Melpa, settlements may not be so large and consolidated as among the Ndika.

The result is that the simple contrast between main clan settlements which possess dancing grounds and branch settlements without dancing grounds does not appear.

On Map 3 I have shown the position of fifty-three ceremonial grounds within a few miles of Mbukl. The record of grounds is complete only for six clans (those of Kawelka tribe, the Tipuka Kitepi–Oklembo pair, and

TABLE 3 *Association of group-segments and big-men with ceremonial grounds*

Grounds associated	Also associated with big-man	Not associated with big-man	Totals
3a. Detailed account			
A. 1 with a tribe	—	1	1
2 with two clan-pairs	—	1	1
3 with a clan-pair	1 (weakly)	—	1
B. 1 with a clan	2 (weakly)	2	4
2 with a clan and one of its clan-sections	2	—	2
3 with clan+clan-section +sub-clan	1	—	1
4 with clan+sub-sub-clan	1	—	1
5 with clan+sub-clan+ sub-sub-clan	3	—	3
C. 1 with clan-section	4	—	4
D. 1 with sub-clan	8	4	12
E. 1 with sub-sub-clan	10	2	12
	32	10	42

Category	Associated with big-man	Not associated with big-man
3b. Summary		
A+B$_1$	3 (weakly)	4
B$_{2-5}$+C+D+E	29	6
	32	10

Minembi Yelipi clan) and it is these which I use for testing the association of groups and big-men with moka pena of varying importance.

Many ceremonial grounds have multiple associations. They may be used by groups of varying span or sometimes by a pair of groups; and at all levels they may also be identified, either more or less strongly, with big-men. I call such an association of a pena with a big-man 'strong' if it is almost always referred to as 'his' and he uses it for moka prestations which he himself makes or in which he is the most prominent contributor and leader. Two big-men may share a strong association with a pena. The association is less strong if the big-man simply happens to live in the

TABLE 4 *Strength of association of ceremonial grounds with big-men*

Category of pena as in 3a	Strongly associated with major big-man	Strongly associated with minor big-man	Less strongly associated with big-man
4a			
A+B (higher order groups)	2	1	9
C+D+E (lower order groups)	19	1	8
	21	2	17
	Total: 40		

Category of pena	Associated with major or major+minor big-man	Associated with minor big-man
4b		
A+B	9	3
C+D+E	19	9
	28	12
	Total: 40	

Pena associated with	Category of pena	More strongly associated	Less strongly associated
4c			
Major big-man or major+minor	A+B	3	6
	C+D+E	16	3
		19	9
Minor big-man	A+B	–	3
	C+D+E	4	5
		4	8
		Total: 40	

manga puklum at the head of the ceremonial ground and the ground itself is usually referred to as one which belongs to a group-segment.

Table 3 shows the general pattern (in 1964–5) of the association of ceremonial grounds with big-men and group-segments. Table 4 investigates the link between big-men and grounds in more detail. In Table 3 certain pena which are outside the territory of the six clans for which data are complete have been omitted; as have a few pena now disused. In Table 4 some of these are included.

From Table 3 it can be seen that pena associated with a clan and/or lower-order groups outnumber by far those associated only with groups of higher order. Clan-sections, sub-clans, and sub-sub-clans thus often have their own pena or else on occasion make moka independently on a pena which is also at times used by a higher-order group. Significantly, pena associated with lower-order groups are more likely also to be associated with big-men (Table 3*b*).

Table 4*a* indicates that pena belonging to higher-order groups are likely to be less strongly associated with big-men; those associated with lower-order groups more strongly. 4*b* shows that, overall, pena are more likely to be associated with major than exclusively with minor big-men;[1] and that where higher-order pena are linked with a big-man, here too it is likely to be a major big-man who is involved. 4*c* gives a synopsis of all the facts, indicating that major big-men also tend to be more strongly associated with their pena than are minor big-men.[2] The conclusion suggested by all these points is that major big-men are most likely to build pena of their own or to be the chief managers of an already existing pena; and that these grounds are ones which are also associated with subdivisions within clans.

The distribution of these smaller pena within clans varies with the clan's size, the number of segments within it, and the numbers of its big-men in different segments. These factors are potentially independent of each other, to some extent; so that, for example, it is possible to find clans which are now small but are heavily subdivided or have a good number of big-men belonging to them. Nevertheless, overall, there is a correlation between clan size and numbers of moka pena (Table 5). The eleven clans in Table 5 have a total population of 2,841 and a mean of 258. Clans above the mean have an average of five moka pena; those below it only 2·7. More extensive, and randomly sampled, figures would be required for statistical testing, but the direction of the figures is clear. On the other hand, the smaller

[1] My distinction between major and minor big-men follows the categories used and judgements made by clansmen of the big-men in question. Minor big-men are more numerous than major ones.

[2] A disused and a current pena of a single big-man are allowed to count as two instances of association in my tables. Strictly the disused pena should not be included; but its omission would not make a significant difference to the figures.

Ceremonial grounds

TABLE 5 *Distribution of ceremonial grounds within eleven clans*

Clan name	Population	Nos. of moka pena	Nos. of sub-clans
1. T. Kitepi	463	6	5
T. Kengeke	448	4	4
K. Membo	360	6	2
T. Oklembo	350	5	5
T. Kendike	276	4	4
		25	
2. K. Mandembo	250	4	3
K. Kundmbo	250	3	5
M. Yelipi	203	3	3
M. Mimke	126	1	3
T. Eltimbo	70	3	only lineages
Kombukla Monggopokae	45	2	5 (shrunken)
		16	

clans each divide into almost as many sub-clans as the larger ones.[1] The processes of growth and decline of clans which underlie this situation are complicated: briefly, a clan which expands quickly, such as Membo clan, may proliferate its ceremonial grounds before its formal segmentation changes; conversely, a clan which has recently declined may retain a number of segment names and ceremonial grounds which later will become defunct. Thus, the tiny Monggopokae clan still has five (shrunken) sub-clans within it and two ceremonial grounds; but the clansmen always act as a single group and use a single ceremonial ground in practice, more especially since the death of one big-man who had his own pena.

These figures, however, do not give the *actual* distribution of ceremonial grounds within a given clan nor the details of their use during 1964–5. I shall describe, and contrast, the situation in one of the smallest clans, T. Eltimbo, and some of the larger ones, for example T. Kitepi.

The Eltimbo in 1964 numbered fewer than twenty adult men; and half of these were living away from the Buk area at a settlement near to the Gumant river, to which they have recently returned after their earlier expulsion in warfare. At Buk they have no territory of their own, but share ground with Kitepi–Oklembo and with the Kawelka. Yet in 1964–5 there were three pena closely associated with them and a fourth which in 1965 was converted back to garden

[1] The five larger clans contain twenty sub-clans (in some cases a section which is divided only into sub-sub-clans is counted as a sub-clan, and this helps to explain the situation), or a mean of four per clan; the six smaller ones nineteen sub-clans, or 3·2 per clan.

land. (It belonged to a big-man, who finally decided to live at the Gumant only, and gave up his settlement near to Buk.)

The strength of the Eltimbo in moka and their separate existence as a group seems largely to depend on the influence of a major big-man, Kot. He has his own ceremonial ground at Buk (Waimorong 2, no. 28), which he laid out himself. During 1964 he collected twenty-five pigs in moka from a cross-cousin who is a big-man in T. Kengeke clan, and a further twenty-one later from T.

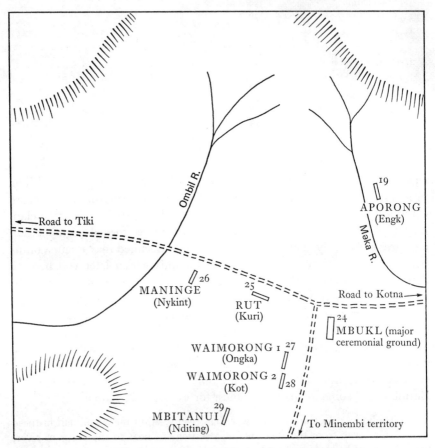

Sketch map of ceremonial grounds near Mbukl

Oklembo partners. Kengeke and Oklembo men gave also to clan-mates of Kot, in particular to Ruk, who appeared to be a rising young big-man. Both Kot and Ruk live as neighbours of men in the larger clans which were involved in moka relations during 1964–5, and their little group would become absorbed in the others if they did not remain vigorous in moka. Their maintenance of separate moka pena has obviously been a part of their struggle for separate existence, and in 1964–5 the weight of this effort lay on Kot, their acknowledged leader. After what I call the 'moka chain' of prestations was completed in 1964–5, the main Eltimbo pena was allowed to fall into disuse; and in 1968 it was partly turned into garden land.

In this example, then, the creation and maintenance of ceremonial grounds is a crucial sign of the corporate existence of a small clan; and its participation in exchanges as a group of the same order as the stronger clans around it depended entirely on the eminence of its leader, Kot. From another point of view, Kot's own position in the moka chain depended partly on his ability to muster Eltimbo men in his support; and the struggle was hard for him precisely because his group was small and divided in residence.

The T. Kitepi ceremonial grounds illustrate a different point; for the Kitepi, rather than having to struggle in order to maintain a single clan pena, actually have two, one which they share with Kawelka clans and one nearer the centre of their territory (nos. 24 and 10). No. 24 is used for moka prestations between Kitepi–Oklembo clan-pair and Membo–Mandembo of Kawelka. It is set among a number of settlements of Kitepi and Kawelka big-men, each with his own pena (Kuri at no. 25, Nditing at no. 29, Engk at no. 19, Ongka at no. 27 and Nykint, sister's son of Kuri, at no. 26, cf. accompanying sketch map). Since the Kawelka gave refuge to the Tipuka men who live near Buk, it is likely that the close exchange partnerships between big-men who live at these various pena have in fact sprung from the host–refugee relationship. Certainly, in 1964–5, it was evident that Kuri and Nditing, major big-men, were heavily committed to their moka with the Kawelka. But the Tipuka as a whole have alliances facing east as well as west, with the Kendipi tribe as well as Kawelka. For a planned prestation to the Kendipi in 1965 preliminary transactions and discussions in which Kitepi men took part were held, not at Mbukl pena but at no. 10, Nunga; and a special men's house to accommodate Kendipi visitors was also built at Nunga.[1]

This example shows how more than one ceremonial ground may be associated with a whole clan. The two main Kitepi grounds are used for prestations to separate sets of allies, the Kawelka and the Kendipi. Nunga was built much earlier than the Mbukl pena, as the size of its casuarina trees testifies; Mbukl has become a focus for Kitepi big-men only since they were driven there as refugees in warfare some forty years ago.

In other cases ambiguity about which is 'the' clan ceremonial ground reflects not divergent alliances of the whole clan but the separate activities of its sections, fostered by big-men. In K. Mandembo clan, for instance, each of the two sections has one or more pena of its own, and neither acknowledges the pena of the other fully as that for all the Mandembo. The two 'rival' grounds are nos. 26 and 27, and it can be seen that each is associated with a big-man. In about 1960 both sections combined to pay a death-compensation to K. Kundmbo clan on pena no. 26. This was not long after the pena was first laid out. Ongka had already

[1] The final prestation, involving all the Tipuka clans, was made at no. 7, a very large, old-established pena closer to Kendipi territory than no. 10.

built no. 27 for himself at Waimorong. Previously, the two sections had simply used the main Mbukl pena together; separately, Kurupmbo section had made moka at the settlement of an outstanding big-man of their group, Mel (disused pena, no. 30); while the Ngglammbo had made separate moka also, at no. 20, high on the hills of the Jimi divide. With the establishment of no. 26, ostensibly as a pena for all the Mandembo, but in fact as a mark of the leadership of Nykint, the Kurupmbo big-man who has emerged as successor to Mel (Mel died also about 1960, when no. 26 was made), Kurupmbo and Ngglammbo have become more separate. In May 1966 the Kurupmbo made a substantial death-compensation payment at no. 26 *without* joint action by Ngglammbo: instead, the latter simply subsidised them by making a prestation to them which helped them to make their own gift later. This was arranged by Ongka and Nykint. While separating themselves, these two big-men rigorously avoid internecine competition; in fact, as the last example shows, they explicitly arrange things together. Both payments mentioned were obligatory; what is arranged in these cases is the *timing* and *sequence* of the prestations, as we see in later chapters.

In this case, then, the two big-men have managed to separate the activities of their sections amicably enough. In other cases there is more conflict, as three further examples will show.

1. In 1964-5 competition and a measure of hostility were building up between two leaders within a *single sub-clan* of M. Yelipi clan. Previously these two had shared a single ceremonial ground. In 1964, to accommodate the pig-stakes[1] of both, a new section of ground was levelled, running out from the old ceremonial ground, and the separate stakes of the two rivals ran out from the poklambo in opposite directions. A third faction in the clan made their own gifts at a further pena. In an attempt to hide the breach, all the Yelipi combined to dance at one pena and then moved in procession to the other to make their speeches; but the atmosphere was bitter, for one of the big-men had been forced into making moka before he was ready. (This case is treated in more detail in a later chapter.)

2. Fig. 1 shows the internal subdivisions of T. Oklembo clan. In 1965, when the Oklembo were making pig-moka, three small *rapa* groups (sub-sub-clans) whose men all live near to Pokløndi ceremonial ground (no. 14) refused to bring their pigs over to the ground of their clan-section's acknowledged leader (no. 12, Marorong).[2] Instead, they gave their pigs away separately, the ostensible aim being to 'hurry the others up'. A young big-man who lives at Pokløndi was at the centre of the dispute, and he seems to have been challenging the older leaders of his clan-section, who live at Mararong. After violent words, and a little physical buffeting, the rebel agreed to bring his pigs for a final ceremonial transfer at the main pena the following day.

---

[1] *Kng pup*. These are strong stakes driven in rows into the ceremonial ground. To each a pig is attached by a piece of rope when live pigs are given away in moka. After a moka, the stakes are removed.

[2] This pena was visited, according to informants, by J. L. Taylor on his way back from the Jimi Valley during an early expedition out from Mount Hagen. Its name has subsequently appeared on various maps of New Guinea.

Ceremonial grounds

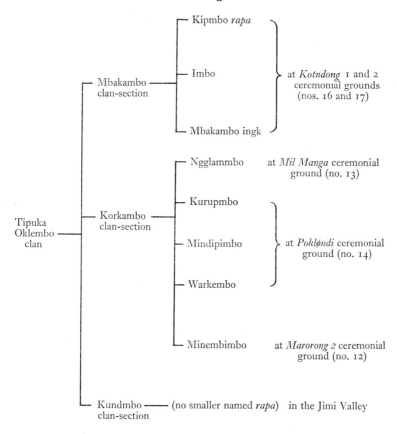

Fig. 1   Tipuka Oklembo segmentation

3. Within Ngglammbo section among the Kawelka there was conflict in 1965 between Ongka and an old big-man, Roklpa, who lived at the earlier Ngglammbo pena, no. 20 (mentioned before). Ongka in 1965 proposed to complete a moka long before Roklpa and his sons were ready to join him in doing so, and they refused to give him any help. Instead, they cleared no. 20, which had not been used for many years, and made their own moka at it separately some time after Ongka finished his. Ongka commented that he did not wish to upset his section-mates, but he was used to 'going it alone' without their aid.

The rivalry of leaders, then, precipitates disagreements within the clan, which centre on *when* and *where* a moka is to be made. The status of segments is not altered immediately by such disputes; and groups which act separately in one context may act jointly in another. But there is little doubt that such rivalry over moka does influence patterns of segmentation

49

E

and fission over long periods of time. Fission, for example, seems to be developing in Mandembo clan as a result of the activities of Nykint and Ongka.

Segmentation of a clan can also occur in connection with exchange activities, but need not necessarily be a direct precipitate of rivalry between big-men.

Well within the lifetime of contemporary old men, Kawelka Kundmbo clan consisted of two segments only, Kumapei and Roklambo. Men of the two segments lived close together, partly for defence in warfare. Internal fighting broke out between the two, which one old informant explained as 'because the place was full and there was not enough ground for us to live on'. It seems likely that this is an example of the 'irritation coefficient' which Rappaport (1967: 116) has suggested for the Maring: living close together, men were more likely to quarrel over thefts, damage done to gardens by pigs, seduction of women, and so on. The two sub-clans solved this problem by combining to drive out a small neighbouring clan (Monggopokae) of the Kombukla tribe which was living isolated from the main body of clans in its tribe: the Roklambo moved out to occupy the defeated clan's territory. Some years later a minor big-man of T. Kitepi clan was officiating at a distribution of cooked pork to mark the end of a period of mourning after a death. In the course of the distribution, he recognised the new expansion of the Kundmbo by calling out a number of separate names for sets of men living at different settlements. The names and groupings were adopted and have remained, so that Kumapei and Roklambo are now clan-section names, and each contains a number of sub-clan names. The choice of sets of men, however, probably in the first place related to the followings of a number of big-men within Kundmbo.

Although a big-man can, and, in fact, must, base himself on an external network of partners as well as on a following within his own clan, separate segments do seem to emerge with growing numbers, whether each segment initially has a leader or not. However, even if each segment is not the creation of its own big-man, eminent big-men may decide names of, and the allocation of persons to, a number of segments. One big-man (Ongka) told me: 'We make our small men's house names when we have five or ten men here, five men there, and five men elsewhere.' He was speaking particularly of the very small subdivisions inside his own clan-section, but gave this as a general statement of how small segment names are created. Other big-men added to this point that they often exaggerate the size of their group by dividing it into segments and telling outsiders: 'We are numerous, give separately to each one of our named groups.' The division is often made on the basis of settlement-affiliation rather than lineage membership, although there is often congruence between these two criteria, particularly as new lineage names and groupings are created from time to time to fit with patterns of residence and the followings of big-men.

To sum up this section: big-men are important both in creating and in strengthening group-segments within the clan. Segmentation does not take place simply through the growth and branching of lineages, but is determined by splits in residence and in the support-groups of big-men. Big-men foster both the opposition and the effective separation of segments. Nevertheless, segments can come into being and continue to operate without a big-man of their own; and big-men, because they can rely on an external network of exchange partners, do not need to have clear and exclusive command of a particular segment in their clan. Big-men often have their own ceremonial ground, or are prominent users of a sub-clan or sub-sub-clan ground; but neither they nor their segments *need* have a ceremonial ground which is exclusively their own. Major big-men, however, are very likely to have laid out their own ceremonial ground; after their death, or if they move elsewhere, these grounds are likely to be abandoned: that is, enduring groups do not always crystallise round the moka pena made by individual big-men.[1] It is probable that with the cessation of warfare big-men have been able to establish small settlements and moka pena of their own more easily, and the fluidity of their support-groups may also have increased. One general point is that, if big-men's sons were always their successors, one would expect to find a more rigid pattern of association between lineages of leaders, clan-segments, ceremonial grounds, and processes of fission. As it is, big-men may appear within any of the lineages and settlements of a clan, and do not necessarily have direct successors. Clan-structure is, in fact, very different from systems in which rank or political headship is confined to single lineages, or a number of specified lineages, by rules of succession. In such systems clans may be conceptualised as consisting of core or high-ranking lineages, around which cluster junior segments or accretions to the authentic stem. In Hagen, and in the other New Guinea Highlands societies, no such conceptualisation occurs, for there are no true offices of political headship

---

[1] Ten out of twelve grounds associated with sub-sub-clans or small lineages were also described as the grounds 'of' big-men. Seven of the ten were in fact *most* strongly associated with the big-man and not with his whole sub-sub-clan. Two were previously used corporately by sub-sub-clans when their members lived close together in times of warfare, but are now becoming disused. Only one was described as a true sub-sub-clan pena in 1964.

governed by rules of succession around which such a structure could be created.

Big-men are, however, partly constrained by their clan's past alliances and exchanges with other groups, and in the next chapter I shall discuss warfare, alliances, and exchanges based on compensation for killings. I shall argue that there was a definite distinction between minor and major enemies, which is highly relevant to exchanges made nowadays; but that big-men may transcend this distinction by extending moka relations to ex-major enemies.

4

WARFARE, ALLIANCE AND COMPENSATION

'We would stop fighting only when we were all tired and heavily wounded.
A big-man would stand up and speak of the marriages between the groups
involved. So we would decide to exchange cooked pig-meat and make
peace.'   Ongka, a big-man of Kawelka Mandembo clan

THE GENERAL STRUCTURE OF WARFARE RELATIONS

Anthropologists have often written of the importance of warfare in New
Guinea Highlands societies before their pacification by Europeans, and
from these writings one gains the impression that Highlanders are excitable,
proud, and physically aggressive men. Barnes (1962: 6) has contrasted
African and New Guinea societies in these terms, suggesting that in New
Guinea there is a greater stress on individual prowess in killing and less
emphasis on traditional alliances between segmentary groups.

There is much truth in this picture, yet it needs correcting in a number
of ways. In the first place, it is scarcely possible to make a block contrast
between Africa and New Guinea in terms of male aggressiveness. An
emphasis on personal strength is, in fact, common in acephalous, segmentary societies throughout the world.[1] Evans-Pritchard (1940) for
example, speaks of the Nuer as proud, independent men, quick to fight
if they were offended or their interests were threatened.

Second, the stress on warlike prowess varies in intensity throughout
the Highlands. It is very strong in some of the fringe Highlands societies
and in Central Highland societies of West Irian (e.g. the Hewa, Steadman
n.d., and the Mbogoga Ndani, Ploeg 1965). It is strong also in some of the
Eastern Highland societies, for example the Kamano (Berndt 1962), the
Bena Bena (Langness 1964), and the Tairora (Watson 1967). Men of
violence – whom Salisbury (1964) has dubbed 'despots' – seem to have
arisen sporadically in a number of other Highlands societies also. But in
many of the large, central Highland areas, where population density is
heavy, men of violence were not necessarily the important political leaders.

[1] Nor, of course, is it confined to them. I am *not* here arguing that aggressiveness is a
precipitate of a particular kind of political structure. The amount of aggressiveness
regularly displayed, however, may well be a *correlate* of certain kinds of territorial and
political systems.

And this is correlated with the fact that in these areas there were well-developed inter-group alliances, gradations of enemy relationships, controls on the escalation of fighting, and means whereby big-men could arrange truces and compensation payments between groups.

Further, big-men were precisely the ones who fostered alliances and controls of this kind. Warfare was what decided the ultimate balance or imbalance of physical power between territorial groups; but there were, and are, other ways in which competitive spirit and aggressiveness could find expression. Pre-eminent among these 'other ways' is ceremonial exchange. In many cases in the Highlands (e.g. the Siane, Salisbury 1962) exchange institutions effloresced and developed to a larger scale when Europeans banned warfare. This was not simply a result of a blockage on traditional means of gaining prestige and power; rather, it was an expression of the interests of big-men in pursuing an avenue of self-aggrandisement which was more effective and less hazardous than warfare itself. Thus it is that we find Kyaka big-men (Bulmer 1960a) urging groups which were still fighting to give up warfare and join in the massive cyclical exchange ceremony, the *tee*, instead. In Hagen also one still hears frequently statements of the type: 'before we fought and killed each other, and this was bad; now a good time has come, and we can pay for killings and make *moka*.' Although such statements are *post hoc* evaluations, they do reflect the fact that *moka* and warfare are seen as two different ways of asserting group and individual prowess.

Against the picture of the fearsome, individualistic man of violence, then, we can place that of the big-man operating in and on a context of group alliances and striving for status through the accumulation and dispersal of wealth.

What, then, was the pattern of warfare in Hagen? I have suggested that there were relatively stable alliances between groups and that these are still important in exchange relationships nowadays. We need to be able to state whether these alliances are of the classic, segmentary kind which Evans-Pritchard first identified among the Nuer. Paula Brown, writing of the Chimbu Highlanders (Brown 1964), has remarked that a study of Chimbu warfare leads to the identification of a segmentary pattern of alliances, but the pattern seems to have been very fragile. Chimbu military alliances, in other words, were not very stable or predictable. It is possible that the further away in time the period of endemic warfare becomes, the more informants are likely to simplify warfare patterns, or to make them more rigid, or to attribute actions to whole groups which in fact involved only certain individuals of the groups; and my own work in Hagen,

Warfare, alliance and compensation

unlike that of the 'first wave' of anthropologists in the Highlands, was done twenty years or more after warfare had been stopped. A further danger is that informants may project back onto the past features of their current political situations so that, while their ostensibly historical account is covertly valid for the present, it is invalid for the period which it overtly purports to describe. Nevertheless, I think it is possible to identify certain main processes in Hagen warfare, and to state how military alliances worked.[1]

Two basic distinctions are important: first, the distinction between major, traditional enemies (*el parka wuə*, = 'red bird of paradise war man', i.e. the man who fights you with his full war-apparel on), and minor enemies (*el øninga wuə, el namb wuə*); and, second, the distinction, in any particular bout of warfare, between combatants who are the 'root men of war' (*el pukl wuə*) and those who are their allies (*kui wuə* = literally 'dead men', from the fact that allies might die fighting for the 'root men's' cause).

Given these two distinctions, a small number of propositions can be made. First, except in the case of very large tribes, such as the Ndika and Mokei, there are no true major-enemy relationships within the tribe. In the very large tribes such a relationship may hold between major sections, but not between clans within a major section. Second, it is often the case that a tribe has a single other tribe as its traditional major enemy. Third, since tribes are often joined in pairs, it may emerge that one pair is opposed to another. In this case, in a particular war, it is likely that one tribe in a pair will become involved in fighting against its own major enemy first; and the same for its enemy. Its main ally is likely to be the tribe with which it is paired, and its leading men will call on men of this tribe to help it. The two tribes thus stand in the relationship of *el pukl wuə* and *kui wuə*, and when the particular bout of warfare is over, the 'root men' must pay their allies for any losses they have sustained. Failure to do so would mean defection of the ally or an open attack from its men. In practice, not all the clans of the tribes involved would actively fight on each occasion; but the relationship is still potentially one between the tribes as a whole. Fourth, within the tribe, between paired tribes, and between clans in additional ally-relationships, only minor warfare takes place. In minor warfare there is no attempt made to annihilate the opponents. They may be chased from their territory but not permanently disseized of it. Moreover, it is always expected that minor warfare will end in explicit peace-making and will be followed by direct compensation for killing between the enemies. Fifth, such minor enemies are likely to be

[1] It is an aid here to have the much earlier work of Vicedom (1943–8), who was working at Ogelbeng long before large parts of the Hagen area were pacified.

allies on other occasions, typically in battles against major enemies, either those common or those specific to each other. When they are allies they stand in the *el pukl wuə/kui wuə* relationship, each in turn occupying the role of the 'dead man', who is owed reparations. Minor enemies thus have two reasons for making war payments to each other: as direct compensation for reciprocal killings, and as reparation for reciprocal services in major warfare. Finally, clans which are paired as allies do not normally fight en masse against each other at all, although they may threaten to do so on occasion; so that such pairs usually form solidary cores of alliance in particular wars.

Although these propositions hold in the main, it would be a mistake to imagine that warfare proceeded automatically in the terms which I have suggested. In some cases allies might be reluctant or unable to help, because of other military commitments. Certain men might not turn up because they had quarrels with individual men among the group requesting aid. Kinsfolk and affines of the group immediately embroiled were those most likely in general to help. In addition, further allies might be called in for an important battle: either clans whose help was specifically obtained for hire, or the allies or other kinsfolk of one's immediate allies. Wars could thus escalate; or, if allies were hard to obtain, they could remain the affair of two principal antagonist groups only. Although the system of alliances made it possible in many cases for groups to hold their own against each other without gaining much advantage, in other cases there were defeats and migrations of the conquered from their original territory, either as a whole group or as scattered individual refugees. Such an upset in the balance of power could result from the split-up of a pair of allied clans, which might leave these not only opposed to each other but without any other effective ally. The weaker of the two was then likely to be dislodged from its territory.

SPECIFIC ACCOUNTS OF WARFARE

Specific examples of warfare and alliances within and between tribes will enable me to illustrate and modify the analytical sketch I have given in the previous section, and to draw out the significance of what may be called 'fields of warfare'.

First, I shall consider the configuration of relationships within the two largest tribes in the Northern Melpa area, Tipuka and Minembi, in order to show the *de facto* strength of clan-pairing and the degree of opposition between tribe-sections. Both tribes number well over 2,000 persons;[1] the distribution of

[1] These population figures relate to 1962, and are now out of date. In a neighbouring area Administration officers have estimated a net increase of 1·7% in population per year. If this holds, the Tipuka by 1968 must number about 2,721, and the Minembi over 3,000.

Warfare, alliance and compensation

population between their main segments is shown in Figs. 2 and 3 (see pp. 61 and 63). The two tribes are traditional major enemies.

In discussing the relationship between clan pairs I ask a number of questions about their friendship or hostility:

1. Are paired clans closely intermarried? (In some cases I rely on informants' own statements about this, when I have no census details. In further cases, the two clans form a single exogamous unit.)

2. Is there overlap between their territories, as a result of their giving refuge to each other in the past or of current grants of land claims?

3. Did they always help each other when one became involved against an enemy?

4. Was there in the past internal warfare between them?

5. Have there been quarrels between them over compensation and reparation payments?

6. Have they ever been on opposite sides in a battle, as allies of other groups?

7. Have there been accusations of poisoning between them?

Affirmative answers to the first three questions indicate positive alliance; to the last four questions they indicate a degree of hostility. In Table 6 I have summarised answers for the Tipuka tribe. In the case of the Minembi I give a more discursive account, to bring out points which cannot be shown schematically.

Affirmatives are represented in the Table as +; negatives as −.

TABLE 6   *Relationships between clan pairs in (a) Tipuka, (b) Minembi tribe*

(a) TIPUKA

Pairs	Questions						
	1	2	3	4	5	6	7
Kitepi (and Eltimbo)–Oklembo	+[a]	+	+	threatened	+	−	−
Ndikmbo–Wanyembo	+?	−	−	threatened	−	−	+
Kengeke–Kendike	+	+	+	once[b]	+	−	once
Kelmbo–Waembe	now one[c] exogamous unit	+	+	−	−	−	−

[a] Eltimbo and Kitepi are especially closely linked. Some Eltimbo men say they can no longer intermarry with Kitepi, there are so many marriages between them.

[b] This arose from a single poisoning accusation, and is spoken of as a matter of shame. One sub-clan of Kengeke joined the Kendike as a result of the fighting and now intermarries with both Kendike and the other Kengeke sub-clans.

[c] The Kelmbo are very numerous. Waembe is being incorporated into Kelmbo as a sub-clan, instead of being pair-clan of Kelmbo.

(b) MINEMBI

Andaoukam section

Papeke–Yelipi: 1. Till very recently the two were a single exogamous unit. Only since their physical separation and estrangement have they begun to intermarry. In 1964 two marriages had been contracted.

2. No. There may have been in the past, but the Yelipi have changed their territory. Cf. 6.

3. No. Papeke did not help Yelipi when they were involved in warfare as allies of Tipuka Kengeke clan. Cf. 6.

4. No. The two had no direct 'root of war' with each other.

5. After fighting, in which they were ranged on opposite sides, direct death-compensations between them were made. Both sides were anxious to take these up, but, owing to suspicions of poisoning, the only Yelipi men who could act as go-betweens to arrange payments were a pair of brothers, who had been brought up among, and were cross-cousins of, Papeke men.

6. Yes. The Yelipi were attacked by a neighbouring section of the Engambo clan, and were driven out from their old territory, which the Engambo took over. In the fighting the Papeke and the Engambo's own pair clan, Kimbo, helped *against* Yelipi, who were left without allies. Yelipi men scattered, but later re-formed in a new territory granted them by maternal kin of one of their big-men, Kambila. The maternal kin were of Tipuka Kengeke clan. Subsequently an alliance between Kengeke and Yelipi developed, *across* the supposed disjunction of major enemy relations between the Tipuka and Minembi tribes.

7. Yes. It was these which caused the split between the two clans. It is possible that Yelipi were, until the split, only a sub-clan within the Papeke clan. The Yelipi speak with bitterness of their 'betrayal' by the Papeke and the loss of their old territory.

Engambo–Kimbo: 1. Yes.

2. No.

3. Yes. For example, Kimbo helped Engambo against Yelipi, and Engambo helped Kimbo against a Kombukla clan, the Monggopokae.

4. Yes. Neither side gained an advantage.

5. No severe quarrels.

6. No.

7. ?Yes. Note: there is a poorly remembered dogma of agnatic linkage between these two, which is preserved in the Minembi origin myth.

Andakelkam section

Nambakae–Ropkembo: I cannot answer each question here. Ropkembo is practically an incorporated group within Nambakae. Ally-payments, however, are still made between the two. Nambakae are the most distant of the Minembi tribes from the Tipuka and Kawelka tribes, their major enemies, and were probably involved in warfare relations with clans closer to Ogelbeng.

Mimke–Napakae: 1. The two are a single exogamous unit. Their spatial separation and separate names are explained as follows:

(*a*) A Mimke man stole a pig belonging to a man of the Nambakae, and Nambakae, aided by one of the clans of Kombukla tribe drove them out for this. They lost many men, and others joined different clans as refugees. That is why Mimke are now so few. The Engambo allowed Mimke to settle on land to which they themselves held claims, and now there are difficulties over this settlement.

(*b*) Mimke and Napakae are reported in the Minembi myth to have been brothers. Napakae was only a little boy, but he ate up a large quantity of pig-meat, and for this his elders boxed him on the ears, whereupon he announced that he could no longer be the same as Mimke but must be called 'the greedy one' (Napakae). The story is clearly a way of describing the growth of the Napakae sub-group into a unit big enough to claim shares of its own in distributions of meat.

2. Previously, not now. Cf. 1(*a*).

3. Yes, except when they could not reach each other in time, since Papeke clan territory divides them.
4. No.
5. No.
6. No.
7. ? No.

Komonkae–Ruprupkae: 1. Yes.

2. Yes, the territories are closely intertwined.
3. Yes.
4. No.
5. No.
6. No.
7. No. These two are closely allied. They are a numerically weak pair, and have had to co-operate to ensure their survival. They live in the Baiyer Valley, at an altitude below 4,500 ft a.s.l., in an area which is hot and harbours death-adder snakes. Groups living there have all been decimated in warfare and further reduced by sickness. Many have been driven there as a place of refuge, not wanted by more powerful groups. Komonkae–Ruprupkae were faced with the expanding Membo clan of Kawelka tribe on their eastern borders, and maintained close unity against this enemy. They were widely separated from the bulk of the other clans of their tribe, and were at odds with their neighbour Minembi clan, the Kimbo.

The *de facto* strength of alliance between paired clans thus varies considerably, from a situation of close co-operation in all areas of social and political activity, through a situation of mutual aid in warfare against others together with a certain uneasiness resulting from quarrels – which could arise over thefts of pigs or valued garden produce, or over adulteries and seductions – to a situation of definite estrangement and antagonism, when the relationship may be broken off. The middle situation is the most common one. The first is a product of adversity; the third is an ever-present possibility, especially if the groups are unequally matched in size and one can dominate the other. The weaker clan, or clan-segment if the two have not yet split, may detach itself or be driven out, and search for a new territory and a new set of alliances, perhaps becoming more closely involved with a clan of a different tribe. Such cross-tribal alliance pairings occur, as in the case of the Minembi Yelipi clan, in response to imbalances of power within the tribe. Another example is the alliance pairing between one of the Kawelka clans, the Kundmbo, and the Minembi Kimbo. There are only three clans within Kawelka tribe, and two of these are allied in opposition to the Kundmbo. These two – Membo and Mandembo – could outnumber the Kundmbo, so the latter's alliance with Kimbo was a matter of expediency. As in the case of the Yelipi again, this alliance cross-cuts the disjunction between major enemy tribes. Cross-tribal alliance and imbalances within particular tribes thus complicate any attempt to analyse warfare patterns in terms of balanced build-ups, following lines of segmentation within tribes. However, one factor did limit the escalation of minor warfare: minor enemies would not be able to call in their own major enemies as allies against each other. Instead, the proposition works only in the reverse direction, minor enemies acting as allies against each other's major enemies. Groups which were major enemies would rarely act as allies of each other, except when they could find a cause which suited the interests of them both. I suggest – although I cannot show this from informants' statements – that the balance of power was again a consideration here. Clans of a single tribe do not make major enemies of each other, for otherwise they might not be able to face other tribes united, and their traditional major enemies might overthrow them. In the very largest tribes, each major section could hold its own against almost all-comers, and effective alliance between the sections thus broke down. Where warfare between clans of a tribe approached the bitterness of major enemy relationships, it is interesting to note that the clans involved often buttressed their position with cross-tribal ties. The alliances of Yelipi and Kundmbo clans are instances of this. I shall examine the configuration of fighting within the Tipuka and Minembi tribes again, in order to place my analysis further into its context.

There are three main blocs within Tipuka tribe, and all three fought each other in minor warfare. The fighting was particularly bitter between Kitepi and Kengeke clans, and the two still do not make direct exchanges of war payments. Instead, Kengeke men give to Eltimbo and Kendike clansmen, who in turn give to Kitepi. This was one factor in the moka chain which I observed during 1964–5, and which will be described later. Kengeke clan also brought in its allies, Yelipi, against the Kitepi who responded by calling in *their* cross-tribal allies from the Kawelka.

Reference to the Tipuka segmentary paradigm (Fig. 2) shows that the sections are not of equal size. Akelkae are the least numerous (but, incidentally, the most united) with 519 persons, Kengeke–Kendike have 724, and Anmbilika have 1,176, but are the least united, for two of their clans, Ndikmbo and Wanyembo, live mainly in the Jimi Valley and were in the recent past imperfectly integrated with the other pair, Kitepi–Oklembo; the latter two together number 812. Kengeke–Kendike+Yelipi (724+250 = 974) would thus be a reasonable match for Kitepi–Oklembo+helpers from two of the Kawelka clans.

It is evident, however, that any two of the sections could outnumber the third. The maximum case would be Anmbilika+Kengeke–Kendike *versus* Akelkae; the minimum Kengeke–Kendike+Akelkae *versus* Anmbilika. Of the possible combinations only the minimum one seems to have occurred. The maximum case would be unlikely, given the hostility between Anmbilika and the Kengeke–Kendike pair. Similarly, Anmbilika were very hostile towards Akelkae, who had many links with major enemies of the Anmbilika, the Wəlyi tribesmen. Here we find a situation familiar in minor warfare: clans do not regularly arrange crushing alliances against each other. One reason for this is the incidence of independent quarrels between single clans. Each clan, or each pair of clans, would often be involved in some fight of its own, and thus would not be able to enlist *en bloc* in another bout of fighting. Because of these independent commitments the full possibilities of bloc warfare were never played out within the Tipuka tribe; and this holds for other tribes also. Generalising, we can say that controls on warfare within the tribe were largely a result of the difficulty of making effective alliances *for minor warfare only* beyond the level of the clan pair. Blocs of two

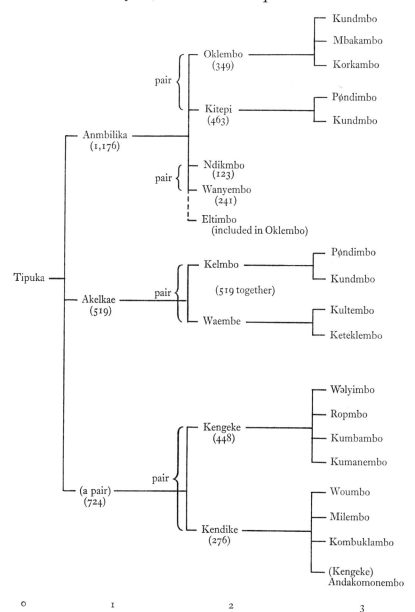

The paradigm is taken to the sub-clan or clan-section level only. Population figures are from the L.G.C. survey. The exogamous groups are at level 2, the 'clan' level.

Fig. 2   Tipuka segmentation

clans versus two others regularly emerged, but escalation did not proceed to a higher level.

It is true that there could be a certain amount of escalation in minor warfare, in that some men at least from clans of neighbouring tribes were drawn into fights internal to the Tipuka; but large numbers could be called in only from cross-tribal paired clans, and, as we have seen, the aid given by these tended to cancel itself out. The scope for build-ups was small, for the edges of possible escalation were defined by the presence of major enemy clans along Tipuka borders. Within the Tipuka themselves, the all-round enmity between the three different sections precluded the likelihood of a stable combination of any two against a third. Moreover, the 'gains' from such a bloc offensive would have been doubtful. Had one Tipuka clan been driven out, the other two would have had to face their major enemies with depleted forces.[1] Before I look at inter-tribal warfare more explicitly, I shall compare the internal situation among the Tipuka with that for the Minembi.

The Minembi (Fig. 3) are divided into two major sections, both rather larger than the Tipuka sections, and neither seems to have formed an effective bloc in warfare. As with the Tipuka, the effective alliance-units are clan-pairs. Within Andaoukam section (cf. Table 6(*b*)) there are two such pairs. Papeke–Yelipi and Engambo–Kimbo. If segmentary relationships proceeded on a simple calculus of escalation, one would expect to find the two pairs on occasion ranged with each other. In fact, this did not occur. In the first place we have seen how the Papeke–Yelipi pair broke up and three of the clans combined against Yelipi, the fourth. Second, each clan was involved in affairs of its own with clans of the opposite major section and of other tribes. The dispersal of their military interests meant that all four clans never came together as a whole section, either against the Andakelkam or against outside clans.

Within Andakelkam section there are three pairs, of very unequal size: Nambakae–Ropkembo (741) persons, Napakae–Mimke (267), Ruprupkae–Komonkae (177). The first and last pairs are widely separated by intervening clan territories (cf. Map 2 on p. 24), and never came into direct conflict. Mimke–Napakae successively fought the Nambakae (and were defeated, as could be expected, for even then they had fewer men than Nambakae), and a section of the Engambo clan in the opposite major division of the tribe. Komonkae –Ruprupkae, with help from their neighbours of a different tribe, the Klamakae, struggled against the drive outwards of the expanding Kawelka Membo clan.

---

[1] I am speculating here on the situation. I do not know if Tipuka men specifically thought the matter out in this way. It is not enough, however, merely to say that the situation resulted from the strength of dogmas of 'brotherhood' between different clans of the tribe. 'Brother' clans or sections of them *were* on occasion driven out: as when some Kitepi were forced up to Buk, and the Wanyembo were chased over into the Jimi Valley, by Kendike. Yet the Kendike did not push their victory into a complete domination of the Kitepi. I suggest both that no group was equipped to rule another large group in this way and that the Kitepi were valuable to the Kendike on occasion as allies against their common major enemies.

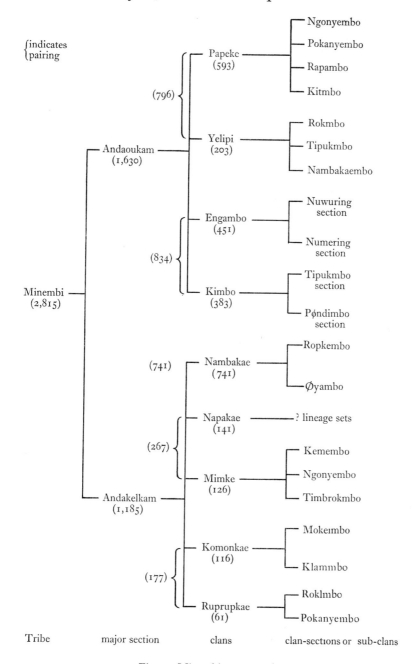

<table>
<thead>
<tr><th>Tribe</th><th>major section</th><th>clans</th><th>clan-sections or sub-clans</th></tr>
</thead>
</table>

Fig. 3   Minembi segmentation

In Andakelkam section also, then, there is neither bloc warfare nor a regular segmentary build-up of oppositions. Andakelkam clans fought with, and were allies of, both each other and Minembi clans in the opposite section. Clan and clan-pair appear as the significant units of solidarity and alliance.

Moreover, the two major sections never emerged as blocs against each other. Their divergent inter-clan affairs drew them away from any such engagement. And, although the tribe as a whole is linked in alliance with Kombukla tribe, its total complement of clans never seems to have mustered for battle in the major warfare against the Tipuka–Kawelka pair. By contrast, Tipuka and Kawelka on occasion did combine as whole groups. Possibly the greater size, as well as the geographical spread, of the Minembi helps to explain this situation.

This analysis of warfare within two tribes thus reveals that the segmentation paradigm of a tribe does not necessarily give the key to segmentary political relations within it. Political relations do not necessarily follow the apparent major lines of 'cleavage' in the tribe, nor does warfare escalate simply along lower lines of cleavage to the higher ones. Instead, if we are to understand the actual patterns of warfare, we must concentrate on individual clans and clan-pairs. Although the system is segmentary in the broad sense that clans opposed in minor warfare would unite for major warfare, it does not follow all the features of segmentary political structure which Evans-Pritchard propounded for the Nuer.

As my discussion has also indicated, major, inter-tribal warfare was also not so simply structured as might be supposed from the initial explanatory comments of informants. In making these, informants tend to speak of whole tribes as units. Thus they will generalise that two paired tribes are allies against each other's major enemies and that between the two themselves there is only minor warfare. For example, Tipuka and Kawelka are said to have helped each other against each other's major enemies. In practice, however, build-ups to the level of one tribe-pair versus the other were inhibited by cross-cutting alliances and areas of neutrality.[1]

Thus, an engagement between two clans belonging to opposed major enemy tribes would not necessarily result in all the other clans joining in. When the Kawelka clan-pair, Membo–Mandembo, attacked their Minembi foes, Komonkae–Ruprupkae, the other Minembi clans did *not* come to the latter's aid. On the contrary, one of the Minembi clans, Kimbo, actually helped the two Kawelka clans, who were on other occasions their opponents in major warfare. Given this unusual alliance, other Minembi clans would have been risking a great deal had they travelled through intervening clan-territories to help the isolated Komonkae–Ruprupkae pair. This cross-cutting alliance of Kimbo with Kawelka

---

[1] Throughout the discussion which follows I deal with warfare as an affair between solidary groups of men. But it has to be remembered that there is a certain artificiality in this. In practice, on many occasions only those men who had strong ties with the men of the principal combatant group (I borrow this term for the *el pukl wuə* from Rappaport 1967) would actively go to their help as allies; and conversely men who had maternal kin or close affines in an *enemy* group to their own would either opt out of fighting that group or would at least avoid killing their close relatives in an engagement.

1 *a*   A big-man (Kawelka Nykint)
        harangues his clansmen

1 *b*   A big-man (Tipuka Kele) runs
        his eye over pigs at a moka

2a Moka among the Kuli (E. Melpa): men parade in *kanan*
2b Moka among the Kuli (E. Melpa): women perform *werl*

was founded on two circumstances: first, the Kimbo were independently enemies of one of the groups which did help Komonkae–Ruprupkae; and, second, they were firm allies of one of the Kawelka clans, the Kundmbo – an alliance which, as I have mentioned, was contracted by the Kundmbo in order to hold their own against the other two Kawelka clans in the first instance. The four clans together – Kundmbo–Kimbo and Membo–Mandembo – were much too strong for Komonkae–Ruprupkae and their allies (members of other small clans local to the Baiyer), and the result was a defeat for the latter with temporary dispersal and severe losses. Membo clansmen took over some territory before occupied by the Klamakae, main allies of Komonkae–Ruprupkae. This example of a special alliance made between erstwhile major enemies indicates two things: first, there is no automatic solidarity within a tribe. There are many enmities between a tribe's constituent clans, and if it suits their interests clansmen will even combine with their major enemies to fight against clans of their own tribe. The usual motive cited is a desire to obtain revenge for past killings. Second, when an alliance of this kind is made, equilibrium can be destroyed. One side gathers more powerful forces, and a definite defeat is inflicted. While the fighting does not 'escalate' so as to involve large numbers of clans, this should not be taken to imply that killings are thereby kept to a minimum. It is clear, in fact, that if only other Minembi clans *had* helped Komonkae–Ruprupkae in this sequence of fighting the Kawelka advance would have been contained. On the other hand, the absence of escalation meant that the Kawelka were never faced with a full trial of strength against all of the Minembi; had this occurred, the whole Kawelka tribe would certainly have been defeated and perhaps forced to disperse.

Effectively, then, the bulk of the Minembi clans remained neutral when Komonkae–Ruprupkae were attacked by the Kawelka. The same kind of process can be seen in minor warfare between Tipuka and Kawelka clans. Fighting is most likely to break out between groups which are neighbours, since contiguity provides the occasions for theft, seduction, and encroachment on territory which spark off aggressiveness. In this case Kitepi–Oklembo are the Tipuka neighbours of Kawelka Membo–Mandembo, and they were alternately their allies in some of their bouts of major warfare and their minor enemies in fights over local upsets of the kind I have mentioned above. This bloc of four clans represented the strongest area of mutual interest between Tipuka and Kawelka clans. Other clans of the same two tribes did not necessarily become involved if one of these four clans was involved against, or as an ally of, another one.

Nevertheless, allies of allies were sometimes called in, and the scale of combat could rise in this way. Sometimes this creation of alliance strings could result in a balance of power being maintained; on other occasions it meant that the balance was broken. I shall give an example of each outcome.

After their retreat to a new territory, the Minembi Yelipi clansmen continued to fight with the Engambo, who had initiated the action to drive them out. Their hosts and new allies, the Tipuka Kengeke, were also hostile to the Papeke and Mimke clans in the Yelipi's own tribe. Kengeke–Yelipi could thus be faced with an alliance of Papeke, Mimke, and Engambo, which would outnumber

F

them. However, because the Minembi as a whole (except for Yelipi clan) were regarded as major enemies by Tipuka and Kawelka clans, two further blocs could be called on by Kengeke–Yelipi to help them: Kitepi–Oklembo of Tipuka and Membo–Mandembo of Kawelke. As a result, their opponents in turn were in danger of being outnumbered, but they called in the Engambo's pair-clan, Kimbo, and also the small Komonkae–Ruprupkae pair, and further helpers from a neighbouring tribe, the Kope. (Kimbo and Komonkae–Ruprupkae were thus allies in this sequence of fights, whereas they were enemies in the sequence described earlier.)[1] The total array was thus:

(*Tipuka* Kengeke+*Minembi* Yelipi)+(*Tipuka* Kitepi–Oklembo)+(*Kawelka* Membo–Mandembo) *versus* (*Minembi* Papeke+Mimke)+(*Minembi* Engambo–Kimbo)+(*Minembi* Komonkae–Ruprupkae)+(some *Kope* helpers).

Six of the ten Minembi clans were thus involved on one side of the battle, and it is clear that a considerable string of alliances was mobilised around the initial opposition of Kengeke to Papeke and Yelipi to Engambo. Yet not *all* of the clans belonging to the tribes involved joined in. In particular, one Kawelka clan, the Kundmbo, could do nothing, for it had ties with both sides; and other clans of Tipuka and Minembi were more distant from the area of battle and preferred to remain neutral. Neither side on this occasion gained a particular advantage.

An example from the Nebilyer Valley provides a case where the outcome was different. The Elti–Penambe tribe-pair were driven from this area up to the Ogelbeng Plain by a powerful coalition of enemies. For the Elti the major enemies were sections of the Mokei tribe, for the Penambe the Kope.[2] This forms a familiar pattern, for Mokei and Kope were allies of each other. Elti–Penambe became involved in a series of increasingly bitter fights against these two. The Mokei are a powerful tribe, and they and the Kope eventually made a special pact with all the other surrounding groups to launch a massive attack on Elti–Penambe, who were left without leeway to contract counter-alliances.[3] Some of the Penambe were enabled to escape through warnings received from friends in the Ndika tribe, with whom they took refuge just in time, carrying off their shell valuables and their children in the night before the attack came. (Many of their pigs had earlier been agisted with relatives living in neutral areas – this, of course, was one crucial reason for agisting pigs in this way: to prevent them from becoming spoils of war.)

Old informants of Elti–Penambe in 1965 could remember the names of more

---

[1] Dating sequences of warfare in relation to each other is very difficult. Most of the fights and alliances which I describe certainly took place within the last fifty years. It would be illuminating to know more about the number of fights that occurred about the same time and the ways in which men were actually mustered for battle; but precise information of this kind is hard to obtain.

[2] Not those Kope who live near to the Minembi and were involved in the battle-sequence just outlined, but a separate tribe, living near to the Mokei.

[3] Elti–Penambe seem to have lacked staunch allies. A similar defeat was suffered by the Kulka tribe, who treated their allies poorly and found themselves routed by their major enemies when their allies, instead of helping them, turned to thieving and rape in their settlements behind the battle-front. Allies were expected to behave in this way when aggrieved.

than a hundred men and women killed by the Mokei and their allies in this battle. In most engagements in minor warfare women would not be killed, although they might be abducted or raped by outsiders while their men were fighting. By contrast, in major warfare the aim was to destroy or drive out the enemy; women and children were killed, houses were burnt, pigs were slaughtered, and territory was over-run, at least temporarily.[1] Following this battle, some of the Elti were forced into the forest above their territory, and the Mokei kept watch night and day to prevent them from harvesting their gardens. The refugees survived through receiving small gifts from individual 'friends' (i.e. relatives, probably, or moka partners) in a nearby tribe, and by eating forest shoots and vegetables.[2] Such a watch to prevent besieged enemies from obtaining food would never be maintained in minor warfare. Similarly, in minor warfare the victors would ordinarily allow bodies to be recovered for burial; but major enemies, by contrast, would forestall burial by hacking bodies to pieces, stuffing them with stones and throwing them into a river, or burning them on pyres at the borders of their territory where the clansmen of the dead could see what was happening. These examples help to indicate what major warfare was like. It is scarcely surprising that groups were roused to furious efforts in order to defend themselves or to obtain revenge for depredations, and that equilibrium between major enemies was not always maintained.

FIELDS OF WARFARE

At the cost of some simplification, the situation of different clans in warfare can be represented in terms of 'fields', within which there is a recognisable structure of relations.

From the point of view of the men of a single clan, all other clans fell into one of the following categories:

1. Pair-clans: usually a reliable ally in both minor and major warfare, unless one's own clan were actually fighting it, or the relationships were broken by previous fighting.

2. Minor enemy clans: some of these might be allies of one's own clan in certain sequences of fighting, especially against a common major enemy.

3. Major enemy clans: with these there was never a direct, and only rarely an indirect, military alliance.

---

[1] Hageners do not seem to have set sorcery-traps against invading enemies as the Kuma (Reay 1959: 53) used to do; nor was there a specific taboo on victors immediately occupying the territory of those defeated, as there is among the Maring (Rappaport 1967: 144). Invaders were, however, afraid of the ancestral ghosts of men, buried in a defeated clan's territory (cf. Reay 1959: 53 again for a Kuma parallel), and Vicedom (1943–8, vol. 2: 161) mentions that a defeated clan's ceremonial ground might be destroyed, to drive its ancestor spirits away. Destruction of houses and gardens, and ensuing retreats from territory of those defeated could also occur at times in minor warfare.

[2] Later they migrated and took refuge with one of the Ndika groups, Opramb, with which they had affinal and maternal ties.

4. Neutral clans: these were outside the area of one's own clan's effective commitments in warfare. Occasionally they might be hired for pay to fight for or against one's own clan in some large-scale engagement. Most often they were neutral.

With clans of categories 1 and 2 there was frequent intermarriage; with those of 3 and 4 marriages were more rarely contracted. Thus, major enemies and neutral groups were both people with whom one had a minimum of friendly interaction.

What is more difficult to represent is the extent to which a number of clans were mutually involved in relations of warfare and alliance. To represent this, even partly, I have to restrict myself to the main contexts of minor and major warfare. An example would be what I call the dominant field involving the Tipuka–Kawelka and Kombukla–Minembi tribe-pairs among the Northern Melpa, whose activities I have discussed in the previous section. This I have represented in Fig. 4. In the Figure, the vertical axis divides traditional enemies, the horizontal (dotted) one paired tribes. Tribes horizontally opposed are the ones which were each other's chief major enemy. The two clans whose names are placed *across* the vertical axis are ones which, as we have seen, belong to one tribe but are paired with a clan of a nominally major enemy tribe to their own. There are no such interstitial clans between Kombukla tribe and Tipuka–Kawelka, and this is in fact reflected in the absence of intensive moka exchanges between Tipuka–Kawelka and Kombukla nowadays (except for moka between Kawelka Kundmbo clan, and the tiny, isolated Andakelkam section of Kombukla, which is widely separated from the main body of Kombukla clans).

As we have seen, not all of the clans in these four tribes were equally involved in the field. That is why, in fact, I call it a 'field', *within which* more specific alliances and oppositions emerged. It does, however, depict the main structural constraints influencing these more specific events.

What must be considered in more detail is the extent to which different clans of these tribes, or the whole tribes, were involved in other fields besides this one. Geographical distribution is important. Clans fight or ally themselves with groups whose borders are near to their own; but they do not do so with *all* their neighbours, since some of these fall outside the fields of warfare in which they themselves are involved. This can be shown if we consider each tribe in turn.

Kawelka: Kawelka clans were not involved as principal combatants directly against any clans other than those in this field. Membo clansmen live close to groups involved in another field, to their west, but did not fight in it. Kundmbo clan was not on the best of terms with the Kope, but never fought them directly. (Here there was another factor: Kope men were allies of Kundmbo's own allies, the Kimbo.)

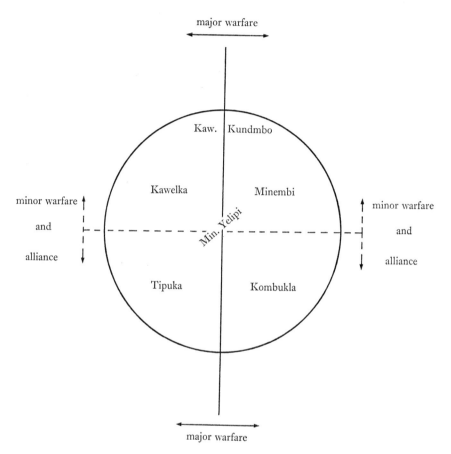

Fig. 4   Fields of warfare 1

Tipuka: The whole of Tipuka tribe was also involved in major warfare against all but two of the clans belonging to Wǝlyi tribe on its eastern borders. To defeat the Wǝlyi they contracted an alliance with clans of Kendipi tribe who hem in the Wǝlyi, from the east, and the Wǝlyi were forced to flee into the Jimi Valley. This field hardly cross-cuts the field shown in Fig. 4 at all. Only a few Kawelka men helped in the fighting against the Wǝlyi; and it was not till after their defeat that some of the Wǝlyi arranged privately with Kombukla men to kill some of the Tipuka in revenge; an arrangement to which the Kombukla, as major enemies of Tipuka, were amenable.

69

Kombukla: Kombukla clans also fought against the Kendipi on their own account. Their opposition to the Kendipi fits with the Tipuka–Kendipi alliance. One can see in these battle sequences an implicit quadripartite field emerging, consisting of Tipuka–Kendipi *versus* Kombukla–Wəlyi. But in fact this potentiality was not realised, and Tipuka gained the advantage by driving out some of the Wəlyi clans.

Minembi: The only two clans which fought in major warfare against clans outside the field in Fig. 4 were Nambakae and Napakae. Both of these clans border with Central Melpa groups to their south, and it was against these that they fought. Correspondingly, Nambakae and Napakae were less involved in warfare against Tipuka–Kawelka. A long mountain ridge separates the rest of the Minembi clans from the Central Melpa groups, and this effectively insulated them from attacks and conflicts of interest with groups to the south of the range other than Nambakae and Napakae themselves; whereas the latter two live on the edge of the grasslands leading over to the Ogelbeng Plain and were directly faced with some of the Central Melpa clans.

One small tribe, the Klamakae, was interstitial between the field given in Fig. 4 and one of the fields in the Baiyer and Jimi Valleys, and this situation I illustrate in Fig. 5. In field A (which represents a particular set of alliances within the field shown in Fig. 4, Kimbo here appearing as interstitial) the Klamakae helped side 2 against side 1; in field B they aided side 1 against side 2. The Kawelka, by contrast, were never engaged against the Andakapkae or Epilkae.

Further complications and overlappings could be shown with the aid of more diagrams, but these two examples are enough to indicate that clans were *variably* involved in the fields which I have described. Nevertheless, these fields were areas of central concern for at least some of the clans involved in them. The warfare relations which were contained within the field given in Fig. 4 are also paralleled nowadays by a complicated crisscrossing of moka relations between the Minembi, Tipuka, and Kawelka tribes.

ORGANISATION AND LEADERSHIP IN WARFARE

Structural analysis of alliances in warfare does not give much insight into its actual organisation or into the 'feel' of warfare to its participants; so in this and the following section I shall discuss briefly organisation, leadership, and the ways of taking revenge for deaths inflicted by enemy action.

As I have pointed out, allies did not always come out in force to the aid of a clan which began a fight; only those more strongly committed to individual friends among the principal combatants would turn out immediately. Others might follow later if one of their clansmen, acting as an

Warfare, alliance and compensation

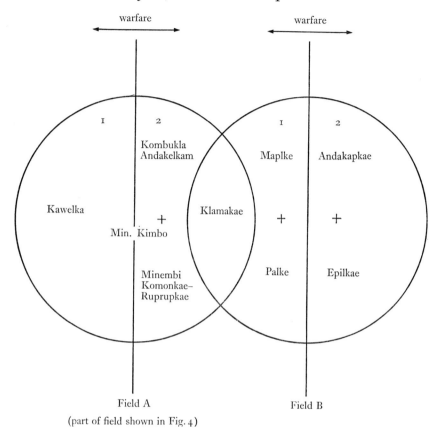

Fig. 5   Fields of warfare 2

ally, were killed. Big-men could influence others to follow them. This was in fact how the Kendipi became involved in helping the Tipuka against Wəlyi tribe, as the following account indicates.[1]

The reason why the Tipuka are making reparation payments to the Kendipi is as follows. A man of the Kundmbo section of Tipuka Oklembo clan went to stay at the place of his mother's brother of Kopembo sub-clan in Tipuka Kelmbo clan. The man's name was Nggor and his mother's brother was Mɪtɪpa. The Kelmbo became involved in fighting against the Wəlyi, and Nggor was killed while helping them. Mɪtɪpa was upset. Two days later they went out to fight again, and Mɪtɪpa also was killed. Now Mɪtɪpa's father's sister had been married to a man of Kendipi Timbokambo clan, and her son, Mele, was now grown up and had become a big-man. Mele spoke to all

[1] The source is a letter written to me by a friend after I had left the field in 1965.

71

the Kendipi, saying that the Wəlyi had killed first Nggor and then Mɨtɨpa, and he called on all the men to fetch their spears, bows and arrows, and shields, and go to help the Tipuka. This was done, and in the long fights that followed Mele himself was killed. The fighting continued, and the Tipuka killed many of the Wəlyi's men. Tipuka and Kendipi joined forces, routed the Wəlyi and drove them out. The Tipuka were principal combatants here, and because Mele had died the Kendipi became *kui wuə* ('dead men') to them, and so they have to be paid for their losses.

Here we see the big-man, Mele, exhorting his clan-mates and others to help him avenge the death of his cross-cousin among the Tipuka. He and the Kendipi may have had other motives also; but to my informant, at any rate, the desire for revenge seemed paramount.

The intensity of minor warfare, the amount of time spent at it, and the total duration of a sequence of fighting until truce negotiations were made, were all highly variable. Minor warfare in some cases was similar to feuding between Nuer groups (Evans-Pritchard 1940). The aim in it was usually to repay some specific insult, theft, seduction, or killing, and once balanced reciprocity had been achieved, fighting might end. But in other cases it could be more severe than this. Fighting could continue, off and on, for many months. Pseudo-offers of making peace were sometimes used to trap and kill selected men among the enemy. Several deaths might result from particular engagements and sometimes groups would refuse to pay compensation for these, even though minor enemies were expected to do; and this in turn raised resentments further and made the likelihood of renewed conflict greater. Nevertheless, women and children were not massacred nor were settlements destroyed in the ordinary course of minor warfare. In major warfare, as we have seen, there were no such restraints. Even in minor warfare the victors might dislodge their opponents and make them flee, not wishing to have them as troublesome neighbours. For example, the Kitepi clan among the Tipuka was dislodged in this way by Kendike clan and had to migrate some three miles westwards; a few Kitepi big-men found refuge with their Kawelka kin, and subsequently became king-pins in the intensive moka relations between Tipuka and Kawelka.

A particular account of treachery will show that revenge could be taken by either public or private action:

A man of the Roklaka tribe was living as a refugee with the Kawelka Kundmbo. Men of Minembi Engambo clan, neighbours of Kundmbo, approached him privately with an offer of pigs and pearl shells if he would entice a certain man of Tipuka Kengeke clan, whom they wished to have killed for purposes of revenge, up to the Kundmbo territory, and assassinate him, handing the body over as proof. The Roklaka man agreed, and tied up some ashes from the fire in a bundle to make them look like ash-salt from the Enga area, a trading valu-able. He then went on a visit to his home tribe and on the way back he called in on the Kengeke man and promised him the bundle, if he would come up later to fetch it. The Kengeke man did so, and was duly struck down. Informa-tion, however, had leaked out; the Engambo were suspected, the Roklaka man was thrown out by the Kundmbo, and Kengeke men demanded compensation from Kundmbo for the death. A payment in pigs and shells was put together and offered to an assembly of Kengeke men at a ceremonial ground lying between the territories of the two clans. A big-man of Kundmbo rushed down the row of wealth objects as a prelude to marking the transfer with formal oratory, when one of the recipients took aim with his cassowary-claw-tipped spear and killed him. The Kundmbo were unprepared for battle and, snatching their big-man's body, they fled. The Kengeke pursued them for a short distance, and wounded another Kundmbo man with an arrow in the ribs; the man died at a nearby settlement-place before reaching home. The rest of the Kundmbo mustered in their main cemetery-place and readied themselves for defence. But the Kengeke did not pursue the matter further once their revenge was taken, and they returned to their own territory. The treachery involved here on the part of the Kengeke was a reflection of the Kundmbo's ambivalent political position: they were partly identified with the Minembi, major enemies, and thus the Kengeke treated them in a way they would never have employed against the other two Kawelka clans.

Mustering in the cemetery-place of the clan was a favourite action before men undertook major warfare, or whenever they were hard pressed in a particular fight and their enemies had forced them back in their own territory. In the cemetery-place they would make a sacrifice to clan ancestors, asking for strength to avenge deaths. No woman could enter the cemetery or share the sacrifice-meat on these occasions, for women's polluting influence would weaken men's weapons; men also decorated themselves with a few feathers and charcoal, or smeared themselves with clay,[1] if they were already mourning a loss, before they went out to fight. Preparing themselves, they would halloo and kick up their heels in a dance which nowadays they repeat when they are celebrating their achieve-ments as donors at a moka.

Such a retreat into a clan cemetery-place certainly often occurred in minor, as well as major, warfare. Ongka, a pre-eminent big-man of the Kawelka, told how a retreat of this kind was forced on the Kawelka in a battle against the Tipuka Oklembo:

[1] Strathern A. J. and A. M. 1971.

73

Oklembo Kømnga died, and the Kawelka were accused of poisoning him. 'But the Oklembo are our maternal kin and cross-cousins, how could we poison him?' the Kawelka protested. But the close lineage fathers of Kømnga said, no, the Kawelka killed him, they sent poison and it was given to him by one of his wives.[1] The Oklembo laid out Kømnga in his house, and then made their way up to a ceremonial ground, Maninge, in Kawelka territory, to ambush a man, Mara, there. They pushed open the door of his house and looked inside. But as it happened Mara was suffering from dysentery and was away in his lavatory, so they missed him. Some of the Kawelka saw the Oklembo go and began to suspect that their brothers were being killed, so they brought out their weapons and rushed to Maninge. Battle followed until all our weapons were broken and night-time fell, but no-one had been killed, and the Oklembo went back to their houses. The Kawelka went off to a settlement-place high up in the hills, Kiningamul. In the morning the Oklembo came up in force again and began to ruin gardens and houses and kill pigs. The Kawelka came down from Kiningamul and took refuge inside one of their cemeteries, surrounded by the Oklembo. The Kawelka then burst out, shouting, and killed an Oklembo man, Kongrui, with an arrow through his face. The Okiembo carried him off by a path leading near to Kiningamul, and there an Oklembo man, Ok, killed Klønt, a big-man, the father of Membo Kont (a current big-man). The Kundmbo section of Oklembo came over from the Jimi and made an attack from the hills above Maninge, while the rest attacked the Kawelka from below. The Kawelka fought on both fronts, trying to keep their old men in the middle. Other men also joined in. Klamakae men came up from the Baiyer and killed two Kawelka men who were wounded and hiding in a settlement-place in the hills. Little men (i.e. unimportant men) from the Minembi and other Tipuka clans came and raped women, ruined gardens, fired houses. The Kawelka all took refuge in the high forest. They made a roof for themselves of *kunai* grass, supported on poles, and surrounded this shelter with shields. They had no food, and eventually had to retreat into the Jimi Valley. The Oklembo were afraid too, and they all went to live at the place of Oklembo Kundmbo. The two sides stayed, both nervous of each other, and then they fought again. This time we chased the Oklembo and killed those of them who had accused us, and this was right, for their accusations were wrong. That is why the Oklembo and we have exchanged death-compensation payments since then.

This account indicates that the amount of destruction involved in minor warfare could be considerable, particularly since men from other groups with grudges against the main combatants or men with an eye to obtaining some of the spoils of warfare sometimes came to take advantage of the combatants' preoccupation with battle. The account corrects

[1] He had two wives, both from clans within Tipuka which were minor enemies of Oklembo. Hence it was quite likely that these wives would be suspected of administering poison to him.

the notion that in minor warfare destruction of property and killing of men were minimised. In the excitement of battle and the need to defend oneself against sudden ambush, there is no doubt that strongly aggressive feelings were roused. Yet this is not to deny that conflict in minor warfare *was* limited in certain ways and that cross-cutting ties of kinship and affinity between the opponents, given substance by exchanges of wealth, were important in determining how the limits were set.

Fighting was also sometimes conducted in open spaces (although these were not specially prepared or reserved for warfare), when spearmen formed up in lines behind large, painted shields, and advanced under covering fire from bowmen. At close quarters and in ambushes and assassinations the stone axe was employed as well as the spear. A special type of blade, larger than that for the work-axe and thicker than that for ceremonial wear, was used.

Fighting ability is often nowadays listed as one of the ideal capacities of big-men, and especially of major big-men, although it is agreed that these were matched by fighters who were not big-men at all.[1] One old man, who had certainly himself fought as a youth, insisted that in his group all men fought equally hard in pitched battles, and there was no-one who was pre-eminent over the rest as a warrior. Vicedom (1943–8, vol. 2: 147 ff.) partially confirms this point. He remarks that there were no real fight-leaders, although an orator might marshal men initially for a pitched battle in open country. Important big-men (perhaps those who were growing old?), far from leading the ranks, might actually keep away from the fighting, since they were especially attractive targets. (The reason for this, we may interpolate, is that the big-man is regarded as both a planner of group policy and a source of strength for the group through his contact with ancestor spirits. When a big-man dies, his kinsmen claim they feel physically weak and at a loss for direction; and this is one of the major burdens of funeral songs.) Vicedom also mentions that although big-men were not always leaders in battles they did at times incite their clansmen to war, in order to humble neighbouring clans and prevent them from holding successful moka festivals. The death of a big-man would create an occasion for warfare also: if he was held to have been poisoned, or had been killed in warfare, he had to be avenged, even if his clan were weaker than that of the reported killer. Retaliation by poisoning or by hiring an assassin was often resorted to in this circumstance. Or a big-man might take it on himself to gain revenge by raiding enemy territory:

[1] Informants here imply, correctly, that fighting ability alone could not give a man a claim to being a *wuə nyim* ('big-man'). Financial and oratorical ability were also required.

Men of one of the Kawelka clans, Mandembo, had contracted a truce with their enemies, the Kundmbo, but felt that the latter were killing them off by poison, through the agency of a man who was a maternal parallel cousin of a big-man of Mandembo. Such a maternal kinsman should have been trustworthy, but the Mandembo suspected him. One day the big-man, Komb, forayed into Kundmbo territory, found his cousin, and seizing hold of him broke his neck. He took the body to a river on the border between his clan's area and that of the Kundmbo, and hid it in a hollow tree. The Kundmbo suspected foul play and attacked, pinning the Mandembo inside a central cemetery-place at Mbukl. The big-man deliberately came out, and when they seized him and asked him about the death, he asked them in return 'What would you pay me if I gave him back to you?' (implying that he had taken the man prisoner). In their surprise at this they momentarily loosed their grip, and he struck one of them down. His clansmen, watching from inside the cemetery, were emboldened by this, and, rushing out, drove their enemies off. The big-man commented, in telling this story: 'We do not usually kill our matrilateral cousins, but I did so on this occasion because of the bad feeling and anger between my clan and his.'[1]

However, in addition to the occasional importance of intrepid exploits of this kind, there were more long-term aspects of fighting. Big-men could especially help not only to secure allies, as we have seen, but also to pay for their services. Further, they were important in peace-making. Vicedom (1943–8, vol. 2: 173) emphasises that peace could be made between two groups only if their most recent debts in deaths were squared; but elsewhere (*ibid.*: 158) he records how, even if this were so, the control of peace-making by outstanding big-men was necessary, to prevent further disputes from flaring up. The problem arises: how could major big-men influence events in this way? The answer is two-fold: first, because they are men who have developed to a high degree the rhetorical arts of persuasion and of focusing attention on themselves in debates; so that, although they may have no physical sanctions behind them, they can dominate events in which they take part. And, second, they exert control because they offer the power to organise alternative channels of competition through moka activity: they offer a positive alternative to warfare. The history of pacification throughout the Highlands reveals that big-men seized upon the Administration's arrival and the influx of shell valuables which accompanied it as the occasion for expanding their exchange activities (cf., e.g., Salisbury 1962).

It is difficult to say to what extent Hageners have re-fashioned their past as well as their present life in response to Administration actions, but it is at any rate a favourite saying among Hageners nowadays that their

---

[1] The big-man himself gave me the story, and his clansmen concurred in it.

big-men were *møi keap*, 'native equivalents of Administration officers'. However, their resources of power were not as great as those of the Administration. They relied on bringing about peace by exchanges of wealth rather than by imposing it with superior force.

Hageners link this view of big-men's actions with their concepts of *noman* and *popokl*.[1] Both concepts can be glossed in a number of ways. *Noman* is social consciousness, thought, feeling, intention; *popokl* is frustration, anger, sometimes desire for revenge. The *noman* is said to reside in the chest region. When it lies straight against the wind-pipe it is in a good condition and action proceeds correctly or rationally; when it lies crooked, this is likely to be because the person is popokl and cannot act as he otherwise would. Hageners say that men who are always quick to take revenge are men who are *popokl-mundi*, 'they become frustrated'; whereas the big-man does not suffer from popokl, but comes to terms for compensation instead of taking revenge. Popokl is held to weaken a man and to make it likely that he will become sick. Moreover, some men become popokl too easily, and this incapacitates them for action. Big-men are supposed to avoid such a condition. It can be seen that the Hageners' theory is not dissimilar to Read's characterisation of successful leaders among the Gahuku–Gama as 'autonomous', i.e. men who have control over themselves (as well as others) and can make independent choices of action (Read 1959).

This view is perhaps somewhat idealised, and it should be taken as an ideal statement. Stories about actions of big-men in the past may be coloured by this ideal; but there may be some truth in them also, and I shall give some examples of such accounts.

The first is a panegyric by a current big-man of Ndika Pangaka clan:

Nɪmb was a major big-man of my clan, and he married five wives. He was a great peace-maker. The reason why he was able to make peace was that he made all men afraid. He was like Tom Ellis.[2] When all the Mokei clans fought against the Yamka, he forbade them to carry on, and they stopped. He protected the Mundika tribe and the Nengka Kwipanggil. [Some 1,500 persons!] He used to present shells and pigs to those threatening fights, telling them not to quarrel, since they were all sisters' sons and brothers of each other. He broke up fights just when they were starting. He held the talk, and all the others depended on him. When he died, it was as if our leader had been removed and we did not know from whom to take our talk. By contrast, my own father was a bad man, who killed people when he met

---

[1] For a detailed exposition on these see Strathern A. M. 1968*b*.

[2] i.e. the present Secretary of the Department of the Administrator, who was then District Commissioner at Mount Hagen.

them along the road. Nɪmb told him to stop this and to take up paying compensation for deaths instead, but he would not listen. He wanted to gain his revenge for the deaths of his brothers.

Whatever the degree of historical accuracy in this account, it does clearly show the dichotomy between the ideal type of the peace-making big-man and the ideal type of the violent man, who preferred revenge-killings to compensation payments.

The second account[1] concerns the activities of a big-man who lives at Mbukl, Kuri, of Tipuka Kitepi clan: Kuri was one of those who came to Mbukl as refugees, chased there by enemies of Tipuka Kendike clan, perhaps in about 1925. After his arrival he married women from each of the Kawelka clans, in whose territory he was living, and announced to every-one that they should stop fighting and begin making moka properly. He does not seem to have succeeded at once in this, for fighting continued until the time of pacification several years after his arrival. Yet it is true that after warfare had been stopped he vigorously extended moka ties, mainly with the Membo–Mandembo pair of clans which are especially allied to his own.

A similar statement, in general form, was given to me by another major big-man, Ongka,[2] and a shortened version of its beginning appears as the epigraph to this chapter:

> We would stop fighting only when arrows had lodged in our chests, arms, and legs and our whole bodies were tired. Unimportant men could make no moves towards negotiation, but a big-man would stand up and speak of the fact that they had given their sisters as wives to the men they were now fighting and had received wives in return. Now these women had borne children, so that they and their enemies were cognatic kin to each other. They wanted to see the faces of their sisters and sisters' children again; and so they decided to cook pigs and present them to the other side, which agreed to do the same. Only a big-man on either side would make speeches at the time of the exchange; others would think only of fighting on, until the big-men suggested a truce. The cooked meat was presented in an uninhabited part of the boundary area between the two principal combatant groups. Both sides ate together at the place as a sign that now they were to be friends; but this could not happen if the two sides were major enemies.

[1] This is pieced together from remarks by himself, one of his sons, and various Kawelka men.

[2] Ongka, like many other big-men, was once an Administration *luluai* and is now (1969) a Local Government Councillor. Clearly his views on the functions of big-men have probably been coloured by his experiences since pacification. They may also represent what was always an ideal but was not always practised. One can only say that the picture which informants give is fairly consistent, while admitting that much of the information is drawn from big-men themselves.

78

Warfare, alliance and compensation

In such a case no cooked meat could be offered between them either, but a big-man would set a taboo-sign (*mi*) on one of the pathways used by warriors; and, standing at a distance, he would call out to the enemies that now they were all tired of war, let each go back to his own place and carry on making moka, obtaining wives, and tilling gardens. The truce would then last for a while; but later a woman would be seduced or a pig stolen, and so men became popokl again and brought out their weapons to obtain revenge. And this continued till a big-man suggested a halt again.

Here the big-men appear as initiators of peace, but only when it was clear that the rest were also tired of fighting. Other accounts indicate that big-men – and not, it seems, others – took the initiative more definitely on some occasions. Ongka, for example, claimed that he used to intercede even in disputes between Tipuka clans, making speeches and knocking sticks aside when, say, Kitepi and Kelmbo clans were quarrelling – a risky action for an outsider to undertake, but one for which Ongka's intrepid temperament and his occasional gift for humour made him well suited. Similarly, the same big-man of Mandembo clan whose aggressive exploit against the Kundmbo clan I recorded earlier also arranged for peace-making between the two groups:

> When the White men were at Hagen and we thought that the aeroplanes were going to eat us, three of the Kundmbo big-men threatened that they would attack again and kill all the men of Kurupmbo section (in Mandembo clan). One of our minor big-men was ready to fight, but Komb said no, and he gave him a leg of pig-meat to eat instead. Komb himself took one of his wives and her baby son with him over to the place of another Kundmbo big-man, Roltinga. Roltinga wondered if Komb had come to kill him, but, instead, he proposed peace. Roltinga cooked a pig and presented it to him and gave him pearl shells also, and in this way the talk of fighting between Kurupmbo and Kundmbo was stopped. Later there were larger-scale exchanges between our two groups.

Here it was Komb's audacity and Roltinga's ready adjustment to this that helped to transform open fighting between the two groups into moka relations.

To sum up this section: while it is true that big-men were not military commanders, they could still influence events in warfare. They took the initiative, often, both in aggressive and conciliatory action; and they urged on their clansmen decisions to support other clans or pay compensation for killings or to start a further bout of warfare. At least some big-men had enough force of personality to break up minor battles, when these were just beginning. Ongka, the most important Mandembo big-man, linked this ability to the fact that big-men could 'find things'; that is, they could obtain pigs and shells to pay compensation as an alternative to pursuing revenge. A switch from attempting to 'get even' with an enemy by taking revenge, to demonstrating superiority over him and at the same time formally making him into a friend, is indeed highly significant. In the next section I shall consider revenge procedures in more detail, as a preamble to showing how revenge is most likely to be replaced by exchange between minor rather than major enemies.

REVENGE PROCEDURES

Hageners recognise five immediate causes of deaths: old age, sickness, sorcery, poisoning, and physical violence. Persons who reach a very old age and become weak and helpless like children are sometimes said to die *we*, that is, for no further reason; but often their death is complicated by some sickness which is held to have brought on by an upset in their relationships with kinsfolk. The upset makes them popokl, and they become sick. In this kind of circumstance, and in others also,[1] sickness is held to be sent by dead spirits, usually close relatives of the sick person, and sacrifice is made, to appease the spirit involved, and, if appropriate, as a sign that relationships between living kinsfolk have been repaired. If death occurs from such a sickness, and no other cause is identified, revenge procedures are not, of course, undertaken, for one does not take revenge against ancestral spirits.

Other spirits can make men sick and sometimes kill them: wild spirits of forest places, and the Male and Female spirits which are the focus of important cults in Hagen. A further agency is the substance *kum*. Hageners say they are afraid of kum stones, which can leap up from the bed of a stream at which a person is drinking, lodge in his throat or belly and kill him. Kum also appears as a flickering, nocturnal light. It may be directed by wild spirits of the bush, especially those which come from the Jimi Valley.[2]

True sorcery appears to be less important in Hagen than poisoning. There is a technique, called 'fastening and planting the soul' (*min pup poromen*), which is known at least in the Central Melpa area;[3] but Melpa

---

[1] Cf. again Strathern A. M. 1968b.

[2] For further details cf. Strathern A. J. and A. M. 1968: 194, and Strathern A. J. 1969c. Among the Kuma, eastern neighbours of the Hageners and speakers of a closely related language, the word *kum* clearly refers to witchcraft substance (Reay 1959: 135–9).

[3] The sorcerer obtains pieces of the hair, apron, excrement, etc., of his victim, and puts these in a phial which he hangs over the fire in his house. As the fire heats the phial, so the victim will become ill with a fever. After a while the sorcerer takes the phial and buries it, covering it with a special leaf, to fasten the soul inside it. Unless a ritual expert diagnoses the cause and recovers the soul, the victim, it is thought, will die. A knowledgeable old informant, Wundake of Elti tribe, was able to cite only two cases of this type of sorcery being diagnosed in his area.

3 *a* Recipients lead
away pigs

3 *b* Laying down shells
for display at a
ceremonial ground

4a A big-man (Kawelka Ongka) examines shells due to be given him in moka

4b A young man (Kawelka Ru) dances *mørli* (with a girl whom he later married)

and Temboka speakers mainly fear as sorcerers peoples who live to their north and south. Northern Melpa men fear the *Mongaemb wamb*, who live north of the Jimi River and are alleged to project stones into men or to turn themselves into stones, enter the anus of a victim, and kill him; and an informant of the Ulka tribe in the Nebilyer Valley told me that Kambia (= Kaimbi) men, who live south of the Kubor range, obtain pieces of clothing, hair, excrement, or fingernails from an intended victim and throw these into certain ponds. As the pieces are swallowed up by the water, the victim dies. Kambia old men, in their studied denial of knowledge on this point, directed me to the Aua (Imbonggu) area south of the Kaugel River as the true home of classical sorcery techniques.

Questions of revenge and compensation arise most often when death is thought to occur by poisoning or by direct physical violence on the part of human agents. The Melpa terms which I translate as poison are *kopna* and *konga*. Both are also names for ginger (*Zingiber* sp.) which is employed in a number of magical rituals.[1] Apart from this usage, the terms have three connected but separate applications:

1. 'lethal poison'. E.g. *kopna ming*, 'small bamboo phial for carrying poison'; *konga rok mek anderemen*, 'they carry poison about and kill us'.

2. 'love-magic', most often called *amb kopna*. It comes in many different forms (e.g. as pieces of sweet-smelling cinnamon), and is most often proferred to a girl at a courting party, secretly sprinkled over a cigarette.

3. 'magic' or 'magical', as in *konga ku/kopna ku*, the terms for different kinds of magical stones, employed to draw in shells, pigs, and women to a man's household. The stones are most often pieces of volcanic iron, black river stones, natural crystals, or prehistoric artefacts made by earlier inhabitants in the Highlands.[2]

Hageners state that lethal poison may be gathered from certain roots, leaves, and fruits, from the tails of deadly snakes, from corpse fluids, and nowadays from 'benzine', i.e. petrol. In the Nebilyer I was told of how poison was 'originally' discovered among the Koka–Milika, who live on the foothills of the Kambia area: 'High in the forest two men, Apa Kerua and Kng Kerua, found a stone from which water dropped and all the plants around it were withered. The two realised the water was lethal, and collected it in a long bamboo. Later the substance was traded out to other

---

[1] Ginger is perhaps taken as the prototype of sharp or strong-tasted things, into which category poison also falls; but this is only a conjecture.
[2] Cf. Bulmer 1963, 1964.

G

groups.'[1] Poison is considered to be directly lethal, without the inter-
vention of spirit agents, and it is thought that it must be consumed by the
victim along with his food or drink.

Hagen men also claim that they greatly fear menstrual blood, and that
if a man eats a piece of this with his food or takes it into himself through
his penis during copulation, he will waste away, his skin will become slack
and pimply, and eventually he will swell up, putrefy, and die. Wives
married into a clan from enemy groups or whose mothers came from enemy
groups are suspected of slipping poison into their husbands' food at the
suggestion of their natal kin. Similarly it is thought that phials of other
poisons may be given to them for admixture with a proposed victim's food.
In the past, if a man died and his wife came from an enemy group (especially
if this was a major enemy), the wife would often escape to her own kinsfolk
in case she should be punished for poisoning him.[2]

The wife is the first to be suspected because she prepared food regularly
for her husband. Persons who visited not long before a death are suspected
also. The visitor is supposed to slip poison from a phial into a sweet potato
which he has scraped and hands to his victim; or to slip it into a bamboo
drinking-tube. Poison acts more quickly than ordinary sickness, and an
apparently healthy man who dies suddenly is likely to be considered a
victim of it.

Counteraction against suspected poisoning consists of both treatment
of the patient and attempts to discover who administered the poison-stuff.

Specialists for removing menstrual blood are usually men or women of
the victim's own clan, or wives married into it. They are paid with pig-
meat (or shells/Australian currency). They recite spells and perform
actions which are described as 'drawing the blood into a bamboo tube'
applied to the patient's belly. They also give the patient ginger, mixed
with pig's blood and liver, to eat. The same specialist may have the skill
of removing other types of poison. He sucks at the patient's skin, either
directly, via the bamboo tube, or through pieces of sugar-cane peel laid
over small cuts in the skin, and applied to the cheeks, thighs, knees,
calves, forehead, chest, and back. He then spits on a heated stone to see
the black particles of poison-substance remaining after the spittle has
dried.[1]

[1] Informant Rumb, of the Ulka tribe.
[2] On the other hand an accused wife might be spared if she had borne many children
for her husband's group. His clansmen were 'sorry' for her, and would give her in marriage
to another man of their group (if she stayed), while quietly taking steps to kill off men
of her natal clan, who were presumed to have suggested she kill her husband.
[3] Each of these methods is clearly open to some manipulation.

Warfare, alliance and compensation

It is men who are considered the prime targets for poisoning, for it is they who fight, make exchanges, and thus ensure the strength of their clan, and poisoning is reckoned to be part of the pattern of aggression between enemy clans. And it is particularly the deaths of big-men which are likely to be interpreted as due to poisoning.

Traditionally an autopsy or a divination-sequence was held to establish who had poisoned a man; both methods have now been abandoned owing to Mission influence. First, the autopsy method: when a man fell sick, his close clan kin visited him and asked him if he was sick because of popokl or because ancestral ghosts were popokl with him over a wrong. If not, they questioned him closely on where and with whom he had eaten within the last few days. When he died his body was laid on a platform in the grave, and covered with a layer of leaves and earth. His stomach was cut open and a hollow bamboo tube was set upright in it so as to protrude from the grave's surface and allow the stench from the corpse to escape. Later, when the body had dried up, the grave was opened and the contents of the stomach were examined for traces of poison, recognised by their black colour. The investigators match the fragments of food in which they find the poison with the dead man's earlier account of his recent meals, and decide who is guilty on this basis.

Divination was conducted either by the taro or the fire-thong test. The first[1] was employed if a member of the dead person's settlement was directly suspected. Each person was required to choose a taro corm, and these were then cooked in small separate ovens. The one whose taro remained raw when all the others were cooked was convicted, for the ancestors of the dead man were supposed to reveal his guilt in this way. Those found guilty might be seized at once and killed; but if they were only visitors from another place, compensation had in turn to be paid for their deaths. The fire-thong test was used when the dead man's kin had captured someone from another group whom they suspected. In one case a clan inveigled one of their minor enemy groups up to their ceremonial ground with promises of cooked pigs as a peace offering, then closed in and forced them to try the test: if they could not make fire, they were to be pronounced guilty. Fighting broke out before much was established by these means, and the visitors fled.

In addition to these specific methods, a dead man's clansmen watched

[1] Cf. also Meiser 1938. As with many such tests one is left wondering how it was in practice manipulated. What, for example, if the test pointed to an important man of the group, or to the deceased's own father or mother as the guilty party? Similarly if everyone's taro were cooked when the ovens were opened, or if several taros remained uncooked.

to see if any of their major enemies were holding celebrations: putting on fine feather head-dresses, greasing their bodies with pork fat, singing and playing drums and courting girls. If they did so, this was taken as a sign that they had caused the death and were jubilant over it. It is possible that a strong group might hold celebrations in this way as an insult to the bereaved and a challenge to open fighting.

A further possibility, but one not often taken, was openly to accuse those suspected and to request compensation. In one case the accusers burnt a special fire in a pathway between their territory and that of the accused, surrounding it with a rim of hardened ash. Such a fire is a sign of peaceful accusation. They requested cooked pigs as compensation for the death, but were refused, and at this point they switched over to violence, and took up their shields for a full-scale fight. In another case, the accusation of poisoning was not made until twenty years after the death, when it was treated like any other pretext for conducting inter-group exchanges, and the accused paid up in return for initiatory gifts. This took place well after the two groups were under Administration control. In earlier such cases accusations were simply denied and accusers had to resort to direct individual revenge-killing, hiring an assassin, full warfare, or counter-poisoning.

A person convicted by one of the tests I have described might be seized, tortured, and killed at once. Besides the dead man's widow (if she came from an enemy clan), a co-resident cognatic kinsman who was also a rubbish-man (man of low status) might be seized. It is often said that rubbish-men are jealous of big-men – whether both are agnates of their clan or not – and that they may be willing to accept bribes from enemies to slip poison into their food. Like wives, such rubbish-men often ran away as soon as a big-man in their settlement died, in order to avoid immediate seizure by his clansmen.

Even if someone was identified as the immediate poisoner and killed, this might not be held to solve the matter. It is thought that poison can be passed on from hand to hand by arrangement and may eventually be administered by a person who does not even know who originally marked the victim. Usually it is assumed that men of major enemy groups have initiated the chain of conspiracy, and have offered pay to their helpers. The immediate poisoner is supposed to knot a piece of cordyline leaf taken from the rear-covering of the victim and send this back along the chain of people who have passed the poison on, as a sign that he has been successful. Big-men in debates often drop hints about big-men in other groups having in this way 'received the cordyline' for the death of men in their own clan:

such remarks are part of the claims and counter-claims which groups make against each other.

Sometimes it was not necessary to hire a poisoner, for someone might volunteer:

In the Nebilyer Valley Penambe and Kope tribes were major enemies (as we have seen earlier). A Penambe man died, supposedly of poison, and the Kope were suspected. His Kope wife had been in the menstrual hut at the time and so she was freed of suspicion, for it was agreed that her husband would not have taken food from her while she was polluted by menstruation. Nevertheless the Kope were thought to have been jubilant over the death. Another Kope woman married to a Penambe man mourned at the funeral; and her immediate brother, saying he was 'sorry' for his sister's apparent grief, came and offered to poison a specific man of another Kope clan to gain revenge for the Penambe. The brother's action here was accepted as genuine, since his own clan had helped the proposed victim's clan in warfare but had not received reparation payments for losses incurred and was angry over this. At all events the man marked as a victim later died, and the Penambe put this down to poisoning and celebrated the death.

A short account (from a young big-man) on how to gain revenge by hiring a poisoner shows that revenge was pursued most assiduously against major enemies:

If a good man of ours is killed, we hold a meeting and ask what is to be done. Who has a friend close to the place of our enemies? Would he take this thing (poison) which we can give him? We have cassowaries, young nubile women, fat pigs and pearl shells. If we can find a road, we are willing to give all these away. If the man chosen agrees, we send the poison to him and he passes it from hand to hand until it kills a big-man at the place of our enemies. When their big-man is dead, they are at a loss, for he showed the way to them and without him they are weak. Now then, we close in on them and finish them off in fighting and take their ground for nothing. We pay the poisoner in secret, and we defeat our major enemies. This is called *el kløngi*.

The informant here emphasised that big-men are the targets for poisoning; and that poisoning a leader could be a prelude to attacking his group. On the other hand, if a group was *not* strong enough to launch attacks on a major enemy, its men could nevertheless maintain they were killing the enemy off by poison; and nowadays, when warfare is stopped, poisoning between major enemies is a matter of frequent debate. It is in this way that depleted and weakened tribes can think of themselves as taking revenge on vastly more powerful groups which in the past drove them out of their territory. It is not even necessary to kill a close kinsman of a man who has killed or is supposed to have killed one's own kin: any man of the killer's clan will do. Hence, sooner or later a death occurs in one of the enemy clans to which one's own clan has 'sent poison', and this death can be claimed as a result of one's poison. Since each revenge-group keeps its activities secret, it is clear that the same death can be 'claimed' in this way by a number of different groups. The likelihood is that there are sufficient deaths for a number of groups to feel that their poisoning activities are successful.

THE INCIDENCE OF POISONING ACCUSATIONS AND SUSPICIONS

Poisoning suspicions do not arise at random. In this respect they are similar to accusations of witchcraft and sorcery which anthropologists have studied extensively in Africa.[1] For example, I have mentioned that wives from enemy clans, and rubbish-men whose position and presumed loyalty were both weak, were both liable to be accused and killed in the past if a big-man of their settlement died. Otherwise suspicions were projected right outside the clan-parish[2] group. I now sketch the incidence of accusations and suspicions in a little more detail.

Within the clan it is an explicit ideal that there should be no poisoning. The ideal is kept to in practice, with two exceptions. The first we have already seen. Unimportant marginal men might be accused, especially if they had switched their affiliation from one clan to another during their adult life. (Sisters' sons incorporated in their mother's clan from an early age were not suspected in this way.) Even in these cases extra factors are usually present which help to explain why a particular man is accused. I have only a few cases from Kawelka clans, and one of these illustrates the point.

There was a man of little importance in Membo clan. He had no immediate brothers and no close lineage mates. When his wife was seduced by the son of an important big-man in the other sub-clan of Membo to his own, he was furious, but the seducer refused to pay compensation. Soon afterwards the big-man's son died and there was an outcry: he was a young man and had died suddenly – who had poisoned him? Suspicion turned on the aggrieved 'little man', and he had to flee for refuge with a distant cognatic kinsman in Mandembo clan, the big-man Ongka. He became a 'helper' of Ongka, looking after pigs for him, and he lost his membership of Membo clan group.

The other circumstance in which accusations arise within the clan is when a clan has divided into sections and the sections are becoming independent of each other:

[1] E.g. Marwick 1965.
[2] I.e. the clan-group of men plus their co-resident wives and children.

Warfare, alliance and compensation

The Kawelka Ngglammbo suspected a Kurupmbo man – of the opposite section within their clan – of poisoning a minor big-man. The accused man's sisters were married to Kombukla and Minembi men (major enemies), and it was thought that they had brought him offers of pay from their husbands if he would do the poisoning. An Ngglammbo man challenged him to eat a piece of the Kawelka divination substance, a type of cordyline leaf, as a test of his innocence, and he complied. Later his testicles swelled up and he died, so he was affirmed guilty. The Ngglammbo then asked further for compensation for the death of their big-man, but Kurupmbo at first refused, and they engaged in stick-fights over the issue from time to time. Eventually they decided to exchange cooked pork and pearl shells and made the peace.

The case is interesting, as it shows how within the clan tests of innocence could be conducted through the medium of the tribal *mi*, or divination substance. If a guilty man perjured himself while holding and eating a piece of the *mi*, the *mi* would later 'eat him from inside' and he would die.[1]

Between pair-clans there is a similar ideal of 'no poisoning' to that which holds within a clan; but the ideal is more often broken, in that the relationship between pair-clans can become disturbed: for example, as between M. Papeke and Yelipi clans, whose conflict I have described earlier. Poisoning suspicions both preceded and followed the major battles in which the Yelipi were driven out into a new territory.

Minor enemies accused (and still suspect) each other of poisoning frequently enough, whether they belong to a single tribe or not. In the past, open accusations were often the signal for warfare to develop between them.

Within blocs involving two sets of pair-clans, only two out of the total of four clans would be 'principal combatants' (*el pukl wuə*), and only these two would frequently accuse each other of poisoning. The two who were merely allies of the principal combatants were in fact not thought of as directly fighting against each other. Fig. 6 shows how this situation applied in the case of the Tipuka–Kawelka alliance. K. Membo and T. Kitepi clans were thus simply allies of the two principal combatants; and this fact is often repeated in moka speeches nowadays as a reason for a closer exchange-alliance between these two than between Mandembo and Oklembo; for in the moka relations which have developed over the years between these clans the two principal combatants give to each other, and the two 'allies' do likewise.

---

[1] Strauss (1962: 206–79) has discussed thoroughly the functions of the *mi* in disputes of this kind. It is tempting to see the *mi* as a particularly clear example of an 'externalised conscience'. Each tribe's *mi* is an objectively existing substance; but the substance is closely identified both with the ultimate origins of the tribe and with each current individual member of it. It is notable also that the divination test involves *eating* a piece of the *mi* substance.

Big-men are often willing to volunteer generalisations about which clans their own clan had 'reasons for fighting', and which were suspected of poisoning activity. Their generalisations do not always square with actual cases gathered from other informants, but they do give a reasonable picture of the main expectations in relationships. Table 7 summarises some of the statements they made to me in response to the questions 'Were there poisonings between these two groups?' and 'Did these two groups

	Kawelka side	Tipuka side
principals	K. Mandembo (especially Kurupmbo section)	T. Oklembo
allies	K. Membo	T. Kitepi

Fig. 6   Tipuka–Kawelka relations

have a cause of war (*el pukl*) against each other?' It should be noticed that the two informants whose accounts I have used are likely to have presented an optimistic picture of Tipuka–Kawelka relations, as both live at Buk within Kawelka territory and were in 1964–5 highly important exchange partners of Kawelka men. Both belong to the T. Kitepi clan.

In the case of major enemies expectations are clear and simple. All major enemy clans with which one's own clan had a 'cause of war' in the past are regularly suspected of poisoning activities. Allies of major enemies can also be suspected, but the suspicion is less intense. Thus, in the Tipuka–Kawelka–Kombukla–Minembi field of warfare (Fig. 4) there were in the past cross-cutting alliances between Minembi and Tipuka clans; and these have subsequently been extended in moka relations.

COMPENSATION FOR DEATH

In the preceding sections I have described how sequences of fighting arose and were terminated between groups. The only satisfactory way of establishing either a truce or a more long-lasting peace was by making exchanges of valuables as formal payments for deaths. Such payments I described in general as war payments. They are made either as compensation for killings to a minor enemy group, or as reparation to a group which has acted as an

TABLE 7 *Ideal statements on Tipuka–Kawelka fighting and poisoning relations, made by two big-men, Kuri and Nditing*

F = *el pukl* in warfare between the two
F = no *el pukl* in warfare between the two
P = poisoning in warfare between the two
P = no poisoning in warfare between the two

Gaps in the cells indicate that information was not specifically given. In some cases it can be inferred from other entries.

(a) Within Tipuka tribe

	Eltimbo 'clan'	Ndikmbo clan	Wanyembo clan	Kitepi clan	Oklembo clan	Kengeke clan	Kendike clan	Kelmbo clan	Waembe clan
Eltimbo	—	—	FP	FP	FP	FP	—	FP	—
Ndikmbo	—	—	—	FP	FP	F	—	—	—
Wanyembo	FP	—	—	—	FP	FP	FP	F	F
Kitepi	FP	FP	—	—	F (once only) P	FP	FP	F	F
Oklembo	FP	FP	FP	F (once only) P	—	FP	FP	FP	FP
Kengeke	FP	F	FP	FP	FP	—	FP (special cases)	FP	—
Kendike	—	—	FP	FP	FP	FP (but still close allies)	—	FP	P
Kelmbo	FP	—	F	F	FP	FP	FP	—	—
Waembe	—	—	F	F	FP	—	P	—	—

(b) Tipuka–Kawelka

	Membo	Mandembo	Kundmbo
Eltimbo	—	FP	FP
Ndikmbo	P	—	—
Wanyembo	—	—	—
Oklembo	FP	FP	FP
Kitepi	FP	FP	FP
Kengeke	FP	FP	FP
Kendike	—	FP	—
Kelmbo	FP	—	FP
Waembe	—	—	—

89

ally. Typically, after fighting between minor enemies, the opponents not only compensated each other but also paid reparations to their allies.

Besides these payments for specific killings, it was expected that after *every* death some form of compensation would be made to the maternal kin of a man or to the natal clan kin of a wife. Such compensation is known as *kik kapa rui*, 'to wipe off the dusty ashes' (which are plastered over their heads and bodies by mourners at a funeral): that is, the compensation is paid because the maternal kin 'feel bad' and ruin the healthy condition of their skin in mourning, and the aim is to make them 'feel good' again. Death-compensation payments thus divide as shown in the accompanying diagram.

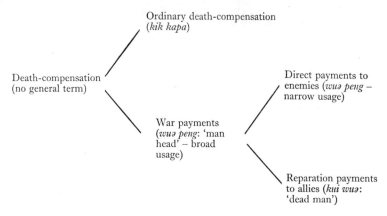

I give some notes on *kik kapa* in Appendix 5, and shall describe the content of war payments in more detail in the next chapter. Here I concentrate on the contexts in which war payments are made.

Informants at Mbukl maintained that in the past no war payments were made to major enemies, only to minor enemies, with whom it was expected that peace could be made and who might be one's allies in a different sequence of fights later. It is with these minor enemy groups that many of a clan's marriages are made, and the individual relationships between in-laws are said to form a 'path' (*nombokla*) along which men can send their ceremonial gifts. With major enemies it is expected that there will be few marriages and hence the 'paths' for these gifts are fewer. Major enemies it is said, 'do not see a road' linking them.

If payments were not made to allies, these had an accepted means of protest, called *el kaep*. The aggrieved ally would rush into the territory of the 'root man', to destroy gardens, steal bananas and pigs, burn houses, and rape women. Far from defending their property, the 'root men' were supposed to stand by and exclaim: 'I ate his man (i.e. his man was killed while helping us), and now he's come to eat us' (i.e. to steal pigs and copulate with women). The destruction could be stopped only by an immediate offer of the reparation payment which was owing. Between regular allies this kind of licensed aggression was clearly an alternative to full-scale attacks. It was, in fact, a means of preserving the alliance while giving satisfaction to the feelings of the aggrieved party.

A milder version of protest-behaviour is *ui-mel* ('mud-thing'). Allies unpaid by their root man may plaster themselves with white and orange clays in the guise of mourners (for the man they have lost), and go to dance before their debtors. They cut down banana-trees also, but do not turn to rape or arson. Clearly, *ui-mel* is performed when feelings are more under control.

Protests of this kind by allies agianst root men can be made between different sections of the same clan, and in the past took the form of stick fights and fisticuffs which were supposed to be non-lethal. The root man/ally relationship continues up the segmentary scale between pair-clans, clans which were alternately minor enemies and allies in major warfare, and whole tribes which acted as allies to each other on occasion. Most payments are in fact made between clans which were minor enemies, since these may owe each other both reparations and direct compensation payments; and there is also a marked degree of rivalry between them.

In recent years, however, largely through the agency of big-men, there have been extensions of payments to groups which are traditionally major enemies. These new payments, leading into reciprocal exchanges, are moves to widen the scope of ceremonial activity, largely directed by big-men.

For example, it may be remembered that when the K. Membo clan, aided by the two other clans in its tribe and also the M. Kimbo clan, defeated the M. Komonkae–Ruprupkae pair, its men moved closer to the Komonkae, taking over land vacated by the losers. In time a friendship developed between two major big-men on opposite sides who were now neighbours to each other, Membo ∂ndipi and Ruprupkae Pakl. ∂ndipi encouraged his clansmen to pay pigs to Pakl, so that they could live in peace with him.

The alliance with the M. Kimbo was also made an occasion for ally-payments, of cooked pig-meat, and the link was revived in 1965, largely by the big-man of K. Mandembo, Ongka. He gave a large number of pearl shells as 'man-head' payments to partners in one section of Kimbo clan, declaring that this was to safeguard his clan's young men who go to work at a plantation along with Kimbo men: the recipients must now 'feel good' and not poison Kawelka men.

Such occasions remain an exception, although they are highly significant from the point of view of understanding the actions of big-men in increasing their exchange networks. Other prestations which involve apparent 'major enemy' groups are either similarly the result of special arrangements made by big-men, or they are examples of the cross-cutting alliances which were analysed in earlier parts of this chapter. Often, they are facilitated by the fact that the exchanging clans had no direct cause or 'root' of war with each other, but were merely allies of two principal combatant clans. The bulk, however, of the payments which I observed in 1964–5, were made between clans which were allies in the past. Table 8 shows the pattern in more detail.

TABLE 8   *Prestations observed near Mbukl, 1964–5*

NOTE. The definition of 'a' prestation is difficult. What I am counting here as separate prestations are gifts from one *clan* to another (or one segment of a clan to another) which have a separate basis in past relationships. For example, if clan A makes gifts separately and for different reasons to clans B, C, and D, I count this as three prestations.

A. 1. Prestations within the clan	3	
2. Between pair-clans	5	
3. Between other allies who were not also minor enemies	2	25
4. Between allies who were also minor enemies	15	
B. 1. Between minor enemies who were not also allies	2	
2. Between ex-major enemies whose relationship had become more friendly	5	8
3. Between direct major enemies	1	
C. 1. War payments to distant groups	3	
2. Other payments to distant groups	4	7
		40

CONCLUSION

In this chapter I have described warfare and alliance in Hagen, and have related certain patterns of warfare to the incidence of compensation payments. In addition, I hope to have shown the importance of big-men, in instigating war, forging alliances, making peace, and extending the range of ceremonial activities. In the next chapter I shall give an outline of the various forms of moka exchange, as a preliminary to discussing big-men and groups in action on specific occasions.

5

MOKA TRANSACTIONS AND MEDIA OF EXCHANGE

DEFINITIONS

Hageners use the term moka in two ways: first, as a general word for the whole complex of their ceremonial exchange system apart from bride-wealth (and a few other types of payment which I list below); and second, more specifically to refer to all ceremonial gifts in which one partner makes a prestation which is greater in value than the simple debt which he owes. It is strictly this increment in excess of debt which is the moka element in the gift and which brings prestige to the giver.

In addition, there are some categories of payment which can, if the parties so wish, be used as a vehicle for making moka. For example, at bridewealth occasions there are exchanges of pigs, shells, and Australian money between the groom's and the bride's kin. Within these, there is always a distinction made between gifts which are for bridewealth proper (*kuimø*) and those which are designed to initiate moka partnerships between the affines.[1] The same holds for growth-payments made on behalf of a child to its matrilateral kin when it is newly weaned, and when its hair is first cut.[2] A big-man may decide to make these payments a depar-ture-point for moka gifts. Gifts to maternal kin continue when a person grows up, and a man takes them on himself, continuing his father's earlier payment on his behalf. Such gifts are called *mam-nga pukl kaklp ngond*, 'I straighten my mother's root and give', i.e. 'I straighten my relationship with my mother's people'. Where there are big-men involved, such gifts to maternal kin may be made a basis for extended moka relations between a span of men connected to the close kinsmen. The same holds for death-payments to maternal kin (*kik kapa*, cf. Appendix 5), which are in effect the final stage of *mam-nga pukl* payments.

---

[1] For analysis of the categories of exchange in bridewealth payments cf. Strathern A. J. and A. M. 1971; and for a more lengthy account Strathern A. M. 1968a.

[2] The two payments are called *wakl te kng*, 'child faeces pig', i.e. a pig paid to maternal kin when a child's faeces become firm as a result of his eating solid foods; and *peng ndi rop tımmın*, 'they cut the head hair'.

The most important type of prestation which is likely to become converted into a moka exchange is the war payment. In the previous chapter I divided this category into *wuə peng* = 'man head' payments, i.e. payments to an enemy group for the killing of one of their men; and *kui wuə* = 'dead man', i.e. payments to an ally for the loss of a man fighting on one's own group's behalf. The first I have called *direct compensation* payments, the second *reparations*.

Both types of payment are preceded, some months in advance, by a *wuə ombil*, 'man bone', payment. The victim's (or ally's) group makes this to the killer's (or root man's), as an initiatory gift. Those who share in the man bone payment are obligated to take part in making the main return gift later. Thus this earlier gift mobilises the groups involved, and through it is settled who the individual partners on each side are to be.

It is said that the killers or root men have 'eaten' the victim, and are now willing to hand over his bones in return for a payment. The ideas here are metaphorical: eating stands for killing; the bones stand for wealth which will be handed over in the main gift. The metaphor is likely to be referred to when the victim's group bring the gifts for *wuə ombil*. The visitors say: 'You killed our man, but you did not really eat him or taste anything sweet; so now we have brought you this cooked pork, so that you may eat it, feel good, and pay *wuə peng* to us.' The form and size of the *wuə ombil* gift indicates to the main donors how much the victim's group expects to receive in return: if live pigs are given, live pigs are expected, and so on. Often it includes live pigs, shells, and cooked pork as well. Special items may be added as an encouragement to the main donors: red pandanus fruits and cassowary eggs, for example.

If the main gift includes shells (nowadays almost exclusively pearl shells, as I shall explain in the next section), the standard form for each transaction is that the donor gives to his partner or partners one or more sets of eight shells. It is said that no material return need be made for this, since the whole gift is a payment for losses in warfare. In practice, as we have seen, the main gift is preceded by an initiatory gift from the recipients-to-be; the direction of gift may be reversed later; and there is also a special arrangement whereby two shells may be added to each set of eight. These extra two are then met by the gift of a small pig, called *kng tembokl rui*, 'pig for killing', which the main donor is expected to cook and distribute to those who have brought him decorations just before the dance to celebrate the final transfer of the concerted main gift is held.

Similarly, if live pigs are given, the main gift is preceded by a *wuə ombil* initiatory gift, and each transaction is in practice conducted in accordance

94

with moka rules. Moka gifts must be reciprocated, and this is what formally ensures the continuance of payments of this kind between groups over time. The motives for continuing these payments will emerge more clearly later, but it can briefly be repeated here that the moka system is a major arena for status-competition in Hagen; and war-payments, which have been interwoven with moka-making, provide a neat set of idioms in terms of which the 'war of status' can be carried on.

The large payments which are nowadays made between groups are usually said to have developed out of earlier, smaller transactions. There is in fact an ideal progression of transactions from gifts immediately following a death to ceremonial exchanges many years after it. First, the killers or root men would give *wantəp ka:n kng*, 'pigs for the *wantəp* tree rope'. These pigs were cooked, and given soon after the victim had died, while his coffin of tree-bark was still being bound with *wantəp* rope. The gift was made in the hope of restraining the mourners from taking instant steps for revenge. A second gift, *køya ongom kør kng*, 'pig to cut the cordyline leaf', was presented during the funeral period when mourners were wearing cordyline leaves round their waists as a sign of grief. Cutting, i.e. removing, the cordylines is a sign that the initial period of violent mourning is over. Much later, the first large payment, again of cooked pig, is made, called *wuə metemen* 'they bear the man', that is, pay adequately for his death. If the recipients of this gift have killed a man of the donor's clan, they may make a reciprocal payment of cooked pork in return for the *wuə metemen* gift; and the two groups may continue afterwards to exchange cooked pork.

More often, *wuə metemen* is followed by *wuə peng*, with payment in pearl shells and perhaps live pigs as well. Subsequent exchanges of pigs between the groups are called *kng oa* or *kng nombokla*, 'pig road'. The groups now say they are making 'a road of pigs' between themselves, and exchanges can continue indefinitely.

The full progression from *wantəp ka:n* to *kng oa* is by no means always realised. In the case of some groups the earlier payments are completed through to *wuə metemen*, in order to avert troublesome relations with a victim's aggrieved group, but the gifts are not converted into the more positive alliance represented by moka-style exchanges. In other cases, where there is a rapprochement between formerly hostile groups, *wuə peng* exchanges may be initiated long after a killing, even if the 'earlier' categories of gifts have not been made at all.

Even in the past, little emphasis seems to have been placed on standard rates of compensation for a single man killed. Bulmer (1960*a*), however, reports certain rates paid among the Kyaka Enga, many of whose exchange customs closely parallel those of the Hageners; and Strauss (1962: 250) states for Hagen that 'for each man fallen in warfare the root men must give at least 4 pigs and 4 pearl shells, and in addition certain "extras" such as salt-packs, cowrie ropes, axes, and so on'. I was not told about these rates. It may be that they are particular to the Central, rather then the Northern Melpa, groups; or that they belong to the days when warfare was still continuing. The version that was given to me stressed that the aim of compensation is not to make a standard, exact payment for a death but to make a payment large enough to soothe the anger of the bereaved. The actual amount paid depends on the relationships between the groups, their current commitments, the involvement of big-men, and so on.

Direct compensation for killings, if paid at all, was in the past made by the 'root man' group on the killer's side of the battle to whichever group had been bereaved. Thus, allies were not committed to paying for killings they inflicted on behalf of a root man group, although the latter was committed to paying its allies for any losses they incurred. If on each side in a battle there is a principal combatant group plus an ally, and each group kills a man from each other group, a number of theoretical possibilities for war payments emerge, as shown in the accompanying diagram.

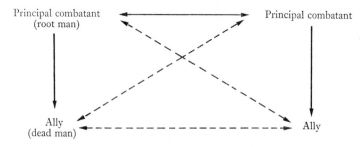

Here the dotted lines represent channels of possible exchange which in the past were less likely to be used.[1] Nowadays, where such sets of four groups form blocs for exchange relations, all the possibilities are realised. It can be seen that if killings were reciprocal, there is a possibility of reciprocal payments. One group may pay *wuə peng* and the recipients subsequently make returns under the same rubric.

[1] Vicedom (1943-8, vol. 2; 155-6), however, notes a case. The Mundika were fighting the Kotumbu tribe, with Ndika clans as their allies. Ndika men were killed, and Kotumbu paid their clansmen compensation with eight cooked pigs and four shells for each man who had died. But the Ndika were not appeased, and took revenge as well. Here the Kotumbu, a small tribe, was faced with a powerful set of clans from the large Ndika tribe, and its direct payment to the Ndika seems to have been an attempt to buy the latter off.

Moka transactions

In addition to these war payments, there are categories of shell-moka and pig-moka which are unconnected with death-compensation.

Shell-moka is described as *moka køi kng*, 'bird-pig moka', or simply as *kin moka*, 'pearl shell moka'. As with the other transactions, it consists of an exchange of an initiatory for a main gift. The initiatory gift consists of a number of unit gifts of two pearl shells plus one pig, and the ideal return for each unit is a set of eight or ten pearl shells. The main gift exceeds the initiatory gift in value. The items in the initiatory gift are all named. The pig is *køi kng*, 'bird-pig', i.e. a pig given to help finance the moka dance, at which bird of paradise feathers are worn;[1] the two shells are *kin pol* (or *por*) *pek rakl*, 'the large and the small shell', since they are supposed to be of unequal size.[2] The whole initiatory gift is called *moka kint*. (The same term is sometimes transferred to the public occasion when returns for these initiatory gifts are made.)

Pig-moka is named simply *kng moka*. The unit transaction here is a return of live pigs or cooked pork for an initiatory gift of 'small pigs', *kng pek*. *Pek* here is sometimes explained as a shortened form of *pendek* = the front leg of a pig, which is less substantial than the back leg or *por*.[3] The initiatory gift may consist of cooked pork and/or live pigs also. Cooked legs of pork may be presented to a partner as a private initiatory gift, or en masse by men of the future recipient group to the main donors, when the gift is called *il okl kng* 'saliva belly pig', that is pork to please the palate of the main donors and to encourage them to make the main gift. A similar initiatory gift of live pigs is called *kng peng kont*, 'pig head alive'. Concerted initiatory gifts seem to be made only within the context of 'moka chains', which I shall describe in the next chapter.

The main gift of pigs may also comprise live pigs or cooked pork. In the first case the gift can take one of two forms. The most common form is 'pig-moka proper' (*kng moka ingk*), in which there are individual gifts between partners, but the donors combine to dance at the final transfer of the pigs. Alternatively, when the gift is passing between ex-major enemy groups between which there are few social contacts, men of the donor group contribute a pig or two each to a block gift which is presented to

[1] Cf. Strathern A. J. and A. M. 1971. The particular feathers referred to here are the Duke of Saxony bird's long crest feathers.

[2] Occasionally – and often, previously, in the Nebilyer Valley area – a third shell is given, called *kin koklpe*.

[3] In another usage *kng pek rui* means to 'ask for more pigs' than one has been offered by a partner. It is possible, then, that *pek* simply means 'solicitory pigs'. In a further usage *pek rui* means 'to scrape away', viz. to peel vegetables. Some informants say this meaning applies in the context of moka also: the recipient 'scrapes away' at the donor's resistance and persuades him to hand over more pigs and shells. Cf. also p. 115.

97

the recipients as a whole group. The recipients then re-distribute the gift internally. Big-men are usually important as negotiators on each side. At a later stage in the sequence of exchanges between the two groups individual partnerships between men of ordinary status may develop; initially, big-men manage the transaction. This type of block gift is called *kng ende*.

Prestations of cooked pork given in moka are described as *kng kui*, 'cooked pig'. If donor and recipient groups are allies, there are individual partnerships, otherwise not. The two groups alternate in gift-giving at intervals of a few years. The theoretical progression in the size of the gift, at least as some informants explain the matter, is x, $2x$, $4x$, $8x$ and so on; but in practice smaller increments are added.[1] The increment alone is taken as the debt for the next gift, so that the situation is controlled, as can be seen from the following scheme:

A gives x to B
B gives $2x$ to A
Thus A owes x to B
Next A gives $2x$ to B
And B owes x to A
Next B gives $2x$ to A
and so on.

When live pigs are given, a number of special categories of gift may be involved. An ideal number of pigs for a single man to give to a single recipient is a set of eight. If this ideal number is realised, the recipient should return a large pig out of the total of eight, 'so that the donor should not be too short of pigs' for his other purposes. A gift of eight pigs is a large one, and the return is made to avoid 'shame', for if the donor gives too much he is said to be making the recipient into a 'rubbish-man' (*təpa korpa mondonom*). The return of a pig in this way is likely to occur only between close friends, who are nevertheless sensitive to their mutual status relationship and wish to preserve their equality. The returned pig is called *kng por*, 'large pig'.

Further, of a number of pigs which a donor gives to a single recipient, one or even two may be exchanged directly for a precisely equivalent pig, so that the superiority of the main gift does not become too great. A similar arrangement can be made for shell gifts. The pigs exchanged directly in this way are called *kng anmbile*, 'tongue pigs'. Tongue here stands by

---

[1] The 'doubling' concept may date only from recent times or be an inaccurate 'native model' of what actually happens. Cf. Drucker and Heizer 1967, pp. 53 ff.

synecdoche for the pigs' heads, which are supposed to be matched and found equal in size.

A final complication is that pigs for the main gift may be handed over either privately, in advance of the ceremonial transfer, or at this final transfer itself. A reason for handing them to partners in advance is that the donor is relieved of the burden of feeding more pigs than his household can properly manage. The recipient in turn may dispose of a pig received in this way to yet another partner, before the ceremony of transferring the pigs to his group has taken place. Should this happen, he is expected to bring an equivalent pig of his own to take the place of the donor's pig at the moka ceremony. Often the donor complains that substitute pigs which are brought are not up to the mark of those he originally gave. On the other hand, if donors badly disappoint recipients, the latter may refuse to bring their substitute pigs. The donors' moka is then spoiled by the appearance of 'empty pig-stakes' (stakes to which pigs are tied on the ceremonial ground).

Pigs given in advance are *ka:n kng* 'rope pig', or *koemb ile porom kng*, 'the pig that goes first'. Substitute pigs are *omong kng*.[1]

Pigs not given in advance are *kng kont*, 'new pigs'. The same term can be used also to contrast with pigs which are paid to meet debts (*kng pund*). In this sense, 'new pigs' are true moka-pigs, representing an increment 'on the back of' (*mbukl-øl*) what is paid to meet debts.

As the categories relating to pig gifts are rather more complicated than those for shells, I have represented them in a key (Fig. 7).

In the key it will be seen that I have included one category not mentioned so far, *nde olka kng*. These are pigs given as 'extras'. The donors bring them out from a hiding place at the final dance and tie them to a large stake made of *olka* wood (hence the term for them). In theory, they are to be cooked and enjoyed by the recipients rather than re-invested in further transactions; in practice this is not always possible, for the recipients may be short of goods for their future prestations. The *olka* pigs are supposed to lie peacefully heaped on each other while speeches are made nearby: otherwise it is a bad omen. The *olka* stake, it is said, should also remain in place at the ceremonial ground until the gift is reciprocated, both as a sign of debt and to inform passers-by that moka has been made by the group which owns the ceremonial place. Much interest centres on these 'extra' pigs; in fact, quarrels invariably break out over their distribution.

---

[1] Literally this means 'leaf pig'. The name refers to the phrase *omong iti*, to grow large, as a leaf unfolds and grows. 'Leaf pigs' should be large ones, just as *kng por* are.

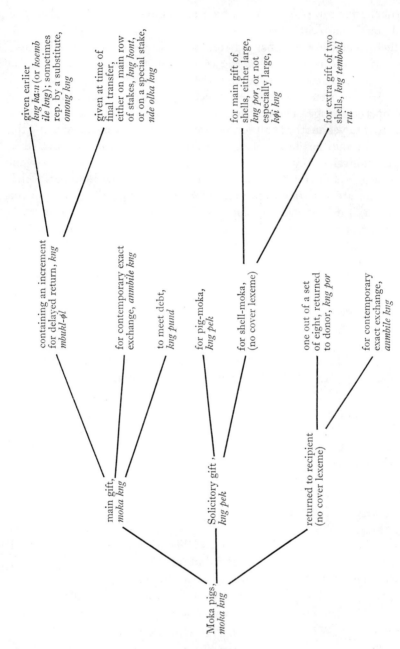

Fig. 7 Categories relating to pig-moka

Other extras are regularly given, and similarly bring increased prestige to the donors at a moka; but less feeling surrounds them. Examples are: live cassowaries, long bamboo tubes of decorating oil, packs of salt, cassowary eggs, pandanus fruits, and nowadays live steers for butchering.[1] Men also talk of giving bicycles or cars, live marsupials, wild pig-meat, and types of edible snake found in the Jimi Valley; but such promises seem rarely to be kept. In the past ceremonial stone axes were given also.

In the next section I shall examine in greater detail the media of exchange used in moka. In particular I shall discuss changing rates of exchange for shells since warfare has stopped and Europeans have settled in the Hagen area.

MEDIA OF EXCHANGE

Items and their use

The main items traditionally employed in trading, bridewealth, and *moka* exchange in Hagen are: pigs, six kinds of shell valuables, bird of paradise plumes and other feathers used for decorations, salt, decorating oil, stone axe-blades and hafted stone axes, marsupial furs, and red ochre paint. Of these, pigs and shells were most important in moka and bridewealth; axe-blades, oil, and salt were significant in determining certain patterns of trade.

Table 9 indicates the six types of shell,[2] and Table 10 the main categories of use for these and the other items.

No clear, multi-referential distinction can be made between trade and ceremonial exchange in the Highlands, although a distinction between these two as ideal types can be constructed. Thus we could contrast immediate and delayed exchange, exchange between unrelated and related persons, exchange of unlike and exchange of like objects, exchanges private to two individuals and those connected with group relations, and a focus on useful objects by contrast with a focus on the creation of friendship. The second terms of all these contrasts correspond to ceremonial exchange as it actually is practised in the Highlands; but trade does not conform to all the first terms, for it often did involve the creation of friendship and

---

[1] Steers are obtained from European plantation-owners; or from men who have begun to keep beef cattle, following Administration schemes.

[2] Vicedom (vol. 1: 107–9) mentions that in the 1930s *Cymbium, Nautilus*, and *Ovula* shells were also found, the last introduced by Europeans. Cf. Berndt 1962: photographs opposite pp. 106, 363, 395, for *Ovula*; Bulmer (1964: 56). Vicedom refers also to *Cypraea tigris*, a type of cowrie.

TABLE 9   *Terms for shell valuables*

Melpa and Temboka terms	English glosses	Conchological terms
1 *Kokla kin* or *mande* (*rumøl* or *tumøl* in T.)	Gold-lip pearl shell	*Pinctada margaritifera* Lightfoot
2 *Kokla køtø* or *ørpi* (*kata* in T.)	Green-snail shell	*Turbo marmoratus* L.
3 *Kokla raem* (*tam* in T.)	Bailer or white-gum shell	*Melo amphora* L.
4 *Kokla ranggel* or *mong* (*tanggel* in T.)	Cowrie shell	*Cypraea moneta*, etc.
5 *Kokla nuin* or *pikti* or *rambe*; in form of mat or headband: *pela øi* or *nggraem*	Nassa or dog-whelk shell	*Marginella* sp.
6 *Kokla poke*	Conus shell	[No specimen collected]

NOTE: I am most grateful to Dr Anna Bidder, of Cambridge University Zoology Department, for identifying specimens of shells, now in the Museum of Archaeology and Ethnology in Cambridge.

TABLE 10   *Uses of exchange media in Hagen, approx. 1930–65*

	Ceremonial exchange, life-cycle payments, payments to experts	Bride-wealth	Sacrifices	Self-decoration	Food	Tools for work
Live pigs, pork and grease	—	—	—	—	—	
Live marsupials, meat, and furs	—	—	—	—	—	
Cassowaries, meat and plumes	—	—	—	—	—	
Pearl shells, bailers, Cowries, nassa	—	—	—	—	—	
Green-snail, conus shells	—	occasionally		—	—	
Axes and axe-blades	—	—	—	—	—	—
Salt packs	—	occasionally			—	
Bird of paradise plumes, etc.	—	—	—	—	—	
Decorating oil	—	—	—	—		
Red ochre				—		

sometimes was conducted by delayed reciprocity. Nevertheless we can distinguish between full ceremonial exchange, especially moka, and occasional transactions for the purpose of obtaining valuable goods by means of

TABLE II *Uses of shell valuables*

(*a*) Moka, trade and bridewealth

Shell	Use in moka	Trade	Bridewealth
Pearl shell	*køi kng* and *wuə peng*	direct exchange for pigs, tree-oil, plumes; previously for salt	standard item: now in decline
Green-snail	previously in *wuə peng* (whole examples, purchased in stores)	minor adjunct to use of other shells	—
Bailer	as pearl shell, but more limited use	as pearl shell; very popular in trade with Ialibu and Tambul	previously: occasional use; not now
Cowries	previously in *køi kng* and *wuə peng*. Not now	previously: exchanged for nassa mats, small nos. of shells used for minor transactions	previously important. Replaced by pearl shell
Nassa	as cowries	exchanged for pigs and cowrie ropes	as cowries
Conus	rare	popular in trade with Ialibu for pigs, etc.	—

(*b*) Decorations

Pearl shell: larger examples, mounted on resin boards are worn suspended over the breast at dances, especially by women and young girls. In the past, the boards were smaller; shells might also be worn in rows, reaching from the neck downwards (cf. Vicedom 1943–8, vol. 2: plate 12). Smaller shells (*kin mapa*) are worn unmounted, low over the breasts by young women, high at the neck by men, as everyday decorations.

Green-snail: pieces are worn by older men tied to the hair behind their ears. Women wear them at their ears also, especially for dancing at moka and one of the spirit cults (*kor wøp*).

Bailer: small bailers and an inside part of the whole shell are worn by boys, women, and girls, everyday. Both sexes wear large bailers over the breast for dancing. Men also wear rounded pieces on their foreheads.

Cowrie: until these went out of use as currency, they were popular as women's decorations, swathed round the body at dances. Men wore them also, in less profusion. They might also be draped over corpses at funerals (cf. Vicedom, vol. 2: plates 6, 7, 8). Old men occasionally wear a few cowries at the neck; boys and girls longer necklaces.

Nassa head-bands, mats, and necklaces: head bands were greatly prized before 1945 and were worn only by important men. The Central Melpa obtained them from Mendi, where they were also valued: hence their scarcity. Bands were often worn only partly covered with shells (cf., e.g., Vicedom, vol. 1: plate 5 nos. 1 and 2). Now they are no longer a mark of status.

Mats were worn by women at dances, suspended at their apron-fronts. They are out of fashion now.

Necklaces were worn by men or women suspended from the ears and running across the cheeks to the nose, where they were supported by pins inserted into holes in the nasal alae (cf. Vicedom, vol. 1: plate 10 no. 3).

Conus: these are favourite wear for big-men. They are inserted into the pierced nasal septum. At dances a whole row of men may wear them. In the past, when they were scarcer, they were a more definite mark of status.

handing over some acceptable exchange goods. Moreover, we can 'distinguish the circulation of goods within an area from the movement of an item along a route from its source' (Strathern A.M. 1966: 119), whatever the mechanics whereby circulation and movement along a route were effected. Both elaborate ceremonial exchange and less elaborate trading transactions may be involved in both processes.

Table 10 gives only a crude picture. We need to know also the relative importance of the items, their value in exchange for each other and how

TABLE 12   *Changes in rates of exchange for shell and other valuables*

(*a*) Shells

Shell	Earlier rate, 1933–49	Devalued rate, 1950 – Central Melpa, late 1950s – Northern Melpa	Cost in trade stores in 1950s onwards
Pearl shell	1 shell = 1 small pig (Ross 1936: 353) traditionally (pre-European times) 1 shell = 1 full grown pig	2 shells = 1 small pig 4 shells = 1 med. pig 8 shells = 1 large pig 1 shell = A$2–6[a]	A$4–12
Green-snail	minor item, not often exchanged	out of currency	A$4–10 (whole example)
Bailer	as the pearl shell	out of currency but valued as decoration	up to A$12
Cowrie	1 rope = 1 medium pig 1 necklace = 1 little pig (Leahy and Crain 1937: 192) 1 rope = 1 nassa mat	out of currency (occasionally given in moka to Jimi groups)	paid only as wages and for food
Nassa	1 large headband = 1 full-grown pig 1 large mat = 1 full-grown pig 1 mat = 1 cowrie rope	out of currency *c.* 1953: 5 mats = 1 full-grown pig now out of currency	paid only for food
Conus	1 shell = 1 small pig	out of currency	up to A$10

NOTES

(1) 1 pearl shell used to be paid for about a month's labour. Leahy in 1934 paid workers 4 or 5 cowries a day; later he raised the rate to 10 a day. Nassa shells were paid at a rate of about a dozen for as many pounds of sweet potatoes. (N.B. some 200–400 cowries are needed to make a cowrie rope; several hundred nassa shells are required for a single mat.)

(2) Combinations of different types of shell were originally used in moka. For example, 4 nassa mats + 4 cowrie ropes + 2 pearl shells could be put together to make up a set of 10 valuables. When exchange rates altered, making different types of shells of unequal value, this could no longer be done.

(3) Pigs are measured roughly by their height. A small pig is below the knee of an ordinary adult Hagen man, a medium one is up to the knee, and a large one is just above it or further up the thigh.

Moka transactions

(b) Other items

Item	History of exchange value
Cassowary	Equivalent traditionally to a long tube of decorating oil or 4 pearl shells and a pig, and still sometimes exchanged for these items. In 1964–5 conventional money value was A$50 for a full-grown, black-plumaged specimen. Young ones bought from Jimi Valley Melpa men, who find them in the forest and rear them, at price of A$10–20. Most often given in *wuə peng* or bridewealth payments.
Decorating tree-oil	See above. Rates for this item have remained fairly stable. Nebilyer men pay 4 shells for a long tube, Northern Melpa men add a pig or a head-dress to this price (they are further away from the main source, Lake Kutubu).[b]
Work-axe blades	1 blade for a pack of salt (unspecified size) from the Enga area. 1 large blade for a pearl shell. 1 small blade for a conus shell or a measure (not a pack) of salt. The blades do not circulate nowadays, as they have been replaced by steel axes. Nebilyer men used packs of salt from Mendi, ex-Enga, to pay for work-axe blades from the Wahgi, and exchanged the blades for conus shells with Ialibu men.
Battle-axe blades, ceremonial axes	1 full-grown pig, 1 pearl shell, 1 large salt pack of 12 lb or more (cf. Meggitt 1956: 102).
Steel axes from Ialibu	1 big pig. This was the rate at which Hageners first paid for blades obtained directly from Europeans also. Nowadays a medium-sized axe blade costs A$1.50.
Salt-packs from Enga, Mendi, and the Jimi Valley	1 pack (large) = 1 pig, 1 stone axe, 1 pearl shell. Men from Tambul used, by their own account, to go to the headwaters of the Lai river, there to make ash salt. They paid the owners of the salt springs with axes, cowrie ropes, and pearl shells.

NOTE: for *axe-quarries* in the Highlands see Vial (1940: 158–63), Bulmer and Bulmer (1964), Reay (1959: 105), Brookfield and Brown (1963: 65), Salisbury (1962: 85), Strathern A. M. (1965, 1966, n.d.), and Chappell (1966). On *sources of salt* cf. Meggitt (1958: 309–13), Maahs (1950), Hides (1936: 124), Vicedom (vol. 1: 228 ff.), Reay (1959: 105), Brookfield and Brown (1963: 65 and 78), Stopp (1963: 17), Rappaport (1967: 106), Godelier (1969), and Hughes (n.d.).

[a] Money rates are expressed in Australian dollars, although the change to dollars from pounds occurred only in 1966.
[b] Cf. Williams 1940: 134. The oil has a sweeter smell than pig-grease, *pace* Williams, who found it unpleasing.

exchange rates have changed over time, and their respective sources and routes by which they entered the Hagen area.

The main items of currency today are pigs, Australian money, and pearl shells. Pigs and pearl shells are the dominant items employed in moka, while all three are important in bridewealth. Stone axes, cowrie ropes, and nassa mats were, at least until the 1940s, important in both moka and bridewealth payments. They were replaced as currency by the pearl shell and, later, Australian money. Cowries and nassa retain a minor place in personal decoration as necklaces and headbands; stone axes, with their large, polished blades and plaited balancers, are still valued both as important adjuncts to dance decorations for men and for sale to European tourists.[1] Other items – green-snail, conus, cassowaries, decorating oil, and native salt – have always been 'extras', or optional bonus gifts, in the moka system, and similarly of optional use in bridewealth. Cassowaries and the long tubes of decorating oil retain these functions; green-snail and conus shells are still popular as ornaments; while salt-packs are nowadays only occasionally seen, and are rarely used in transactions. Tables 11 and 12 summarise information on the main uses of shells, in the past and now and on exchange rates. In the next section I shall consider how changes in the uses of exchange media have come about.

Changes in exchange rates

In looking at changes in the use and exchange rates of items in trade over time, we can distinguish between items which have passed completely out of use, those which no longer function as exchange media but continue to have some other use, and those which are still used in exchanges but at altered rates.

Stone work-axe blades and salt-packs are no longer in use at all. They have been entirely replaced by steel axes and European salt. For a time packs of native salt continued to circulate in moka prestations in Hagen, but by the 1960s they were rarely used.[2]

Among shells, green-snail and conus were always used most prominently as decorations rather than as moka payments. As with the other shells they can be borrowed for dances and later returned to their owners: they are rarely exchanged nowadays, except perhaps for cash. They survive as ornaments. By contrast, cowrie ropes and nassa mats and bands *were* used in moka exchanges; their popularity and prestige-value as ornaments dropped when they ceased to be used as currency. The conclusions from this contrast seem to be that green-snail and conus have an aesthetic effect as decorations which is not duplicated by other items – hence their retention; whereas the value of nassa mats and cowrie ropes as ornaments depended on their value as currency, that is, they were symbols of wealth. When the pearl shell replaced them, they lost their value as decorations also. The same argument should apply to bailers: they are still popular as impressive chest ornaments, although they are no longer used in moka.

---

[1] Cf. Strathern A. M. n.d. (forthcoming in *Proceedings of the Prehistoric Society*).

[2] Ongka, a Northern Melpa big-man of K. Mandembo clan, gave one away to his traditionalist sister's husband from the Jimi Valley in 1965. It was given as an 'extra', along with a tube of decorating oil, some fowls, and a large saucepan.

Moka transactions

Items in which regional trade continues are decorating oil, furs, plumes of all kinds, and cassowaries. Money is used to obtain the latter three items (unless they are being given in moka). For decorating oil men prefer a direct exchange with an adult cassowary. The money cost of all these items is rising as the total volume of cash in the hands of Hageners increases through sale of land, coffee, labour, and vegetable crops. One item whose price has risen steeply is the decorative stone axe: this is because of its potentialities for sale to Europeans. Jimi men now produce blades from soft slate instead of hard hornfelsed meta-sediments, so that the quality of axes falls as their production rises to meet tourist demands.

How did the decline in use of cowrie ropes and nassa mats occur? In pre-European contact times (before 1933) shells of all kinds were much scarcer. Pearl shells came in from the Wahgi and up from the Nebilyer Valley, traded in from Ialibu and Mendi. Hageners had a sufficient supply of stone axes for subsistence, but valued shells highly for use in moka and bridewealth; hence demand was brisk when European explorers, missionaries, and Administration officers brought in shells as payment for labour and food. At the same time as supplying an existing want the Europeans actually increased the demand for shells by stopping warfare and encouraging Hageners to make war payments. Europeans settled first among the Central Melpa and Northern Nebilyer groups, and enriched these with payments for wage-labour. Gradually, the new wealth dispersed outwards in all kinds of exchanges, effecting adjustments in exchange rates both in trade *and* in ceremonial payments and bridewealth. The size of prestations increased, and the unit value of shells dropped. It seems possible that at one time surrounding groups gave more wives than usual to the Central Melpa men, but such a process would also be partly inhibited by traditional enmities and fears of poisoning.

The excitement caused by the arrival of Europeans and the influx of wealth objects is reflected in accounts by old men who were youths when the Leahy brothers and Taylor first came in 1933. One account I have is by Kint, an aged big-man of the Kope tribe, who seems to have made friends with Taylor: 'Before we Kope were involved in fighting, and as all of my group had been killed I went to live with kinsfolk at Kømnga among the Roklaka. One day we had made a fire and were sitting together when suddenly we heard the news that some people had arrived. Kiap Taylor came up and shook my hand, and pulled at my arm. I left my spear and, taking my axe only, I went with him. He showed me some sugar-cane peel, and then put his hand in his pocket and showed me four large cowrie shells. I went back to my garden, cut some good sugar-cane and brought it to him; later I brought him a banana-bunch in the same way. He took me into his tent and gave me plenty of shells, and I covered them with a piece of paper which he handed to me and slipped them underneath my bark belt. My friends standing outside said that Taylor was a spirit and would kill me; but later, when we brought more bananas, he gave us more cowries, plenty of them. "They used to tell the story of a cassowary which laid cowries in a pond", I thought, "but now this white man has come. Never mind the big-men, we ordinary men will go and work for him and we'll get plenty of shells." So I stayed with Taylor. Waklpkae Nykint shouted to me "The white men are like *Tei wamb* [sky spirits; in some stories also cannibals]. They are *tei wamb* who tried to climb up into the sky by a rock, but it was greasy and so they have come back here. Don't kill them. Let them be and give them food!" The men told me to come back and sleep in the men's house with them, but I told my wife: "He gave me some cowries. All my clansmen have been killed, it doesn't matter if I die too. I want to go and see if I can get more cowries". And I gave the cowries to her to look at, in case I should die [through contact with the sky spirits]. Next morning the Roklaka thought "If we kill this company and throw their bodies into the Gumant river we can get their cargo", and they readied their weapons. But Taylor eluded them, and his cargo-line swam across the Gumant, and I followed them ... [At Kelua he met the Leahy brothers and saw how they gave conus and pearl shells in exchange for pigs] ... When I finally left them they paid me with pearl shells, and later I was made a boss-boy, afterwards a tultul and a luluai.'

It seems clear that the influx of shells made these available to men other than those who in the past had dominated the moka by their exchange partnerships. A Northern Melpa big-man[1] listed for me 23 men who were the only ones in the Tipuka and Kawelka tribes to have pearl shells in their possession 'about the time the Europeans arrived': and it is likely that his account actually relates to a time shortly after the arrival of the Leahys and Taylor. His account agrees with that of Vicedom (1943–8, vol. 2), who argues that before European contact big-men monopolised shell moka payments in Hagen. Kint's surprise at Taylor's offer of shells in direct return for food or help related to the fact that such an exchange was unprecedented. Vegetable foods were available to everyone, including less important men, who could thus enrich themselves. Previously, vegetable foods had to be fed to pigs and these raised for eventual exchange with shells, if shells could be found: now food and shells were exchanged

---

[1] Councillor Rokla of Tipuka Oklembo clan.

directly. At one time, it seems some 500 pearl shells per month were flown in by the Leahys.

Eventually this increase in wealth led to inflation. But this was delayed by the strength and elasticity of the demand for shells. In particular, the demand for pearl shells seems quickly to have outstripped that for cowries and nassa.[1] Pearl shells replaced others in the standard transactions of moka and bridewealth. Among Central Melpa groups this process was well advanced by 1950; among the Northern Melpa at Mbukl it was delayed till the middle 1950s, for they were further from European suppliers until a mission station was established in their area post-1950.

With the cessation of warfare after 1945 and the spread of steel axes and bush-knives (cf. Salisbury 1962) exchange activity has greatly increased. Hageners did not initially see the increase in wealth as undesirable 'inflation', but as a means of making moka properly. In moka the more one gives away the greater is one's prestige and credit. But if supplies are inflated demands of partners and their standards of what constitutes an adequate payment increase commensurately, so that it takes more shells to achieve the same amount of prestige. Eventually, if shells become too plentiful, their devaluation is bound to be so great that they will go out of currency.

The earlier replacement of cowries and nassa shells by pearl shells was a result, essentially, of the greater esteem in which the pearl shell was held, traditionally, before Europeans arrived.[2] The current decline in the 'esteem value' and the exchange value of pearl shells results both from the vast increase in their supply and the advent of Australian money, which can be used to obtain new ranges of goods and has penetrated the ceremonial and trade sectors of the economy as well.

Initially, with the increase in numbers of pearl shells, bridewealth payments became huge. In earlier times (pre-1933) only cooked pork, a few live pigs and shells, and stone axes were paid (cf. Vicedom vol. 2: 206-7 and plate 2 no. 2). When steel tools were introduced and warfare was stopped, stone axes were dropped from bridewealth and replaced by pigs, concomitantly with inflation in the numbers of pearl shells. From the mid 1940s till 1960 inflation continued. Big-men paid higher rates in bridewealth than others, in order to maintain their superior status: 60–100

---

[1] For a local fluctuation, however, cf. Ross 1936: 353. Ross (1969: 61) reveals the cash prices of shells which were used to purchase pigs and vegetable foods in 1934: for example, a bailer shell costing about 25 cents would purchase a 200 lb pig. The cost, it may be noticed, is well below the price set on bailers in trade stores during the 1950s.

[2] In Appendix 6 I discuss the evaluation of pearl shells and their preparation for use in exchanges.

pearl shells might be disbursed for a single bridewealth.[1] From 1960 onwards the situation began to change. The Administration no longer favoured the payment of shells for food and labour; cash cropping began, fostered by the Department of Agriculture; Local Government Councils were established, with the explicit aim of speeding up economic development and the introduction of the Hageners to the use of cash. Mount Hagen township began to grow, and stores and vehicles proliferated. More land was purchased for large-scale development. All this occurred as part of a general programme the Administration was following under the aegis and stress of comment from the United Nations. A market began in Mount Hagen, run by the local council, to which vegetables were brought and sold for cash to the growing numbers of indigenous labourers and clerks in Hagen township. People brought produce to the market either on foot or in vehicles purchased by whole clans co-operatively. Council tax rates rose, stimulating the need for cash. Councillors, influenced by advice of the Administration and by what they heard from other areas, also set limits on the size of bridewealth payments. It was argued that high payments encouraged parents to persuade their married daughters to separate from a first husband and re-marry some one who was offering a higher price. (Much of this argument was somewhat inaccurate, since bridewealth involves elaborate *reciprocal* payments between the groom's and the bride's side, but it is true that the bride's side gains a little from the transactions.) When Dei L.G.C. was established in 1962, a theoretical limit of 30 items (e.g. either 20 shells and 10 pigs or 20 pigs and 10 shells) was placed on bridewealth payments. The tribes within the Council are the Tipuka, Kawelka, Minembi, Kombukla, Kendipi, etc., who were the main subjects of my study. Partly as a response to this specific rule – which did not mention Australian money – cash was introduced into bridewealth about this time, and as the amounts of cash required for a single payment rose, so the numbers of shells fell. The numbers of pigs, by contrast, have remained fairly constant. Clearly, money is replacing shells as a scarce, admired, and valuable medium of exchange. The supply situation is changing also: shells are no longer being imported in any numbers, whereas money is becoming increasingly available. Whether the shell currency will eventually recover or whether it will be driven out completely by money remains to

[1] It is worth stressing here that rates changed in the ceremonial as well as the trade 'sector' of exchange. Indeed, as I have mentioned, sharp distinctions between these two sectors would be unrealistic. An important reason for this response in ceremonial exchanges to changes in supply of shells was the enormous *scale* of the changes. In bridewealth, for example, it was likely that rates would rise to prevent too sudden and unstable competition for women.

be seen in the next few years (post 1969). Much depends on whether moka will continue as a valued institution or not and on the degree to which money can penetrate into moka exchanges and bridewealth.

I now return to traditional trade routes and sources for shells.

TRADE ROUTES AND SOURCES OF SHELLS

Of the items used in trade and ceremonial exchange, only one, the pig, is produced throughout the Highlands. Until Europeans brought new strains of pigs, the only type was *Sus scrofa*, which is also 'probably present in feral state in all forest areas of any size below 5,500'' (Bulmer 1964: 48); so that no group possessed a genetically superior strain. However altitude, availability of pastures, feeding, and breeding methods no doubt made some areas richer in pigs than others, so that potentially this could have influenced trade patterns.

Production of many of the other items is more definitely restricted. Furs and plumes can be obtained only from forest areas. Cassowaries breed only in the forest, in particular the Jimi Valley and parts of the southern Nebilyer Valley. Jimi men capture the chicks and rear them. Native salt was in the past produced in the Jimi also and in the Wahgi Valley, but I have the impression that the quantities obtained from the Enga area west of Hagen were greater. Decorating oil is tapped from a particular kind of tree at Lake Kutubu in Papua (Williams 1940–1: 132–3), and is carried up in its long bamboo containers via Mendi to Hagen. The manufacture of stone axe-blades near to Hagen was confined mainly to Chimbu (Dom quarry), the South Wahgi (Abiamp), and a number of sites north of Buk on the Jimi Divide and in the Jimi Valley.

Shells, of course, were not 'produced' at all, but came to Mount Hagen mainly from the Nebilyer Valley ex-Tambul and Mendi. Possibly they also came along the Wahgi from the east. Nassa-shells, one type of conus shell, and green-snails came through to the Northern Melpa groups from the Jimi, but whether they came as an offshoot from Wahgi routes or via some independent route from the northern coast of New Guinea is uncertain.

Although it is true that many different kinds of item were constantly being passed between individual partners in accordance with their particular needs, both along what I have suggested are 'trade routes' and at random to these, it seems reasonable to argue that certain main flows of objects occurred in response to differential needs. Thus the Enga in the west had few axe-factories,[1] whereas the Hageners were short of salt, which the Enga possessed. The Mendi had no axe quarries, but they did control some of the access routes for pearl shells, conus shells, and decorating oil which came into Hagen. In the north, Jimi Melpa speakers had both salt and axes, but they wanted shells and pigs also, and were willing to exchange their products for these.

Rappaport (1967: 106–7) has made the point that the inclusion of valuables with utilitarian goods (e.g. salt and axes) in a single 'sphere of conveyance' helps to distribute the utilitarian objects adequately over a wide area. His argument depends on a situation, realised in the Highlands, in which the production of certain utilitarian goods is restricted to small numbers of local groups. The demand of a single local group for a utilitarian good is limited by its members' consumption needs. If the utilitarian good it produces its exchangeable only for one other scarce utilitarian good, for example, if axe-blades could be exchanged only for salt, the manufacturers of both would tend to produce only enough of their own good to satisfy their demand for the other. The demands of many other groups around them for these same goods would thus remain unsatisfied. Including shells and other valuables in the range of items which can be exchanged for the utilitarian goods solves this problem, since the producers' demands for shells are likely to be more elastic than their demands for utilitarian goods only. In particular, Rappaport postulates, the inclusion of valuables overcomes the difficulties of a chain-like structure of partnerships, and this is precisely the structure which develops where sources of production are few and fairly far apart and political relations between groups make it impossible for men in every local group to have personal ties with men in the groups which control production (i.e. where a web-like structure, in Rappaport's terms, cannot develop).

This argument, propounded for the Maring, holds also for Hagen, with the additional point that to the Hageners *ceremonial* axe-blades and, in some circumstances salt-packs, were *themselves* valuables as well as or instead of being utilitarian objects: ceremonial axes and large salt-packs were given away in moka and bridewealth, and circulated just as other valuables did. One can argue, therefore, that they were not simply included in the same sphere of conveyance as valuables, but were actually converted into the same category of goods as shells, plumes, etc.

Rappaport's argument is relevant also to Salisbury's analysis (1962: Ch. 3) of indigenous economic activities among the Siane into three distinct

[1] Two axe-quarries have now (1969) been discovered in the Wapenamanda–Wabag area, but the extent of their contribution to the supply of axes for the Enga populations is uncertain (Bulmer R. N. H. – personal communication).

nexūs, recognised by the Siane themselves. The three nexūs can be glossed as subsistence, luxury, and ceremonial activities. Each nexus is characterised by a particular mode of reciprocity, by the type of goods employed in it, and by the social relationships to which it applies, thus:

Nexūs	Types of goods and services	Mode of reciprocity	Social relationships
subsistence	vegetable foods help in garden work	generalised	intra-clan relationships
luxury	pandanus oil trinkets	balanced	inter-clan *individual* relationships
ceremonial	pigs shell valuables	balanced	inter-clan *group* relationships

From this initial scheme Salisbury develops the point that the essential distinctions are between the types of relationships and the modes of reciprocity that go with these, not between the types of goods and services. Thus pigs and shells are sometimes distributed within the clan, but if this is done, the distribution takes place on quite a different basis from inter-clan presentations. Conversely, vegetable foods are sometimes presented in First Fruits ceremonies from one clan to another, but they are then treated as if they were ceremonial valuables.

Accepting this modification of the scheme, it can be seen that similar distinctions to those the Siane make appear also in other Highlands societies. But there are problems. *How* important is the type of good for defining each separate nexus? How would salt and axes, as they are used by the Maring, be placed into one or another of the nexūs? From one point of view they are subsistence goods; but from another they are like Siane 'luxuries', in that they must be obtained, on a basis of balanced reciprocity, from individual extra-clan trading partners. Yet, further, they can be exchanged directly for shells, and would thus seem to fall into the ceremonial category. Clearly, in terms of types of goods, the Siane scheme is not replicated among the Maring, although one could argue that the nexūs still exist, and axes are treated differently according to which nexūs of exchange they are involved in at a given time: they are lent for no direct return between clansmen, exchanged for shells between friends in private deals, and handed over ceremonially in public exchanges between groups.

For Hagen, the problems are sharper, for moka relations, based on balanced reciprocity, can be taken up between clansmen as well as between men of different clans. Hence relations within the clan are not wholly

I

characterised by 'generalised reciprocity'. Moreover, there can be sharing, free borrowing, etc., between kinsmen of different clans.

It seems, then, that Salisbury's scheme cannot be exactly duplicated for Hagen. Perhaps it would have been better if he had explicitly taken social relationships as the determinants of his nexūs; one would not then be concerned, even initially, to fit all types of goods into one particular nexus.

Besides considering how shell valuables aid the distribution of utilitarian objects, one can consider the matter in reverse. All along these routes up from coastal sources, shells were probably to some extent retained for internal circulation within particular areas, especially, as in Mendi, where they were highly valued. Peoples at the ends of trade routes would thus receive only a few shells, given a certain scarcity of these, unless they could offer highly attractive goods for exchanges. Control of axe-blades from a number of quarries would be vital here for the Hageners, and it is precisely the axes' superior material and their indispensability for work which is crucial. Given that the primary producers could be stimulated sufficiently, as we have already seen, to disperse axes throughout the Hagen groups, possession of these undoubtedly gave the Hageners drawing power on shells, which otherwise the Mendi might have kept for circulation among themselves.

Another factor which seems to effect an even distribution of valuables, and also salt and axes, over a wide area is the scope of ceremonial exchange systems. In the Enga *tee* system, for example, items, including shells, move from clan to clan across a large part of Enga territory from the Hagen end in the east to Wabag in the west; and, in a different cycle, the items move in the opposite direction. The system thus ensures the dispersion of valuables throughout an area in which these were perhaps relatively scarce, more so than in Hagen. Seen from another point of view, the chain arrangements which the Enga have adopted for their *tee* are a means of maximising the size of transactions, which Enga big-men exploit in order to increase their status.[1] Similar, but smaller, chains which develop in Hagen, will be described in the next and subsequent chapters.

[1] Cf. Strathern A. J. 1969*b*.

6

MOKA CHAINS

'The ropes of moka hang on men's skin and are entangled there. When they
are all straightened out, then the big dance can be held.'

Ru, of Kawelka Kurupmbo group

In preceding chapters I have described group structure in Hagen, sketched
the processes of trade which brought valuables into the Hagen area and
given an account of the valuables themselves. In this and following chapters I shall take up the analysis of moka activities themselves, setting groups
and their big-men into action in co-operation and conflict with each other.

EVENTS LEADING UP TO A MOKA

Many months before a moka prestation can take place, initial arrangements
between individual partners must be made. Many partners exchange with
each other over a long period, and at each prestation the state of play
between them is known and agreed upon. But men contract new partnerships also, and sometimes drop old ones, especially if there has been
defaulting on one side or the other. Before a prestation, then, each prospective donor reviews his partnerships and renews his specific arrangements with each partner. The recipients-to-be make initiatory gifts of
shells, pigs, and legs of pork (*kın pol pek, kng pek, kng tımb*)[1] to the donors.

Initiatory gifts are made either individually and in private at different
times (within a certain period of time), or in concert at a single time. Where
moka gifts are to pass through a chain sequence it is more likely that
initiatory gifts will be concerted. Again, whether a chain is involved or not,
if the moka is taking place under the rubric of a direct death-compensation
payment (*wuə peng*), it is preceded by a concerted initiatory payment (the
wuə ombil or 'man bone' payment, cf. Chapter 5). From the time when this
is brought, or after the bulk of the initiatory gifts have been made privately,
the prospective recipients begin to ask for a declaration of how large the
main prestation is to be.

---

[1] *Pek* gifts are similar in function to the Trobriand category of *kaributu*, which
Malinowski (1922: 99) translates as 'solicitary gifts'. I hesitate to use Malinowski's term,
however, because in the moka it is often the main donor, not the recipient-to-be, who
actually asks for *pek* gifts. Nevertheless, the term clearly implies 'asking for a greater
return', and thus can be taken to mean 'solicitary'. I have compromised by translating it
as 'initiatory': *pek* gifts formally initiate a new phase in an ongoing exchange partnership.

Discussions are held at the ceremonial ground (or grounds) of the donor group. If it is a live-pig moka which is planned, the donors display their initial promises by setting up a number of stakes in a row on the ceremonial ground: each stake represents one pig to be given away. They also clear and tidy the ceremonial ground, perhaps with the help of the recipients, and men on both sides make speeches, ranging over the history of relations between the two groups and the reasons why they are planning this particular moka.

Several meetings of this kind may be held, and the recipient side becomes more demanding as time goes on. Only those on the donor side who are ready to promise a certain number of pigs (and/or shells) to their partners attend the meetings. It is big-men who do the talking and who instigate these occasions, but a single big-man can also hold up the moka by simply failing to turn up to a discussion. No-one can be forced to come.

At each meeting big-men are likely to lead attempts to contract for more gifts. A big-man calls men of his group, including his own close supporters, together, and they walk down the row of pig-stakes. Each stake must be 'taken': that is, one of the donors must state that he will tie a pig to it at the time of the moka. The big-man asks each of his group-mates in turn how many he will give. He counts the stakes in twos, making these into sets of eight or ten, and a supporter keeps a record on his fingers of how many sets are taken: for each set he bends one finger down. Unimportant men are often reluctant to commit themselves. The big-man berates them urgently, and tells them not to hold back their pigs. As the group progresses down the row of stakes he tries to maintain enthusiasm and increase the competitive spirit of his clansmen, insisting that they must surpass gifts they have received before and must set up a longer line of stakes than some neighbouring rival group has achieved on a recent occasion. If men have not come to the meeting, the big-man asks their close associates how many pigs the absentees are known to be preparing for the moka, and he counts these in with the rest. Usually, the big-man who takes a prominent part at this stage is an acknowledged leader, either of his whole clan or of a large sub-clan within it. The recipients, meanwhile, sit quietly at the side of the ceremonial ground, watching carefully as the knot of donors moves down the stakes. Later, when the 'taking of stakes' is completed, and the leading big-man among the donors has spoken about this, leaders among the recipients will reply, arguing that the donors have done well, but they should increase their promises further if they wish to gain prestige.

Many of the individual donors base their decisions on private agreements between themselves and their partners, for such agreements enable the size of initiatory gifts to be arranged and the subsequent disposal of pigs to be planned also. But donors do not publicly inform their individual recipients how many pigs they will give. Recipients have a good idea of what to expect; but they cannot be sure, especially as many private promises are made in a veiled way by means of *tok bokis* (Melanesian Pidgin = 'concealed talk'), and they always hope for more than any number a donor may explicitly state he will give.

If the main gift is to consist of, or include, shells, discussions on the shells are held in a special house, either the men's house at the head of the ceremonial ground or a further shell display-house built beside the men's house.

The climax of all these discussions is the concerted 'showing'[1] of gifts at the ceremonial ground. Once this is completed, the final transfer, accompanied, if the occasion is a large one, by dancing as well as formal oratory, can take place on the next day. Preparations for the showing are always accompanied by delays and disappointments. Successive days are 'marked' for it, but pass by and new days have to be marked; weeks may elapse between the first announcements that the moka is 'imminent' and the actual showing. A concerted showing is also preceded by private displays and discussions at all the homesteads involved in the moka. Recipients walk from settlement to settlement, viewing pigs and making speeches to each of their partners in turn.

At the concerted showing donors, recipients, and parties of men interested in the moka plans of either side, attend. For example, a rival group of recipients may turn up, to see that no pigs or shells which have been promised to them are being given away. Often, also, different segments of the donor group are out of step with each other, and hold separate fore-showings at different times; but all should combine for the final one, and usually they do. Live pigs are lined up on roughly-cut stakes to the

---

[1] 'Showing' pigs is called *kng ndi ngui*, 'to give the hair of the pigs', i.e. to allow recipients actually to see them. For pearl shells the phrase is *kin tepam ngui*, 'to give the *tepam* of the shells'. Hageners are generally at a loss to explain the latter phrase; although there is a lexeme *tepam*, meaning 'father', and one intellectualist informant based a conjectural explanation on this fact. He suggested that the phrase derives by analogy from an abortion custom. If a pregnant woman wishes to abort her child and has failed to do so by tightening ropes round her stomach or pushing herself against a rock, she may call in a female expert. The expert covertly obtains pieces from the woman's husband's head-net and apron and 'shows' these to the unborn child in the woman's belly. She says 'You are refusing to die, but I am showing you these things belonging to your father as a sign that he also wants you to die, so now you must really die'. Later, the woman is supposed successfully to abort. The expert's action is called 'to give the things of the father', *tepam-nga mel ngui*. In the same way, my informant argued, the shells are first shown at a moka, as a sign that the moka will soon 'die', i.e. be completed, and later it is actually completed. This analogy was offered as a conjecture only, and although compressed it is certainly ingenious. (The informant is Ru, of the Kawelka Kurupmbo clan-section.)

side of the formal row of stakes to which pigs will be tied for the actual ceremony of transfer. Shells are arranged in rows on the shelves of the display-house, which is decorated with ferns for the occasion.[1] Fresh red-ochre powder should be sprinkled on the shells' resin support-boards.

When all is ready, big-men among the prospective donors step forward to the *poklambo* tree planted at the ceremonial ground's head, and make formal speeches, explaining why the gift is the size it is and re-iterating how this prestation relates to others in the past and to projected future occasions. Recipients and interested persons reply. Big-men often, but not always, speak first, followed by men of lesser status. There is no office of sub-clan or clan orator, as there is among the Kuma (Reay 1959: 118), but some men are known as good speakers, and these always take part early in the proceedings, although any concrete suggestions they make are not necessarily heeded. The formal oratorical style called *el-ık* ('war-talk') is usually reserved until the final day.

'Extra' items to be given are not displayed at the showing. They are presented on the final day, ostensibly as a 'surprise', though in fact they are often agreed on beforehand.

After the showing the recipients remove all the gifts to their own settlements, unless these are too far away. The donors are thus left free to prepare for the dancing and speech-making which accompany the final transfer.

If the occasion is a big one, the transfer is postponed for a day, and the donors kill and cook further pigs, whose meat they distribute to guests. Some of the guests have helped them with decorations or with items for the moka; but others, especially married sisters and close affines, can come simply to receive pork and watch the dancing. On later occasions they reciprocate in kind, when their own or their husbands' group holds a festival. Big-men, who have more affines and friends than others, must budget to kill perhaps three to six pigs for guests. On the same day, dancers sort out and assemble their decorations, while they wait for the pork to cook.

On the final day, men and women of the recipient-group converge on the ceremonial ground of the donors from soon after dawn till mid-morning. Women lead in batches of pigs, made unruly and suspicious by the stir. Men carry shells in bundles suspended from bamboo poles.[2] Pigs

---

[1] The ferns are Cyatheaceae *Cyathea* sp. (in Melpa *nøng*), and are held to attract valuables to the ceremonial ground.

[2] In the past, shells were brought in dramatically, wrapped in large net-bags. This custom (called *kın wal omb-al menemen*, 'they carry shells in *omb* net-bags') seems to belong especially to the Kaugel and Enga areas, and does not seem to have penetrated to the Northern Melpa. Cf. Strauss 1962, colour plate 1; Bus 1951.

are initially tied to trees beside the ceremonial ground, and shells are laid nearby, to be watched over by the women.

Donors meanwhile decorate themselves,[1] either at their homes or on the ceremonial ground itself. Recipients, and men from groups allied to either side, also decorate themselves and dance for an important moka, particularly if it forms one of a definite sequence of prestations in which they will later be directly involved. The men wear arrays of plumes inserted into their wigs, pearl-shell pendants on their chests and green-snail pieces hung from their ears, and especially fine bark belts and aprons. They rub their bodies with pig-grease or tree-oil, and paint their faces with charcoal and ochre, picking out their eyes and noses in red and white. The men's main dances are *mør* and *kanan*. *Kanan* is a stamping dance used for processional entry into or exit from the ceremonial ground. For *mør* men stand in a long line (or two opposing lines or in a horseshoe), and genuflect gracefully to the beat of drums, and in time with whistling or singing. All fit men of the group, and some young boys, are expected to take part.

Female spectators admire and carefully compare the decorations and bearing of the dancers. If the moka includes a sufficient number of impressively large pigs, wives of the donors may decorate themselves elaborately also and perform a separate *werl* dance to celebrate their achievement in raising the pigs. Otherwise girls and married women put on more informal decorations, without head-dresses, and perform the *mørli* dance, jigging in circles, and shrieking at the crescendo of their songs. They often continue to do *mørli* while the men have moved on to the stage of speech-making, to the men's occasional annoyance. When *mør* is over, young men, both unmarried and married, begin *yap*, a more vigorous version of *mørli*. The men and women thus form rival circles and may sing ribald songs about each other.

Mør dancing breaks up early in the afternoon with shouts that rain is threatening or that it is growing dark. The pigs are now brought rapidly to their stakes and the shells are laid out in a row, on fern, cordyline, or banana leaves. Big-men attempt to direct both activities, calling out that the line of shells is crooked or shouting to their wives that their pigs are fighting each other. Pigs wrap themselves round their stakes and squeal as the ropes cut into their feet and they become defenceless against a snapping neighbour. Women sit beside excitable pigs, fondling them in order to calm them down.

When the gifts are in line the donors mark their achievement by racing

---

[1] For a longer account see Strathern A. J. and A. M. 1971.

up and down the row, crying hoo-aah, hoo-aah. They return to the ceremonial tree at the head of the row, where they perform a war-dance,
kicking up their heels and twirling their axes.[1] If pigs are to be given as
'extras' the donors now rush off to bring them out from nearby bushes.
They rope the pigs to the tough *olka*-wood[2] stake at which they are to be
tied and advance in *kanan* formation, singing loudly. Porcine pandemonium
breaks out as the unfortunate animals are seized and jostled. Once the
stake is set up, the ideal is that the pigs should remain peaceably sprawled
over each other while orators make speeches beside them: it is a bad omen
if the pigs squeal.

If there are no *olka* pigs, men make their speeches at the head of the
ceremonial ground. Orators of all ages show their skill at *el-ık*, striding up
and down in a confined space, twirling their axes, and ending each allusive
phrase with a long-drawn-out o-o-o-o.[3] During these speeches an eye is
kept on the pigs, to see they do not faint in the heat. If this is about to
happen, men cut branches and set these up to shade the pigs.

The final transfer is made either before or after *el-ık*. An orator (not
necessarily an important big-man) counts the gifts, listing the shells in
sub-sets of two and four making up sets of eight or ten.[4] He counts the
pigs singly, kicking each one lightly, and, addressing a prominent man
among the recipients says 'Kill this little person and eat him'.[5] The recipient walks down with the counter and shouts a stylised 'thank you'[6]
for each pig. His own pigs will occupy only a part of the row, and he says
thank you merely on behalf of his group-mates.

Pigs and shells are now rapidly collected and removed by recipients.
The pig-stakes are either knocked down or extricated for use elsewhere.
Their removal marks the supposed fulfilment of the donors' promises.
However, the *olka* stake and a stake smeared with charcoal called 'the boar
stake' should be left standing, as a record that the moka has been completed. Informants explain that visitors passing through the ceremonial
ground might think it was in disuse and that its owning group was a

---

[1] War-dance = *el rangenemen* in Melpa. The ceremonial charge is also called *nombokla
tikring enemen*. At one dance which I saw in the lower Nebilyer Valley on 6 May 1967 the
donors charged holding a frame to which they had attached twelve Red bird-of-paradise
head-dresses, which they were giving away as 'extras' in the moka.

[2] Celastraceae *Elaeodendron* sp.

[3] I give some examples of *el-ık* in Appendix 7.

[4] Eight = 'one hand', i.e. the fingers of two hands together, minus the thumbs. Ten
is eight with the two thumbs down (*pømb rakl pip*).

[5] In Melpa *wamb kel oa rok kui-o*. It is a formal phrase only, since most often pigs
received in moka are not cooked but passed on further in the moka system.

[6] *Akopi ngon eka* = 'now you are giving to me', invariably contracted to *angke*.

'rubbish' group, but companions will point out the two stakes as proof that the group has made moka.

MOKA CHAINS

In the first part of this chapter I have described the sequence of events which leads up to a single moka prestation. But prestations themselves are always part of a further sequence. In the simplest form this consists of vice-versa movements between two partners of two partner groups in a relationship of 'alternating disequilibrium': each partner alternately has the upper hand in the sequence of exchanges, by virtue of the other being in debt to him. More complicatedly, there is a flow of prestations between a number of partners: A gives to B, C to D, D to E, and so on. Whenever a segment of this series is planned out by participants in the exchange system we can speak of an explicit chain of exchanges. Such chains are planned from time to time by participants in the moka, although not on the scale which we find in the Enga *tee* system. Explicit chains are thus parts of the general 'ropes of moka' which Hageners see as linking their groups together. They are one way, in fact, of 'straightening out the ropes of moka', the process which is referred to in the caption for this chapter.

One such moka chain took shape during 1964–5. It consisted of a series of prestations between Tipuka clans within the Məka Valley and their culmination in a gift to the Kawelka Membo and Mandembo clans at Buk. Moka gifts from some clans of the Minembi tribe to both Tipuka and Kawelka recipients meshed in with the main series.

Similar chains certainly emerge in other parts of the Hagen area, but by no means all moka prestations form part of an explicit sequence of this kind. It is likely that the opportunities for planning moka chains, at least on a group scale, have become greater since warfare was stopped, although individual men pursued explicit chain arrangements in the past, as Strauss (1962: 362–73) shows. It is likely, also, that chains organised on a group scale, and chains lengthened in new directions, represent attempts by big-men to expand the scope of their ceremonial relationships. I am not sure, however, that group chains are entirely a post-European contact phenomenon.[1]

All the main prestations in the 1964–5 sequence belonged to the class

[1] Informants usually discuss single prestations as if they were isolated events. Further enquiry sometimes shows that this is misleading: the prestations are part of larger sequences. Similarly, while I was in the field in 1964–5, not all informants thought to let me know that initial prestations I saw would be followed by others: one of the more forthcoming big-men (Kont, who also compared moka to the card game, Lucky) suddenly explained the projected chain for me a few weeks before the main prestations began.

of direct compensation payments for killings inflicted in warfare during the lifetime of the present generation of middle-aged men. Older men remember the killings clearly, and refer to them in their speeches; younger men tend to say 'We are new men, brought up under law; we do not know about war, but we do know how to make moka'. In all cases the groups had exchanged compensation payments before and had gradually built these up into large prestations cast in the mould of moka.

The main gifts employed in the chain were live pigs and pearl shells, items that were durable and could be passed on intact. Cooked meat entered the chain at the stage of initiatory gift-giving, explicitly to 'encourage' the main donors by giving them a taste of pork.

The Tipuka and Kawelka clans involved in the chain are neighbours, and they are flanked also by the Minembi clans which took part. Their other neighbours, the Kombukla and Wəlyi tribes, took no part in the chain at all. These two were principal enemies of Tipuka tribe in the past, and were thus less likely to invest in 'regional integration' with the Tipuka–Kawelka complex[1] of clans.

I distinguish between the main flow which is the moka chain proper, and auxiliary flows, which can be thought as further 'ropes of moka' attached to and feeding into the chain. Minembi clans were involved mostly as 'feeders' into Tipuka tribe. One, however, Komonkae, was supposed to form part of the main chain. Komonkae are a small clan, isolated from the rest of the Minembi apart from one equally small pair-clan, and one of their important big-men has close moka ties with an ageing big-man among the Kawelka: this explains how Komonkae came to be tacked on to the end of the Kawelka in the chain. In fact, however, the size of the Komonkae contribution to the chain was not great; and no major prestation[2] has subsequently been made to them by the Kawelka. Implicitly they have been treated as outside the major focus of exchanges between clans in the Tipuka–Kawelka alliance bloc. Within this bloc there is more participation by ordinary men and the total volume of goods exchanged, along with the total number of partnerships, rises; outside it, exchanges with ex-major enemy groups were in 1964–5 largely engineered and carried through by big-men.

[1] Cf. Harding 1967: 241–4 on the concept of regional integration. I am applying the term to a small-scale area here. The Kombukla clans are to some extent involved with Tipuka–Kawelka: for example in 1965 they combined to hold a festival at which their individual men gave out legs of pork to individual recipients among Tipuka and Kawelka. But they gave no prestations to the latter as a group; and the bulk of their gifts went to their own traditional allies, the Minembi.

[2] In 1966 big-men among them received a few items from Kawelka Kurupmbo partners, who were making a large gift of both pigs and shells to Tipuka Kengeke clan.

Moka chains

Each moka between Tipuka–Kawelka clans and Minembi clans had its specific rationale and formed part of an ongoing or projected series of dyadic exchanges, as well as feeding into the Tipuka–Kawelka moka chain. Many of these gifts which I am here describing as 'feeders' were also part of separate 'ropes of moka' which tied in with the Tipuka–Kawelka chain.

Moka which took place around Mbukl in 1964–5 can in fact be divided into:

1. prestations in the Tipuka–Kawelka chain.
2. prestations feeding into the Tipuka–Kawelka chain.
3. internal prestations within groups, often connected with 1 and 2.
4. prestations separate from 1, 2, and 3, but sometimes part of other ropes of moka.

Here I am interested mainly in 1, 2, and 3, but the charts (*q.v.*) of monthly group-moka activities show a number of prestations either branching off from moka chains or quite unconnected with them: for example, the Kawelka gift of shells to Roklaka men in May 1964, the Tipuka Oklembo gift of shells to Palke men in October 1964, and the money moka which Kawelka Kundmbo gave to Minembi Yelipi men in August 1964. Attempts were made to link some of these unattached prestations to those in categories 1, 2, and 3. Thus, a deputation of Minembi Engambo men came to a big-man of Kawelka Kundmbo late in July 1964 and complained strongly that he had not yet given pig-moka to them; had he done so in time they could have passed his pigs on to the Kitepi to whom some of their group-mates were giving on the same day. Such demands are part of the general effort of gamesmanship which is put into moka relations: recipients try to hasten the moka by claiming that their own creditors are pressing them, while donors maintain that their debtors have failed them and the recipients must wait. Each side knows fairly well how far to insist on their own position: if the donors delay too long they can seriously impede the flow of goods in moka chains, and ultimately this is to their own disadvantage; on the other hand, if the recipients insist on the moka being given prematurely, they are unlikely to receive an adequate number of gifts, and hence they themselves lose. Often, however, the calculations of either side can go wrong, as we shall see in a later chapter.

By August 1964 the extent of the main chain sequence (seen from the point of view of Tipuka–Kawelka clans) had been defined by the passage of concerted gifts in the initiatory sequence (Fig. 8).

The Fig. shows two points. First, the initiatory gifts, as represented, do not form a genuine sequence, for the Kawelka gift to the Kitepi occurs

CHART 1

	Jan.–Feb. '64	March '64	April '64	May '64	June '64	July '64	Aug. '64	Sept. '64	Oct. '64	Nov. '64	Dec. '64	Jan. '65
KAW. Membo												
Mandembo				cp→internally s→Roklaka			p→Kit.–Okl.					
Kundmbo				s→Roklaka			p→Kit.–Okl. m+cf→Yel.					
MIN. Kimbo					p→Me.–Mande					p→Yel.		
Engambo						cp→various gps.				p→Pape.		
Mimke		p→Yel.										
Papeke						p→Keng. cp→various gps.					cp→Kaw. Kund. p→Kit. p→internally	p→Okl., Elt.
Yelipi		p+s→Okl. p→Mimke (adv.)									p+s→var. gps.	
Kom.–Rup. K. Mong.						p→Me.–Mande. p+s→Kaw. Kund.						
TIP. Kengeke			cp→Mande.					p→Elt. p→Kend. p→Maplke		s→Yel.		
Kendike						cp→Keng.		p→Nolka p→Kit. p→Wany.				
Kitepi		s→Me.–Mande. (adv.)			p→Kend.			p→Rammdi				
Oklembo			s→Mande. (adv.)				cf.→Yel.		p+s→Palke		s→Kit.	p→Elt. p+s→Me.–Mande.
Eltimbo												p→Kit.
Wanyembo												p→Okl.

Charts of monthly moka activities, Mbukl, Jan. 1964–Jan. 1965

Moka chains

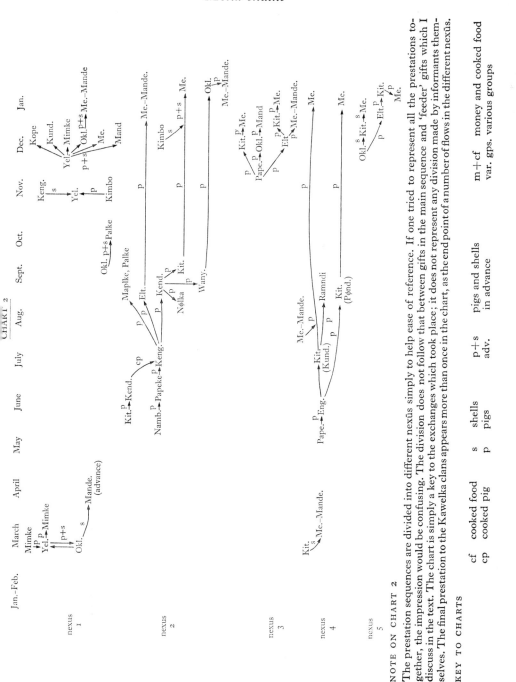

CHART 2

NOTE ON CHART 2

The prestation sequences are divided into different nexûs simply to help ease of reference. If one tried to represent all the prestations together, the impression would be confusing. The division does not follow that between gifts in the main sequence and 'feeder' gifts which I discuss in the text. The chart is simply a key to the exchanges which took place; it does not represent any division made by informants themselves. The final prestation to the Kawelka clans appears more than once in the chart, as the end point of a number of flows in the different nexûs.

KEY TO CHARTS

cf	cooked food	s	shells	p+s	pigs and shells	m+cf	money and cooked food
cp	cooked pig	p	pigs	adv.	in advance		var. gps. various groups

cf cooked food
cp cooked pig

s shells
p pigs

p+s pigs and shells
adv. in advance

m+cf money and cooked food
var. gps. various groups

125

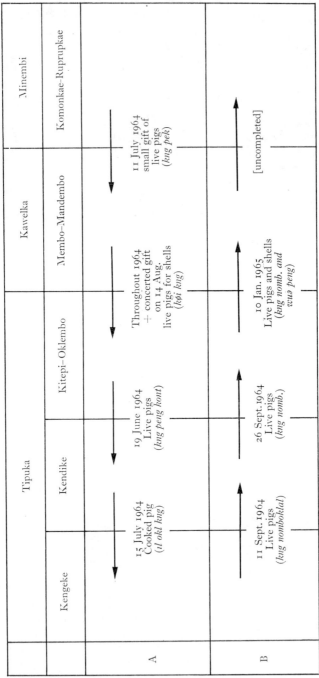

A = initiatory sequence;   B = main sequence

Fig. 8   Gifts in the main 1964–5 moka sequence

much later than the Kitepi to Kendike and Kendike to Kengeke gifts. What explains this apparent anomaly is that in private the Kawelka had passed on a number of pigs long before August and some of these found their way to the Kengeke. These pigs were either brought back to be formally transferred in August, or replacements were found for them by their recipients. In addition, the August gift was a large one (about 130 pigs); many of the pigs at it were given in return for private promises or advances of shells, which were finally transferred to the Kawelka only in January 1965.

Second, in the main gift sequence (B) there is a considerable gap in time between the Kendike gift to the Kitepi and the final stage when Kitepi–Oklembo present pigs and shells to their two Kawelka partner-clans. The fuller moka charts explain this delay. Before the Kitepi–Oklembo gift could be made, moka from the Minembi clans had to be fed into the chain and there were also internal re-shufflings of goods within the Anmbilika section of the Tipuka themselves (cf. Fig. 9). But why had these two further processes to be fitted in before Kitepi–Oklembo could make their moka? For the Oklembo the answer is clear. They were dependent entirely on Minembi clans, especially the Yelipi, for help with raising their gift to the Kawelka. The Kitepi manoeuvred themselves into a better position. Not only were they recipients in the main chain, but they also received more substantial gifts from the Papeke than did the Oklembo, *and* they received internal prestations from the other two clans involved as donors to the Kawelka *before* the gift to the Kawelka was completed. The example of the Kitepi shows that the management of sequences of moka prestations is a very important factor in a clan's political success.

The gap in time before the combined Kitepi–Oklembo prestation also raises the question of *why* these two clans put such an elaborate organisational effort into their gift. 'Political success' is the key here. Figure 10 indicates certain lines of political cleavage between groups involved in the main moka chain. The major line of cleavage runs between blocs A+B+C and bloc D. Moka relations across this line were negotiated by big-men only and were not extensive. Minembi Komonkae and Kawelka Membo are not only traditional enemies but are also specifically 'root men of war' to each other: they were responsible for beginning fights which later involved their pair-clans as allies. Within A+B+C there is a division between A+B and C, corresponding to the division between Tipuka and Kawelka as tribes. At this point the factor of inter-tribal competitiveness is added to the minor enemy cum ally relationship. As a result, the scale of groups involved in the chain was stepped up at this point and the donors

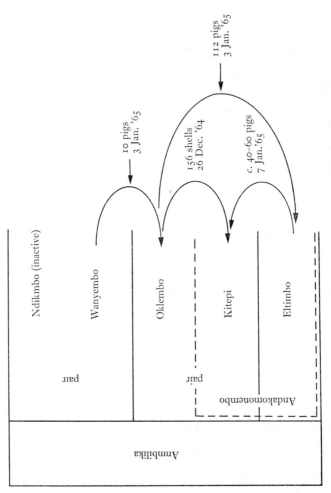

Fig. 9   Relations within Anmbilika section, Tipuka tribe

made greater efforts to increase the size of their prestation. Similarly, in the initiatory sequence it was at this point that the largest initiatory gift was made, and the gift was delayed while the Kawelka sought to ensure that it would be adequate. Kawelka men discussing it in advance explicitly said among themselves that they must make the initiatory gift large in order to see if they could 'beat' their Tipuka allies. Allies are also rivals, competing for prestige through the size of their reciprocal moka gifts.

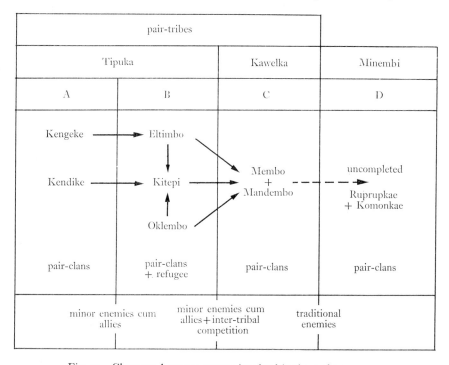

Fig. 10 Cleavages between groups involved in the moka sequence

The competition is not simply for general prestige. I would suggest that the large size of prestations to ex-minor enemies (as, for example, from Tipuka to Kawelka clans) is partly a result of the desire to show temporary superiority and dominance over them, just as was previously attempted in warfare: in this sense, and in this context, moka gifts are a true functional alternative to warfare. Indeed, if one group were overwhelmingly 'defeated' in moka exchanges it could become politically dependent on the victor; hence recipient groups, in order to retain their independence, *must* reciprocate. There is a difference, however, between the game-situation in warfare and in ceremonial exchange, as I have pointed out in Chapter 1.

Large prestations benefit the recipients, whereas heavy defeats in warfare do not do so: while the donors gain credit and prestige, the recipients take the goods, and if they invest these properly they will be able to make adequate returns later. The donors' formally-announced intention, moreover, is often to compensate the recipients for their loss of a man in past warfare, and to make them 'feel good' again. But underneath the formal rubric a good deal of antagonism may show, especially when the social distance between donor and recipient groups is great. This point might lead us to suppose that the largest gifts, expressing the greatest antagonism, would be made to *major* enemies. But in fact this does not happen, for between these there is insufficient trust for groups to risk very heavy investments in each other. On the other hand, there is a prospect of security, but less potential rivalry, between segments of a single clan or between pair-clans. Where rivalry is less pronounced, there is less effort to 'win' over the other group by making a large prestation. The upshot is that most effort is put into prestations to groups which are allies, and are therefore likely to make returns for gifts, but are also in some way politically and socially opposed to one's own groups. Gifts between allied tribes fall precisely into this category.

One way to summarise the situation is by reference to Radcliffe-Brown's definition of alliance relationships (Radcliffe-Brown 1952: 91). Alliance relationships are those which are characterised by an interplay of conjunction and disjunction, by antagonism and yet by mutual friendship and aid. Such relationships occur between persons who are outside the sphere of incorporation relatively to each other, that is outside the sphere of those between whom there is a high degree of regular, enjoined cooperation.

Applying Radcliffe-Brown's concept to the moka system we can describe the field of moka relations as tripartite. The inner part is the clan or pair of clans. Within it relationships of incorporation hold. (This is an oversimplification, for segmentary opposition can proceed right down to the lowest-level segments within the clan in Hagen. Moreover, if pair-clans have fought they become as ex-minor enemies to each other.) Outside this area of incorporation is the primary area of alliance with groups which were ex-minor enemies but also gave military help in the past; while beyond the area of alliance are traditional enemies. With these ties are much weaker, except where they have been partially strengthened by the activities of big-men.

The large moka occasions with groups that are allies test both the financial abilities and the leadership qualities of big-men. In these moka many men contribute on their own account, and the big-man cannot simply rely on numbers of ordinary men in his own group to support him; hence he must arrange extra finances for himself, and this he often does by organising helping moka from groups outside the current focus of exchanges, perhaps from traditional enemy groups. It is in this way that ropes of moka are created and attached to important chain sequences of gifts between allies.

What are the functions of this process of linking prestations together? Very broadly, of course, they effect regional integration. More specifically, they represent political choice: by choosing to exchange under one rubric rather than another, to give to this group but not to that, or to concentrate their gifts mainly in one direction, clans – in particular, their big-men – express, create, and alter their relations with other clans. It is this act of channelling gifts which is both politically and economically significant.

Hageners do not expressly say, as a generalisation, that they make their moka in chains, in the way the Enga make their *tee* exchanges, although they do define and refer to particular chain sequences while these are in progress. They do, however, refer in general to the ropes of moka which run from group to group, and I have suggested that particular exchange-sequences can be looked on as special arrangements of these ropes. The arrangements emerge as a result of negotiation and discussion between groups, especially between their leading men. Why chains pass as they do between particular groups can be explained partly by the traditional (and still continuing) structure of political inter-relations. But their economic advantages and consequences need to be explored further also. If the advantages are sought after and the consequences foreseen by the participants, this may help to explain why chain sequence emerges at all; and such an explanation may help us in understanding the much more elaborately developed form of the Enga *tee*.

I have presented my argument on this problem elsewhere,[1] but will summarise it here. In Hagen each man who participates in moka has a number of partners within his own clan and in surrounding clans. He sends goods to these partners and they send them in turn to men of further groups. If a man's goods radiate out from him into politically and spatially more distant groups, his chances of exerting pressure at the ends of the

---

[1] Strathern A. J. 1969*b*. In this article I examined the hypothesis that the prominence of big-men in Highlands exchange systems is related to the extent to which they substitute credit manipulation for direct control over production. I also contrasted exchange systems dependent on pork and vegetables, perishable goods, as their currency and those dependent on durable shells and live pigs, and argued that where shells and pigs are prominent chain arrangements can emerge more easily.

networks in which he is involved are reduced. Moreover, he must rely on his private inter-personal relationship with his immediate partners in enemy clans, for there is no group alliance between them. If his clan is due to make a concerted prestation, he may find it difficult to raise from his network the items he needs for his contribution to this; at the least he will require considerable time and energy to do so. Moka chains can be seen as attempts to channel and define particular sections of each man's exchange network which are to be activated within a certain period of time. Defining the length of the chain means that the total time required for completion of a sequence can be roughly estimated, and it also means that pressure can be applied effectively throughout all parts of the chain. Moreover, such pressure can be brought to bear by group action: individuals are not left to put pressure on a number of disparate partnership paths within their own personal network. All these factors lead to an increase in the efficiency of the management of finance and in general to security of investment. Chains, however, have to be organised, and it is here that big-men become important. It is they who arrange to attach further 'ropes of moka' to the chains in which they are centrally involved. By their status they are enabled to act as guarantors between traditional enemy groups, so that prestations can flow between them. For example, in July 1964 the Minembi Engambo clan[1] presented seventy-one live pigs as a *wuə ombil* payment to Tipuka Kitepi men.[2] There were only nine donors and six recipients. Four of the participants on each side (eight altogether) were big-men. The Kitepi big-men, each belonging to a different segment of the clan, received from eight to twenty pigs, and each at once redistributed his share to men within his segment. Each big-man would be responsible for the return of pigs to the Engambo later, but in the meantime he redistributed his responsibility to his group-mates. Most importantly, he could not have fed such a large influx of pigs from his own resources. Thus, the big-man requires a set of supporters who can take on pigs which he receives in moka. Given supporters, he can aim at control over transactions rather than control over production. However, in a chain sequence a big-man may not need to redistribute the pigs he receives in this way, because he can pass the pigs on again in a formal prestation fairly quickly. Chain arrangements are thus useful to big-men, for they enable

[1] Strictly, one clan-section of Engambo.
[2] In 1969 I saw some of the main prestations which Kitepi men made in return for this initiatory gift. The interval of five years between the initiatory and the main prestations is explained by the fact that in 1966 the Kitepi participated prominently in a large ally payment to the Kendipi tribe, and they needed time to gather their resources together subsequently.

them to channel a large number of pigs through their own hands without the necessity of their feeding the pigs for long periods or redistributing them to others. Kengeke and Kendike big-men were clearly operating in this way in 1964: thus, the Kengeke gift to Kendike was followed shortly by the Kendike gift to Kitepi. The Kitepi, as we have seen, could not pass their pigs on so quickly because of the further ropes of moka in which they were involved.

Briefly, then, my argument is that, in Hagen, exchange chains provide some measure of economic security in the management of partnership networks and also help big-men to increase the number of transactions in pigs under their control.[1]

Both of these points hold equally well for the Enga *tee* system. But the chains in the *tee* are both much longer and more standardised than are any of the chains I have traced in Hagen. The *tee* links together a very large number of big-men and clans, from the eastern ends of the Enga language area to some hours' walk beyond Wabag in the west. The only explanation for the elaborate form of the *tee* chain that I can suggest is that the *tee* was in the past the major mechanism for transferring both pearl shells and stone axe blades from Hagen and Tambul into the Enga area. A major point of communication between Hagen, Tambul, and Enga populations is Walya, which lies between Tomba and Wapenamanda on the way to Wabag. Through Walya passed a good deal (although by no means all) of the trade between Hagen and the Enga area. Axes flowed mainly east to west, against pigs and other goods; while salt packs flowed from Enga manufacturers into Hagen. It is possible, although I have no evidence of this, that there was a net flow of pearl shells from Walya into the Enga area also. If so, the *tee* was an excellent mechanism for ensuring the distribution of these valuable items over a wide area. From another point of view one could also argue that it was (and to some extent remains) a means whereby big-men could obtain considerable control over the flow of wealth. Here I am looking at Enga big-men in the past as virtual monopolisers of shell valuables, just as many informants state Hagen big-men were. If it is true that Walya was traditionally the most significant entry-point for shells and axes into Enga, this might explain why an exchange

---

[1] The existence of chains also helps to explain two categories relating to gifts of pigs: *ka:n kng* and *omong kng*. *Ka:n kng* are pigs given in advance of a main prestation, often because further recipients within a projected chain would like to see them (in addition the donor does not need to look after them and so can obtain and feed more for the final prestation). *Omong kng* (from the phrase *omong iti*, to become big, as a leaf – *omong* – unfolds and becomes big) are replacement pigs brought by recipients to a prestation when they have already passed on a *ka:n* pig within a chain sequence.

chain was elaborated among the Enga people rather than at Hagen. For Hagen groups received shell valuables and axes from a number of different directions not just a single one, and this may have ensured a regularly more equitable distribution of valuables through the Hagen area. On the other hand, there is little doubt that in pre-European times the major source of pearl shells for Hagen groups was the lower Nebilyer Valley and Tambul. What one finds is, not that a long exchange chain formed from the lower Nebilyer north to Melpa speakers, but that pearl shell moka and its associated customs gradually spread northwards. Northern Melpa groups began making shell moka later than others and without some of the customs practised in the Nebilyer. Perhaps this spread of shell moka is the counterpart of the extension of the *tee* chain into the Enga area; but I can offer this only as a speculation.

Events subsequent to January 1965

For most of 1965 the Tipuka and Kawelka clans made no moka; from late 1965 to the end of 1966 they were active again. After another quiet period two of the Tipuka clans, Kitepi and Oklembo, were active again during August 1969. The major returns for prestations received in the moka chain of 1964–5 have not yet been made, and Kawelka informants estimated that they might not occur till 1971 or 1972.

Events I heard of by letter or saw on return visits to the field were:

1. Late 1965: 3 October. A big-man, Ndamba, of Kawelka Kundmbo clan, and his supporters give 31 pigs to Ongka, a big-man of Kawelka Ngglammbo clan-section (Mandembo clan). By 23 October Ongka organises his resources for a more complicated one-man show in which he gives away 40 pigs and about 184 shells. The shells go to men of Minembi Kimbo clan, traditional enemies of Kawelka. Here we see a big-man extending his moka partnerships beyond the sphere of his own group's alliances again.[1]

In 1969 I learnt that Ongka had now made the return prestation for Ndamba's gift of 1965, although I did not discover how many pigs he gave.

2. Early 1966. There is an internal prestation between Membo clan and men of Kurupmbo clan-section in Mandembo clan. Four Membo men, all of one small segment, give 31 pigs to four recipients of Kurupmbo. The gift was timed explicitly to aid the latter in preparations for a major gift to the Tipuka Kengeke.

3. Early 1966. The Kurupmbo complete a war-compensation payment to the Kengeke, for which initiatory gifts were made in April 1964. My informant accounted for 640 shells given to the Kengeke (17 donors, 13 recipients) and for 53 pigs plus four tubes of decorating oil (12 donors, 12 recipients); also 45 pigs given to men of other groups on the same occasion.

It is interesting to note that this prestation partly 'closed the circle' of exchanges between Tipuka and Kawelka clans: Kengeke clan initiated the main

---

[1] Cf. Strathern A. J. 1969b: 59.

sequence of gifts in the moka chain which ended with Kawelka Membo and Mandembo at Mbukl in January 1965. Now a section of Mandembo gave to the Kengeke. However, informants never spoke of this aspect of the prestation; whereas they had clearly planned and conceptualised the progress of gifts from Kengeke to Kendike to Kitepi to Kawelka in the main chain sequence.

4. Mid 1966. Kendipi men bring 75 pigs and 80 bunches of bananas to Tipuka men as extra initiatory gifts for a large ally reparation payment planned by the Tipuka. This had already been planned, announced, and budgeted for by the Tipuka in 1964.

5. 20 December 1966. The Kawelka Kundmbo clan gives pigs to Minembi Engambo clan. My informant estimated some 200 pigs were given plus two specially-bought European-breed pigs. This prestation is not linked to any Tipuka–Kawelka moka sequence. (Much later, in 1968, the Engambo held a spirit-cult performance, with the aid of this prestation from Kundmbo clan. The Kundmbo are planning a similar performance for the 1970s, and may well demand returns for their gift when they are ready to hold it.)

6. 26 December 1966. The Tipuka complete their moka to the Kendipi. My informant estimates 400 pigs, 50 cassowaries, 8 tubes of decorating oil, and five cattle for slaughtering, were handed over. On 30 December Kawelka and Tipuka clansmen joined together and cooked pigs to celebrate the Tipuka moka, and each man distributed legs of pork to his exchange partners. This event was regarded as closing this particular moka cycle with the Kendipi.

7. Mid 1969. Before I returned to the field the Kitepi clan made returns for the moka they received from Minembi Engambo clan in 1964. No estimate of how many pigs were given.

8. August 1969. Two gifts of pig-moka to Minembi Papeke clansmen. One from a single section of Tipuka Kitepi clan (Pøndimbo), the other from Tipuka Oklembo clan as a whole. In both cases between 80 and 100 pigs were given; both prestations were considerably larger than previous gifts and more recent initiatory gifts from the Papeke.

9. August–September 1969. Internal gifts between Minembi clans; Minembi Engambo give 100+ pigs to the Kope tribe, to help them hold a spirit cult.

This account gives some idea of the scope and frequency of prestations in years subsequent to the moka-chain sequence. In particular, the last but one entry shows that transactions between Tipuka and Minembi clans were not linked rigidly to plans for the return prestations in the Tipuka–Kawelka chain. In 1965 I was told that these 'moka-ropes' with Minembi clans *would* be linked with the progress of return gifts in the chain. Initiatory gifts, it was said, would pass from Tipuka Kengeke through to the Kawelka and possibly on to Minembi Komonkae–Ruprupkae, and the main gift sequence would then proceed in reverse order. At each stage, Minembi clans which had helped Tipuka clans to make their prestations in 1964–5 would receive repayment. But it is clear that this theoretical scheme was open to negotiation and modification. In 1969 the Minembi as a whole were planning to stage a large pig-cooking festival, and Papeke and Engambo asked for returns on their previous gifts before the Kawelka were ready to initiate the reverse chain sequence. Tipuka Kitepi and Oklembo complied, and discussion at these return-moka made it clear that big-men on both sides were attempting to strengthen the Minembi–Tipuka alliance. There were hints of even bigger prestations to take place between the two in later years, possibly after the Kawelka clans had made returns to the Tipuka for the gifts they received in 1965.

In 1969 there was little pressure on the Kawelka to hasten their gift to the Tipuka. It was clear that a number of other prestations would have to take place first; and it was equally clear that the order in which these would occur was not settled. Much would depend on the big-men. For example, in Mandembo clan Ongka could expect to receive from (1) Ndamba, his Kawelka Kundmbo partner; in turn Ndamba could obtain pigs from the Engambo, to whom he had given in December 1966; (2) Mak, his brother-in-law of the Maplke tribe in the Jimi Valley, to whom he had given pigs in October 1965; and (3) Minembi Kimbo partners, to whom he gave shells in October 1965. These will give him pig-moka if he presents them with initiatory gifts. The leader in the other section of the clan, Kurupmbo, could also hope to receive returns from Tipuka Kengeke partners, to whom he and his section gave both pigs and shells in early 1966. Membo clansmen would expect to receive returns from the Roklaka tribe, to whom they were major donors in a shell-moka of May 1964, and to raise gifts from Minembi and Klamakae tribesmen living near them. All these ropes of moka would have to be organised before the Kawelka could make return moka to the Tipuka. Meanwhile the Tipuka, as stable allies of the two Kawelka clans to whom they had given in 1965, were not concerned to push the moka forward. The 'extension of credit' thus seems to be longer between stably allied groups. Where groups are contracting relatively new alliances they call for return moka within four years or so of making a prestation. The organisational reasons for this are fairly clear. Moka between stable allies are large-scale affairs, and require long preparations. In the interim periods, groups make new alliances and call on their new allies to help them with preparations for the larger occasions which they are planning.

In the next chapter I shall consider the detailed patterns and sizes of the gifts in some of the moka which I have mentioned, with a view to establishing the relative prominence of big-men and others as contributors.

7

COUNTING PIGS AND SHELLS

Much of my time in the field was taken up with attempts to discover the details and history of individual partnerships between individual men in moka transactions which ranged clans and whole tribes in relations with each other. From the material which I gathered it is possible to raise, and partially to answer, a number of questions: what is the extent of participation in group moka by adult men? What are the affinal and cognatic ties between the men involved? Do men exchange also with unrelated partners, as they do among the Enga?[1] Is there heavy investment in affines by comparison with other categories of partner?[2]

In particular, details of participation in moka can help us to assess the importance of big-men. Are the big-men more prominent as donors and recipients than others? Is there a distinction between major and minor big-men? Do big-men's partnership networks differ from those of others? That is, do they give to more partners, do they give more to unrelated partners, do they invest heavily in their affines, and so on?

The overall size of moka prestations, the numbers of partnerships activated in them, and the prominence within them of big-men vary to some extent in accordance with the political context in which they take place. We can distinguish at least the following types:

1. Small, 'helping' moka from one big-man to another; or small moka under various rubrics from a big-man and a few associates to another big-man.

2. Larger moka from one traditional-enemy group to another, in which big-men take the part of major participants and guarantors of the new alliance.

3. Moka between groups which were occasional enemies in the past. Big-men's roles in these depend on whether it suits them to invest in such enemy groups.

4. Internal moka, small or large, between sections of a clan or between clans paired with each other; again, big-men are variably important. (Sometimes, type 4 = type 1.)

[1] Cf. Strathern A. J. 1969b: 62, with references given there.
[2] Cf. Bulmer 1960b: 10: 'Not only in terms of frequency but of content the partnerships between affines tend to be the most significant.'

5. Large moka between allied groups. Big-men are prominent both as contributors and as diplomats, but not so dominantly important as in moka of type 2.

I shall take one example of type 2 and two of type 5 for discussion.

The first, of type 2, was the moka from Minembi Engambo clan to Tipuka Kitepi men which was completed late in July 1964. This was, strictly, an initiatory gift only. It belonged to the category of 'man-bone' payment (*wuə ombil*), paid by a group to elicit a war-compensation payment from an ex-enemy. As I have mentioned in Chapter 6, this was one of the gifts which fed into the Tipuka–Kawelka chain of prestations, and Kitepi men took the initiative in asking Engambo men for it, promising to make a main payment in return later, as they did in 1969.

The main account of this moka can be presented fairly simply (Table 13). Big-men were prominent recipients, especially two major big-men, Kuri and Nditing. There is no great density of cognatic and affinal ties between the donor and recipient clans, and many of the partners were unrelated friends. On the other hand, Nditing's specific ties were said to have been important as a point of entry into negotiations with the Engambo. The gifts were block gifts of 4 or 8–10 pigs, which were immediately distributed on the ceremonial ground. Only one pig was given to a man outside the recipients' clan, and this went to Kot, who is a major big-man, a neighbour of Nditing, and was due to give pigs in moka to Nditing before the Kitepi made their prestation to the Kawelka.

In this moka, then, we see big-men as major recipients, drawing in gifts of pigs, and distributing these, chiefly to their own sub-clansmen, in specific preparation for a bigger moka which they are due to make. Major big-men are prominent rather than minor, and it is they who distribute most of the pigs.

The structure of the more developed prestations between allied or ex-*minor* enemy clans is somewhat different, and requires more complicated presentation. As examples I shall take the prestations which were of central importance in the moka chain sequence of 1964–5: the Kengeke gift to Kendike clan, the Kendike to Kitepi, and Kitepi+Oklembo to Kawelka Membo+Mandembo.

My material on the first of these is rather less well-established than on the two others, so I shall simply summarise it, for comparison with the more detailed discussion of the other two: (1) Fewer than half of the adult men in the donor clan contributed, and participation was notably high in a single small sub-clan which contains a high proportion of big-men. Most of the big-men in this sub-clan are also sons of the big-man whose

Counting pigs and shells

TABLE 13 *Main account of the Minembi Engambo gift of pigs to Kitepi men, July 1964*

(a) The initial prestation

Donor[a]	Sub-group of donor	Number of pigs	Recipient[a] (sub-group name appears first)	Relationship
Kaep	Kalnambo	9	Kolkal *Əndipi*	friends
Nøring	Eimkembo	8	Rulke Owe	DH to WF
Yei	Kalnambo	8	Kolkal *Engk* and Numndi	new friends
Ruk and Moka, his FBS	Mimkembo	8	Rulke *Nukint*	new friends
Kakla	Eimkembo	8	Rulke *Nditing*	classificatory MZS
Kakla	Eimkembo	8	Ropke *Kuri*	new friends
Akel	Mimkembo	8	Ropke *Kuri*	friends
Rying	Eimkembo	4	Ropke *Kuri*	new friends
Rokopa	Eimkembo	10	Rulke *Nditing*	WZDH to WMZH
		71		

(b) The division by recipients to their associates

    (i) *Nditing* divided out the pigs nominally received by Owe and Nukint (both men of his own sub-clan), as well as those given directly in his name.

    (ii) *Kuri*'s son, *Pørwa*, made some of the decisions in dividing out Kuri's pigs.

    (iii) I did not account for all the pigs given in the initial prestation: specifically I did not discover where six of the pigs *Nditing* divided out went to.

    (iv) Each man received between 1 and 5 pigs in the division. Most received 1 or 2.

	Nditing	*Engk*	*Əndipi*	*Kuri*	Totals
Taken by himself or left for later consideration	10	5	1	2	18
To sub-clansmen	13	3	7	16	39
To clansmen outside recipient's sub-clan	4	—	1	2	7
To men of another clan	1	—	—	—	1
	28	8	9	20	65

(c) Second leg of the prestation

This was delayed until 7 September, and was much smaller than the first leg. One of the donors expressed this by saying: 'You Kitepi have come to ask us to pay for the bones of our man, Engambo Pakla, whom you killed, but I am really able to pay for a part of his skin only, not his true bones. Before we gave you the backbone of our gift, now I am just adding the head to it.' Donors were Ponom (big-man) 8; Wai+Ui 8. Five Kitepi men divided these out among themselves and eight other men of their sub-group, each man receiving one or at the most two pigs. The donors were all affines of men of the recipient sub-clan.

[a] Names of big-men are italicised.

139

earlier killing was the rationale for compensation payments between the two clans. Their prominent participation was related to this fact. (2) Big-men on either or both sides participated in 34 gifts; in 56 gifts the partners on both sides were ordinary men. Overall, big-men were prominent as donors and recipients; but not all of the big-men were clearly outstanding: gifts made by some ordinary men were close in size to the overall average size of gifts made by big-men. (3) About as many gifts were made to kin as to affines; but those to the latter were on average larger. Weight was placed on immediate rather than classificatory affinal ties.

There is good reason for this last point. Gifts to immediate affines of senior generation, and also gifts to immediate mother's brothers, can be described as *semi-obligatory*. Gifts to affines are an important part of the process which maintains a man's marriage; and gifts to mother's brothers are made to ensure that maternal ghosts do not send sickness or harm the 'skin' (bodily condition) of the sister's son. Other gifts, made to classificatory kin and affines or to unrelated partners, do not have these sanctions behind them, and they can be described as *optative*.

Statements about the participation of big-men in a prestation imply that one can identify clearly who is currently accepted as a big-man and who is not. In fact, however, the situation is not so simple, as Bulmer (1960b: 323 ff) has pointed out for the Kyaka, western neighbours of the Melpa. Informants agree on who are the most prominent and established big-men in their clan and in a few other clans which they know well – these I call major big-men – but they tend to produce discrepant accounts of who the less important, minor big-men are. Basically these discrepancies arise from the indeterminate nature of status-stratification in Hagen. It is true that there are a number of folk-criteria for big-man status, but assignments of such a status to any man are the result of personal evaluations made by his clansmen and others of his ability in relation to these criteria. As Bulmer (1960b: 323 ff) has remarked, we are not dealing with a fixed number of offices in each segment of a clan; although there is some expectation that each small group will have someone who is at least a little more prominent than others in moka-making and can take the lead in their discussions. As a result, the men of a small group can usually – but not invariably – name someone whom they consider to be their leader in certain contexts, although they may admit that he is not a major big-man in wider political affairs. Close agnates are likely to include as big-men some of their young men who are improving their status, but outsiders may not yet recognise this. Sometimes the son of a big-man may be called a big-man by an informant out of courtesy, even if in fact he shows no particular talent.

Counting pigs and shells

My decisions on whom to list as big-men in Tipuka Kendike clan are based on information given by men of three different clans: two acknowledged old big-men of Kendike clan itself, Ant and Kaukla; Køu, a recognised but nowadays inactive old big-man of Tipuka Kengeke clan; Nore, a young Kengeke big-man; and Ongka, a leader of Mandembo clan within Kawelka tribe. As all the informants are big-men, their lists are probably conservative rather than over-generous, and perhaps we can say that they are likely, between them, to include all the best-known big-men while omitting some of those who are regarded internally as minor big-men or men on the way to becoming 'big'.

For Kitepi clan I have interview material from two old men, one a recognised (but now – in 1969 – retired) leader, Kuri, and the other named Tei, who lives away from Kuri with the main body of Kitepi clansmen. The ascriptions of these two old men were checked against the opinions of the Kawelka leader, Ongka, again. For another clan involved in the chain,

TABLE 14 *Names of big-men in six clans*

	Kendike	Kitepi	Wanyembo	Oklembo	Membo	Mandembo
Big-men now old and inactive		*Ok 1* *Ok 2* *Parka* *Rop*		*Køu*		*Roklpa*[d] *Nui* *Akel*
Major big-men leaders	*Ant*[a] *Mek* *Kaukla* *Rying*	*Kuri*[a] *Nditing*	*Tiki*	*Rokla* *Kele*	*ɔndipi*[c]	*Ongka* *Nykint*
Slightly less prominent men, important in their sub-clan	*Nui*	*Engk* *Mara* *Mel*		*Pana* *Waep*	*Waema* *Kont*	
Young men on the up-grade		*Pørwa*[b] *Wai*		*Rokopa* *Nøpil*		
Minor big-men of varying ages	*Ndip* *Møndi* *Tei*	*Kowa* *Ukl* *Tei 1* *Tei 2* *Nøngin* *Rumba* *Tong* *Nukint*		*Engk* *Køi* *Ui*[c] (*possibly Opa*)[e]	*Murli* *Rop* *Ndip* *Pana* *Rui* *Nggoimba* *Ken* *Apil* (*possibly Engk*)	*Rumba 1* *Kuklup* *Møra* *El* *Køpi* *Rumba 2* (*possibly Raema*)

[a] Inactive by 1969.   [b] President of Dei Local Government Council.
[c] Growing old by 1969.   [d] Baptised by 1969 and therefore inactive.
[e] Possibles are not included in later tables.

Wanyembo, I have a similar range of opinion from old, but influential, men. In Appendix 8 I discuss the ascriptions of these informants in more detail; here I shall give a table of ascriptions on which there was general agreement. The particular categories into which I have divided big-men are based on my own impressions as well as those of my informants. I include lists for Tipuka Oklembo and two of the Kawelka clans (Table 14). In Chapter 9 I will present figures for the remaining Kawelka clan (Kundmbo) and discuss the proportions of men in this clan who are big-men, ordinary men, and men of low status. Table 14 is intended only as a key to subsequent discussion in the present chapter, in which I mention the names of big-men from time to time.

TABLE 15   *Participation by donors in two moka*

(a) Participation by Kendike donors in moka to Kitepi and Wanyembo, 1964

Sub-clan of Kendike	Numbers of men in sub-clan	Numbers of men who were donors in moka (+% of total numbers in sub-clan)
Milyembo	39	20 (51·3%)
Woumbo	15	11 (75%)
Andakomonembo	33	16 (48·5%)
Kombuklambo	15	3 (20%)
	102	50 (49%)

NOTE: the low participation by Kombuklambo sub-clan is explained by the fact that this group had recently made a side prestation, to Nølka men, consisting of 57 pigs divided among 10 recipients. All 15 of the Kombuklambo men were donors in this. They were criticised by others for not keeping all their pigs 'inside the Tipuka themselves'.

(b) Participation by Kitepi and Oklembo men in moka to the Kawelka, 1964–5

Clan	Numbers of men (excluding youths)	Numbers of men who gave pigs, shells, or both
Kitepi	115	48 (41·7%)
Oklembo	116	34 (29·3%)
	231	82 (35·5%)

NOTES: 1. Population figures are taken from the Administration tax-census.
   2. The low participation of the Oklembo is explained at least partly by the failure of Minembi Yelipi clan in their prestation to them; partly also by the relative disengagement of Oklembo Kundmbo men, who live in the Jimi Valley away from the Kawelka.

Counting pigs and shells

Table 15 shows the general extent of participation by donors in the two moka we are considering. A smaller proportion of men participated in the second moka: 35·5 per cent of the total numbers as against 49 per cent (54 per cent if Kombuklambo sub-clan is omitted). The reason is not simply that there was less importance attached to the second moka, for this was in fact the culminating prestation of the sequence; but the total potential number of donors in Kitepi and Oklembo clans (231) is far greater than the number of potential adult male recipients in Membo and Mandembo clans (87 + 53 = 140). Hence it was unlikely that so high a proportion of Kitepi–Oklembo men would be involved. By contrast, Kendike (102 men) and Kitepi (115 men) are more evenly-matched; and in addition Kendike men were giving to Wanyembo clan (71 men, although only about half of these were recipients in this particular moka): thus it is understandable that a higher proportion of Kendike men contributed to their moka.

Although these figures demonstrate clearly that only about half of a clan's men participate in even the important group prestations, it does not follow that the other half are entirely inactive in the moka system. Big-men are expected to be prominent on such occasions; but they, and even more so ordinary men, may withdraw their resources from a given moka if their personal plans commit them elsewhere.

Figures which I shall give in Chapter 9 suggest that about a quarter of a clan's men at any given time may be men of low status, who are unlikely to take part in moka. If these were first deducted from the numbers of men which I have given, the proportions of men likely to take part who actually did take part in the two moka would rise considerably.

Table 16 gives an analysis of partnerships in the moka given by Tipuka Kendike clan. Only those partnerships for which I obtained relationship details are included. Table 17 gives some comparative material from the Tipuka Kitepi–Oklembo moka.

For ease of reference I shall label these two moka occasions in the rest of this chapter as follows: moka A (i) Kendike to Kitepi; A (ii) Kendike to Wanyembo; B Kitepi–Oklembo to Kawelka Membo–Mandembo.

The tables suggest at least one contrast between A (i) on the one hand and A (ii) and B on the other: in A (i) the average number of pigs per gift[1]

---

[1] A gift, here and in the following tables, is defined as the actual number of pigs or shells which a donor at a prestation gives to one recipient.

is higher (4·28) than in A (ii) and B (2·58 and 2·52). The difference between A (i) and A (ii) can be explained by the greater strength of the alliance between Kitepi and Kendike than between Kendike and Wanyembo clan: the Wanyembo are a small group, and many of them live in the Jimi Valley away from the Məka Valley where Kendike and Kitepi live; more-

TABLE 16   *Kendike moka: gifts to different categories of recipients*

(a) Detailed statement

Category		To Kitepi		To Wanyembo	
		Gifts	Pigs	Gifts	Pigs
A	1 cross-cousins	1	4	—	—
	2 descs. of c-cs.	2	8	—	—
	3 classific. c-cs.	1	3	—	—
B	1 MB to ZS	4	16	3	4
	2 ZS to MB	—	—	—	—
	3 classific. B1	10	39	4	9
	4 classific. B2	1	4	—	—
C	1 WB to ZH	6	37	—	—
	2 ZH to WB	2	7	2	6
	3 classific. C1 and 2	1	3	—	—
	4 distant classific. C1 and 2	2	7	3	10
D	1 WF to DH	3	14	1	3
	2 DH to WF	1	7	—	—
	3 classific. D1 and 2	4	13	3	8
E	1 H to WMB and vice-versa	—	—	—	—
	2 H to WZH	1	4	—	—
F	1 matrilat-parallel cs.	1	3	—	—
	2 classific. F1	1	8	—	—
	3 WZS to MZH	—	—	—	—
G	unrelated partner[a]	16	67	17	45
H	other[b] relationships	—	—	—	—

  [a] There is often a possibility of choosing to regard a partner as a classificatory kinsman/affine or as unrelated. I follow the participants' own statements.
  [b] E.g. BS to FB, where one man has switched his affiliation away from his father's clan; distant clan ties, arising from similar switches; daughter to mother: women occasionally figure as donors and recipients, for example, if they are widows; DHB to BWM and classificatory instances of this relationship; and FZH to WBS: the FZH is not classified in kin terminology as an uncle but is addressed by personal name and referred to as 'a kind of father' (*tepam-mɪl*), or else as 'a kind of in-law' (*koklom-mɪl*). The former usage is more common.

Counting pigs and shells

(b) Summary

Category	To Kitepi			To Wanyembo		
	No. gifts	No. pigs	Pigs per gift	No. gifts	No. pigs	Pigs per gift
A	4	15	3·75	—	—	—
B	15	59	3·93	7	13	1·86
C	11	54	4·91	5	16	3·2
D	8	34	4·25	4	11	2·75
E	1	4	4·0	—	—	—
F	2	11	5·5	—	—	—
G	16	67	4·19	17	45	2·65
H	—	—	—	—	—	—
	57	244	4·28	33	85	2·58

(c) Immediate versus classificatory links

1. Distinguishing kin and affines[c]

Category	To Kitepi			To Wanyembo		
	Gifts	Pigs	Pigs per gift	Gifts	Pigs	Pigs per gift
Immediate kin	6	23	3·83	3	4	1·3
Classific. kin	15	62	4·13	4	9	2·25
Immediate affines	12	65	5·42	3	9	3
Classific. affines	8	27	3·38	6	18	3
	41	177	4·32	16	40	2·5

[c] I am contrasting the terms 'kin' and 'affines' here. As I mention in the text, I use 'relative' to cover both.

2. Comparing immediate with classificatory ties, and including unrelated partners

Category	No. gifts	No. pigs	Pigs per gift
Immediate kin and affines	24	101	4·2
Classific. kin and affines	33	116	3·5
Unrelated partners	33	112	3·4
	90	329	3·7

over, it was the Kendike who drove Wanyembo into the Jimi in the past. The discrepancy between A (i) and B, however, cannot be explained in this way, since there is a strong traditional alliance between the donor and recipient clans in B. Furthermore, I have argued that donors in inter-tribal moka try especially hard to do well. In this case the difference is probaby related to the fact that the donors were *also* giving away over 1,500 shells,

L

and some of their resources had no doubt been deployed to obtain these. Hence the size of their pig gifts dropped. In A (i) only pigs were given.

Another possible point of contrast, between A as a whole and B, is that more gifts of pigs are made to unrelated partners in B: 43·9 per cent of the total (61/138) as opposed to 36·6 per cent (33/90) in A. The difference is not great, but I interpret it as indicating a greater extension of partnerships between the men of clans involved in A, resulting from their more secure exchange-alliance.

In both A and B the average size of gifts of pigs to unrelated partners is smaller than the average size of gifts to classificatory relatives (I include in this term both consanguineal kin and affines); but the difference is marginal. More markedly, the average size of gifts to immediate affines is greater in both A and B than the size of gifts to other categories. The size of these gifts to immediate affines also ensures that gifts to immediate as against classificatory relatives are larger. The figures thus reveal a pattern similar to that which Bulmer (1960a: 10) identified for the Kyaka.

The shell gifts in moka B (Table 17 (d) and (e)) match the patterns for gifts of pigs. 43·4 per cent of the gifts go to unrelated partners; the size of these gifts is a little smaller than that of gifts to kin and affines; gifts to affines show the highest average size; and gifts to immediate relatives are larger than gifts to classificatory connections.

The overall proportions of numbers (but not sizes) of gifts to affines, kin, and unrelated partners appear in Table 17 (f). The highest single proportions go to unrelated partners; but in no case do these exceed the totals for kin and affines combined. More gifts appear to go to kin than to affines; but the 'preference' is only an apparent one, for consanguineal kin terms are extended much more flexibly and widely than are those for affines. The preponderance of gifts to 'kin' thus comes from the category of classificatory kin rather than from gifts to immediate kin.[1]

THE IMPORTANCE OF BIG-MEN: MOKA A

My information on big-men is more detailed for moka B than for A, so I shall separate material on the two. Table 18 gives some data for A. The

---

[1] Strictly, the significance of these proportions could be determined only with reference to the potential numbers of kin, affines, and unrelated persons in the recipient clans for each donor. But, apart from being difficult, such an exercise would be somewhat unreal since kin terms such as those for 'cross-cousin' or 'sister's son' can be extended very widely. What I am recording here is the way participants themselves classified their relationships; and it seems noteworthy, given the *possibility* of including all relationships under some kind of kin or affinal term, that this choice is not taken and many partners are described as unrelated.

TABLE 17 *Kitepi–Oklembo moka: gifts to different categories of recipients*

(*a*) For comparison with 16 (*b*)

Category	No. gifts	No. pigs	Pigs per gift
A	11	24	2·18
B	21	69	3·29
C	19	51	2·68
D	4	24	6·0
E	9	19	2·1
F	9	18	2·0
G	60	146	2·43
H	5	8	1·6
	138	359	2·52

Cassowaries and goats, which were given as 'extras', are not included.

(*b*) For comparison with 16 (*c*) 1

Category	No. gifts	No. pigs	Pigs per gift
Immediate kin	18	52	2·87
Classific. kin	23	59	2·56
Immediate affines	16	56	3·5
Classific. affines	16	38	2·38
	73	205	2·67

NOTE: Category H is not included. The partnership within it, FZH with WBS, is classified by Melpa speakers either as a kin or as an affinal relationship, and therefore it cannot be fitted unambiguously within the table. It can, however, be fitted into the following table, since it belongs to the category of 'immediate kin and affines'.

(*c*) For comparison with 16 (*c*) 2

Category	No. gifts	No. pigs	Pigs per gift
Immediate kin and affines	38	114	3·21
Classific. kin and affines	39	97	2·48
Unrelated partners	61	148	2·43
	138	359	2·52

(*d*) Comparing kin, affines, and unrelated partners

Category	Pigs			Shells		
	Gifts	Pigs	Pigs/Gift	Gifts	Shells	Shells/Gift
Kin	45	117	2·54	39	388	*c.* 10·0
Affines	32	94	2·94	27	313	*c.* 11·6
Unrelated partners	61	148	2·43	57	548	8·6
	138	359	2·52	123	1249	10·15

NOTE: The FZS – WBS partnership in category H is here treated as a 'kin' relationship rather than an affinal one.

Table 17 *contd.*

(*e*) Gifts to immediate and classificatory kin and affines compared (shells only)

Category	Immediate		Classificatory	
	Gifts	Shells	Gifts	Shells
A	5	51 (av. 10·2)	9	90 (10·0)
B	5	48 (9·6)	12	98 (8·16)
C	9	137 (15·2)	10	102 (10·2)
D	3	28 (9·3)	—	— —
E	—	— —	4	38 (9·5)
F	4	66 (16·5)	4	33 (8·25)
H	1	10 (10·0)	—	— —
	27	340	39	361

Mean size of gift: 12·6 shells
Mean size of gift: 9·25 shells

(*f*) Both moka: comparison of proportions of gifts to affines, kin, and unrelated partners

Percentages of nos. of gifts

Categories	moka A	moka B	
	Pigs	Pigs	Shells
Kin	31·1	33·09	31·3
Affines	32·2	23·01	25·3
Unrelated partners	36·6	43·9	43·4
	100	100	100

total number of gifts considered is not identical with totals in Table 16, since for some gifts I know the relative status of the donors and recipients but not how they would phrase their relationship.

Table 18*a* shows that, overall, major big-men gave a larger average number of pigs than others; minor big-men gave numbers closer to those given by ordinary men. There is also a contrast between A (i) and A (ii): the investment of major big-men in the moka to Kitepi is much greater. This fits the stronger alliance between Kendike and Kitepi.

Table 18*b* shows the prominence of two Kitepi major big-men as recipients. These are Kuri and Nditing (cf. Table 14), who were also dominant in moka B, to the Kawelka. Kuri and his sons were partners of a number of unrelated Kendike men, notably the major big-man Ant, and between them they received 36 pigs in the moka. Again, the gap is between major big-men and others rather than between less eminent big-men and others. A set of ordinary men received the bulk of their pigs from Kendike big-men, and the average number of pigs given to them is in fact greater than that for minor big-men. These recipients were either sons of Kitepi

Counting pigs and shells

TABLE 18   *Contribution and reception of gifts by big-men in the Kendike moka*

(a) Contributions

Status of donor	No. of donors	No. of pigs	Average no. of pigs given by each donor
1. Kendike to Wanyembo			
Major big-men[a]	5	27	5·4
Minor big-men	3	12	4
Others	18	66	3·6
	26	105	4·03
2. Kendike to Kitepi			
Major big-men[a]	5	71	14·2
Minor big-men	2	8	4
Others	28	181	6·4
	35	260	7·4

[a] Some borderline major/minor big-men are included here.

(b) Reception

Status of recipient	Nos.	Nos. of pigs received			
		From big-men	From others	Total	Average
Major big-men	2	19	14	33	16·5
Slightly less eminent men	3	11	8	19	6·3
Minor big-men	6	8	25	33	5·5
Old and inactive big-men	1	3	4	7	7
	12	41	51	92	7·7
Others, who received from both big-men and ordinary men	6	38	17	55	9·2
Others, who received only from ordinary men	21	—	113	113	5·4
	27	38	130	168	6·2

(c) Partnerships

Gifts to big-men from	From big-men donors		From others	
	Gifts	Pigs	Gifts	Pigs
Kin	2	15	3	10
Affines	1	4	5	23
Unrelated partners	4	22	4	18
	7	41	12	51

Total gifts 19; total pigs 92
Pigs from: kin   25, average size 5
           affines   27, average size 4·75
           unrelated 40, average size 5
Average size of gift from big-men: *c.* 6; from others *c.* 4

big-men who were favoured by their fathers' partners or close affines of donor big-men and thus their appropriate exchange partners.

Prominent ordinary-men donors belonged to two types: old men, with long-standing exchange partnerships but no pretensions to leadership, and younger men, who are ambitious and may behave as incipient leaders but have not yet achieved recognition. The top eight among these donors gave 75 pigs to their ordinary-men partners, almost as many as the eight Kendike big-men gave. Their largest gifts went to affines (6 gifts, 39 pigs, cp. 6 gifts, 27 pigs, to kin, 1 gift of 5 pigs to an unrelated partner, and one uncertain case of 4 pigs, total = 75); whereas this was not so for big-men. This suggests that prominent ordinary men invest in their affines rather

TABLE 19   *Contribution and reception of gifts by big-men and others in the Kitepi–Oklembo moka*

(a) Contributions: shells

Clan segment	Contributions of big-men			Contributions of others		
	Donors	Gifts	Shells	Donors	Gifts	Shells
1. Kitepi clan						
Ropkembo	5	16	180	5	6	57
Rulkembo	4	12	153	7	12	117
Kolkal	3	6	77	7	13	107
Pøndimbo	3	4	56	4	4	32
2. Oklembo clan						
Kundmbo	1	2	18	5	5	46
Mbakambo	2	3	42	10	12	94
Korkambo	5	18	165	9	10	95
3. Wanyembo clan	1	2	21	1	1	8
	24	63	712	48	63	557

NOTE: a few more shells are accounted for here than in 17 (*d*): I am not sure of relationship details in all cases.

(b) Shell contributions: big-men and others

Category and nos. in category	No. of recipients	No. of shells	Average shells per donor
Major big-men (4)	19	265	66·3
Slightly less eminent men (3)	6	97	32·3
Younger big-men on up-grade (4)	13	110	27·5
Minor big-men (11)	23	222	20·2
Old and inactive big-men (2)	2	18	9
Prominent ordinary men (5)	14	129	25·8
Other ordinary men (43)	49	428	*c.* 10

Counting pigs and shells

(c) Contributions: pigs

Clan segment	Contributions of big-men			Contributions of others		
	Donors	Gifts	Pigs	Donors	Gifts	Pigs
1. Kitepi clan						
Ropkembo	5	13	64	5	10	32
Rulkembo	3	10	31	9	10	26
Kolkal	3	4	10	9	21	39
Pøndimbo	3	4	5	1	1	4
Roklambo	1	2	8	—	—	—
2. Oklembo clan						
Kundmbo	1	1	8	2	2	3
Mbakambo	2	2	2	7	10	17
Korkambo	6	12	21	7	9	17
3. Eltimbo clan	3	14	43	10	15	27
4. Wanyembo clan	1	1	1	—	—	—
	28	63	193	50	78	165

Av. pigs per big-man: 6·89
Av. pigs per ordinary man: 2·12

(d) Pig contributions: big-men and others

Category and nos. in category	No. of recipients	No. of pigs	Average pigs per donor
Major big-men (5)	22	79	15·8
Slightly less prominent men (5)	6	20	4
Younger big-men on up-grade (4)	8	27	6·75
Minor big-men (13)	26	62	4·8
Old and inactive big-men (2)	3	9	4·5
Prominent ordinary men (12)	32	91	7·6
Other ordinary men (38)	42	74	c. 2

(e) Ranking of recipients in terms of numbers of items received

	Major big-men	Slightly less eminent big-men	Minor big-men	Old big-men	Ordinary men
1. Shells					
80–100	2	—	—	—	—
60–80	—	1	—	—	—
40–60	1	1	3	—	—
20–40	—	—	4	—	7
1–20	—	—	4	1	32
	3	2	11	1	39
2. Pigs					
25–30	2	—	—	—	—
20–24	—	—	1	—	—
15–19	—	2	—	—	—
10–14	1	—	2	—	2
5–9	—	—	4	—	15
1–4	—	—	6	3	25
0	—	—	2	—	11
	3	2	15	3	53

than taking the risk of spreading partnerships to unrelated men as big-men do.

Table 18c shows the distribution of gifts to Kitepi big-men from kin, affines, and unrelated partners of varying status. There is little difference in the overall average size of gifts from kin, etc. Big-men make larger gifts than the others. Unrelated partners are the highest single source of pigs: the pattern here is influenced by the partnership between Kuri and Ant. The prominence of unrelated partners in general reflects the fact that big-men tend to attract 'optative' as well as large 'semi-obligatory' gifts, both from other big-men and from ordinary men.

THE IMPORTANCE OF BIG-MEN: MOKA B

In this moka we have to take into account gifts of shells as well as pigs. I begin (Table 19) with the ranking of big-men and others as donors and recipients, then (Table 20) consider the kin and other ties activated by big-men in their partnerships.

Table 19 confirms in general the pre-eminence of major big-men. The two major big-men who contributed most to the moka were Kuri and Nditing, both of whom were prominent also in moka A, which partly helped to finance moka B. These two belong to Ropkembo and Rulkembo sub-clans, and their influence is seen in the large shell contributions from these two groups; the two were also prominent in pig contributions (Table 19 (a) to (c)). The position of Kuri and Nditing is special: both were driven from Kitepi territory as refugees in warfare and settled on enclaves of land granted them by Kawelka relatives. Since then they have maintained particularly close alliance ties with their Kawelka friends. Several men of Kolkal sub-clan similarly make use of Kawelka land.

In Oklembo clan the performance of big-men in Mbakambo section was poor. This was a result of the failure of arrangements between Oklembo and Minembi Yelipi clan which I examine in the next chapter.

Major big-men were most conspicuous, perhaps, in their contribution and reception of pearl shells. Kuri and Nditing gave 104 and 84 shells respectively. It is only by giving shell-moka that men can add to their status-symbol pendant which they wear over their chests, the *koa mak* or *omak*. In the past only important big-men had sufficient connections and wealth to obtain pearl shells; nowadays, when the shells are not only plentiful but in process of dropping from favour among younger men in the Dei council area, it is still the older major big-men who specialise in their accumulation and display on moka occasions.

Kuri gave 28 and Nditing 27 pigs. Another big-man, Kot, of the tiny

TABLE 20 *Exchange partnerships of prominent Kawelka big-men in the Kitepi–Oklembo moka*

(*a*) Pigs: size of gifts

Relationship of recipient big-man to donor	From big-men			From ordinary men			Overall average
	Gifts	Pigs[a]	Average	Gifts	Pigs[a]	Average	
Kin	5	24	} 3·6	4	10	} 2·3	} 2·9
Affine	9	26		11	24		
Unrelated partner	16	47	*c.* 3	7	16	2·3	2·7
	30	97	3·23	22	50	2·3	2·8

[a] Eight cassowaries and one goat were also given. These were extra gifts, given as prestige items. In 1964 a full-grown cassowary was worth about twice as much as a medium sized pig.

(*b*) Differential status of donors in (*a*)

Status of donor	No. of gifts	No. of pigs	Average per gift
Major big-men + borderline	16	62	3·9
Minor big-men	13	34	2·6
Old and inactive big-men	1	1	1
Sons of big-men who are not themselves big-men	2	7	3·5
Other ordinary men	20	43	2·2
	52	147	2·8

(*c*) Shells: size of gifts

Relationship	From big-men			From ordinary men			Overall average
	Gifts	Shells	Average	Gifts	Shells	Average	
Kin	4	95	} 19·13	5	52	} 8·8	} 12·6
Affine	4	58		8	62		
Unrelated partners	15	153	10·2	3	28	9·3	10·1
	23	306	12·4	16	142	9·0	11·5

(*d*) Differential status of donors in (*c*)

Status of donor	No. of gifts	No. of shells	Average per gift
Major big-men + borderline	13	214	16·5
Minor big-men + younger	9	82	9·1
Old and inactive big-men	1	10	10
Sons of big-men who are not themselves big-men	2	20	10
Ordinary men	14	122	8·7
	39	448	11·5

Eltimbo clan which was hard-pressed in the moka chain sequence (cf. previous chapter), came third with 17 pigs. Kot is a major big-man who also lives within Kawelka territory and is closely allied to the Kawelka. He is rather younger than Kuri and Nditing, and did not involve himself in shell gifts.

Table 19 (*e*) gives a ranking of recipients in terms of the numbers of pigs and shells they received. In the case of shells, the two top recipients are Ongka and Nykint of Mandembo clan, third is Kont of Membo. While the latter two received from immediate relatives who are big-men – Nykint's mother's brother is Kitepi Kuri and Kont's sister's husband is Engk, a 'borderline' major big-man of Kitepi–Ongka had to rely on a number of partners with whom he has only classificatory links. In the case of pig-gifts many of these let him down: he would have been more secure if he had had immediate kin or affines as partners.

One minor big-man who received many shells was Mǝra. He is a younger brother of the major big-man in his group, Nykint, and attracts gifts partly on the strength of this. Another was Ndip, an old big-man who is a wife's brother to Kitepi Kuri and is also married into Kuri's sub-clan.[1] Good placement in networks of kin and affinal relationships thus helps men to do well. Other minor big-men suffered from defaulting partners.

Similar conclusions emerge in the case of pig-gifts. The top two recipients were Nykint (through his tie with Kuri), and ǝndipi, who has a number of partnerships with Eltimbo men.[2] Ndip appears high up, with 21 pigs, 17 from his affines. Ongka dropped to the lower ranks, owing to defaulting by the Oklembo. Ordinary men who did well were connected with Kuri and Nditing.[3] Twelve minor big-men appear low down. In such circumstances they tend to blame their partners for defaulting. Co-clansmen who are recipients in a moka are potentially in competition to

[1] This marriage is irregular: a man and his sister should not marry into the same sub-clan. Irregular marriages are rationalised (1) by saying that the sub-clan is in process of dividing into two, and/or (2) by saying that one of the partners is not a patrifilial member of his or her sub-clan and therefore the marriage does not 'count'.

[2] These are ostensibly his unrelated friends, but in fact his partnerships with them are also based on a traditional 'agnatic' tie. ǝndipi (who is a major and now ageing big-man) is a non-agnate of Kawelka tribe. His father belonged to the Lkalke tribe, which was scattered in warfare and does not exist as a corporate body. After the father's death his mother married a big-man of Kawelka. Some of the Eltimbo men are sons of Lkalke men who joined the Eltimbo as refugees: hence ǝndipi's 'traditional' tie with them.

[3] It should be noted that to activate connections with big-men an ordinary man must plunge into high finance. In one case an ordinary man had to provide as many as 9 pigs as initiatory gifts in order to receive 10 back in the moka. Large initiatory gifts usually mean that their provider must finance himself from a third party, and so he must manage his affairs carefully. His partnership with big-men provides a reasonable guarantee that his finances will work out.

attract gifts from unrelated partners; but recriminations between them are avoided: instead, the blame is always laid on the individual donor for defaulting – not for giving to another recipient. By contrast, passionate quarrels break out between clansmen over the 'extra' pigs given for cooking and eating at the end of a moka, and arguments over these may well provide a release for tension generated by implicit but unadmitted competition for the whole range of gifts.

A prudent big-man, who has the resources, can recover even from a poor set of gifts. In these circumstances the man who can fall back on reserve networks or produce pigs from his own household is the one who survives and is able to pay back men from whom he raised initiatory gifts on loan which he then passed on to the prospective moka-makers. Ongka, for example, received only 11 pigs from his partners. He obtained a few 'extra' ones also, and instead of cooking these he used them to pay back his 'little men' – supporters within his clan-section – in order to retain their good-will. He then used his own resources to finance a moka which he completed in October 1965.

Apart from the minor big-men who did not receive many gifts, there were six Membo–Mandembo big-men who did not receive at all. Two are old and inactive, three live away at the Gumant river where they have established a different set of local ties, and one is of very minor reputation.

The nine most prominent big-man recipients were: Ongka, Nykint, Kont, Ɵndipi, Waema, Mɘra, Ndip, Nggoimba and Pana.[1] In Table 20 I consider the partnerships of these men in more detail.

Table 20 shows the same pattern for both pigs and shells. There is a balance between partnerships with kin and affines and partnerships with unrelated men. More partnerships are made with big-men who are un-related than with ordinary men. The average size of gifts from kin and affines is greater than that of gifts from unrelated partners: here it is the big-men donors rather than the others who cause the difference, and overall gifts from big-men are larger than those from ordinary men (20 (a) and (c)). The largest gifts come from major and 'borderline' big-men (20 (b) and (d)). Finally, more partnerships are made with major and minor big-men than with men of other categories.

These conclusions do not differ much from the pattern shown in previous Tables. The most prominent big-men depend on partnerships with ordinary men as well as other big-men, and on ties with unrelated partners as well as with kin and affines. But particular kin and affinal

[1] Cf. Table 14, under Membo and Mandembo clans. Three are major big-men, two 'borderline' major big-men, and four are minor.

linkages between particular big-men are often important as vehicles for the greatest 'load' of exchanges.

MARRIAGE TIES AS A VEHICLE FOR EXCHANGE PARTNERSHIPS

We have seen that gifts to immediate affines are usually large, and that affines are expected to be exchange partners. Marriage prohibitions ensure that there is no heavy reduplication of marriages between small segments of intermarrying clans, while a preference for marrying into allied rather

TABLE 21   *Marriages between Kitepi–Oklembo and Membo–Mandembo clans extant in January 1965*

(a)

	Oklembo			Kitepi				
	Mbak.	Kork.	Kund.	Ropke.	Rulke.	Kolk.	Rokl.	Pønd.
a. Kawelka men married to Tipuka women								
Membo Oyambo	1	3	—	2	—	1	—	2
Køyambo	—	2	—	—	—	1	—	1
Mandembo Nggl.	—	1	—	1	—	—	—	—
Mandembo Kurup.	1	2	—	—	1	1	—	1
	2	8	—	3	1	3	—	4
b. Kawelka women married to Tipuka men								
Membo Oyambo	—	—	—	1	4	—	—	—
Køyambo	—	2	—	—	—	3	—	1
Mandembo Nggl.	2	1	1	2	1	1	—	1
Mandembo Kurup.	2	—	—	1	1	1	1	1
	4	3	1	4	6	5	1	3
Totals *a* and *b*	6	11	1	7	7	8	1	7 = 48

(b)

Extent of use	No. of cases
1. Link used only by immediate brothers-in-law	5
2. Used by sister's son–mother's brother pair	4
3. Used by father-in-law son-in-law pair	3
4. Used only by classificatory connections of the immediate affines	9
5. Used by father-in-law, brother-in-law, and wife's cross-cousin	1
6. Used by immediate brothers-in-law and by classificatory connections	1
7. Used by sister's son, brother-in-law and classificatory connections	3
8. Used by wife's sister's son and classificatory brothers-in-law	1
	27

(c) Partnerships of a father and son at a single group prestation

Relationship of recipients to Kuri	Kuri		Pørwa et al.	
	Pigs	Shells	Pigs	Shells
Immediate WBs + one WBS				
Kui	—	—	8	—
Kundil	2	10	—	—
b–m Ndip	7	37	—	—
Ketan	3	—	—	—
Lineage WBs				
Tei	4	—	—	—
Kraep	—	—	—	14
Numndi	—	10	—	—
Engk	—	—	7	10
Sub-sub-clan WBs				
b–m Əndipi	—	4	—	4
Tiptip	—	—	—	16
Kngal	—	—	2	8
Sub-clan WBs				
b–m Muri	6	30	2	—
Clan WB				
b–m Rop	—	4	—	4

than traditional-enemy groups ensures that there is some concentration of affinal ties between clans such as those we have been considering in moka B. To some extent individual marriages become a basis on which clusters of exchange partnerships can be established: in a set of partnerships where there were classificatory ties between donor and recipient, twenty-three of the thirty ties involved no greater than lineage or sub-sub-clan extensions of relationships. Where a tie involves an apparently more 'distant' extension, it is often the case that the groups are small and relations between men of their different segments have become somewhat closer than they would otherwise be.

Despite this importance of affinal ties and the tendency to make further partnerships around them, not all marriages are used as a focus for moka activity.[1]

Extant marriages between Kitepi–Oklembo and Membo–Mandembo in 1964–5 were as shown in Table 21 (a). Of the 48 marriages listed 27 were a focus for at least one gift in the moka of January 1965, while 21

[1] In my discussion here I shall deal with affinal ties only in a very limited way. In particular I am not considering the role of women as wives and intermediaries between their kin and in-laws, important as this role is in the actual establishment of exchange relations between affines. Women's roles are examined in more detail in Strathern A. M. 1968a.

were not. Table 21 (*b*) shows the extent to which the 27 marriage ties used in the moka were a focus for clustering of partnerships; and I shall illustrate some of the categories in this table in an attempt to see what factors influence the extent of clustering.

CASE 1: link used by immediate brothers-in-law only.

Kawelka Rumba is married to a sister of three minor big-men of Kitepi Ropke sub-clan. Ropke Rumba gave his Kawelka namesake 8 shells, and Tei gave him a single pig. Earlier, Tei had given 10 pigs to Kawelka Rumba and received 10 back in August 1964. Rumba was now hoping for an increment from Tei and was disappointed when Tei chose instead to give to the major big-man in Kurupmbo clan-section, Nykint, whose mother was of Tei's own sub-clan. Nøngin gave to his son-in-law, Membo Ndip, who is also a minor big-man; and two of Kawelka Rumba's three brothers received large gifts from *their* sons-in-law. The third, Nykint, is of little standing in the moka. The reason for the lack of reduplication here is, then, simply that the related men had further affinal ties with others involved in the same moka occasion. The *reduplication* of marriages between allied clans in fact ensures a *separation* of individual exchange partnerships in cases similar to this one.

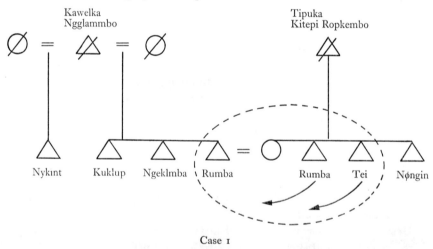

Case 1

CASE 2: link used only by mother's brother and sister's son.

Membo Pana is a minor big-man, with 4 wives and a number of sons. One of his wives is an inherited widow, an Oklembo woman. Her son by her first husband is grown up and married, and it was to him rather than to Pana that her brother Køndikam gave in this moka (8 shells, 2 pigs). The other brother, Wonopa, is old and inactive. Køndikam's partnership with his ZS Ndoa is in fact a continuation of his earlier partnership with his sister's first husband, which he prefers to pursue rather than making ties with her new husband and his sons by other wives.

Counting pigs and shells

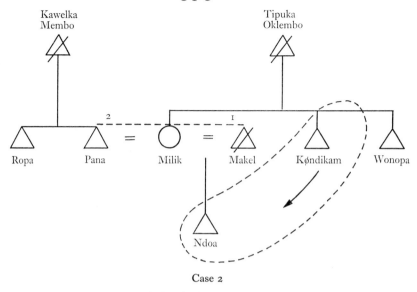

Case 2

CASE 3: link used only by a father-in-law and son-in-law.

This case involves some of the same persons as Case 1. Kitepi Yap, son of Nøngin, gave 10 shells and 4 pigs to his father-in-law Rop at the moka. We have already seen how Rumba, Tei, and Nøngin were occupied; and Yap was unlikely to give to Kaep, who is a timid man and scarcely participates in moka. There are no grown-up wife's brothers of Yap, so his only effective duty was to give to his wife's father.

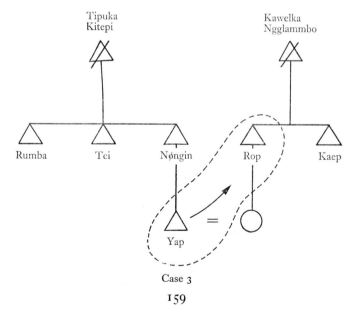

Case 3

159

The Rope of Moka

CASE 4: use of marriage by classificatory connections only.

a. Kawelka Køpi's wife is daughter of Kitepi Mund. Mund is old, and his son *ð*mndi was involved in giving pigs to his own father-in-law, who is also of Kawelka. Nditing, a sub-clansman of Mund and a major big-man, stepped in to take over the partnership with Køpi and gave him 9 shells.

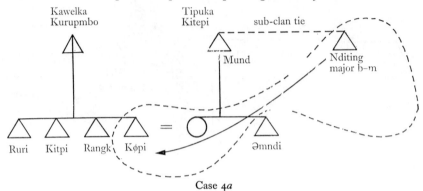

Case 4*a*

b. One of Oklembo Køu's wives is sister of a Kawelka man, Ndoa. But Ndoa is old and lives at a married daughter's place. His son works as a medical orderly and does not make moka either. However, this marriage was used by Koepa and Enga, two sons of Køu, to make gifts to lineage-mates of Ndoa; and by Køu to give to Ongka, leader of Ndoa's clan-section.

clan-section tie   Kawelka Ngglammbo

Mbøndi   Want

Ongka major b-m Køu

Ndoa

Koepa Enga

Anggi   Kwant

Rop   Ndekane

Mel

Case 4*b*

CASES 5 and 6: use of marriage tie by wider sets of classificatory connections.

I select two cases only, as examples from categories 5 to 8 in Table 21 (*b*).

5. Mɨt has been incorporated into his mother's clan by his three mother's brothers, who are minor big-men (Tei, Nøngin, and Rumba – cf. Case 1). He based his partnerships in the 1965 moka around those of his mother's brothers. In the diagram the partnerships of the mother's brothers are shown by dotted surrounding lines, while Mɨt's gifts are shown by arrows. Mɨt exactly duplicates his uncles' ties in two instances, duplicates them in one instance more loosely by giving to a younger brother of one of their partners (Mɜra), and in another case differentiates himself by giving to Waema, his wife's cross-cousin.

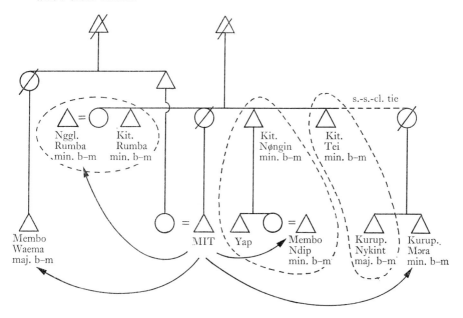

For conventions of the diagram cf. text

Case 5

6. This case shows a much more extensive set of exchange partnerships, created by a major big-man, Kuri. In 1964–5 Kuri was perhaps the most respected and pre-eminent traditional big-man in the Kitepi–Oklembo pair of clans.[1] The chief links he has with the Kawelka Membo and Mandembo clans are two (cf. diagram): one of his wives is of Membo, sister of the minor big-man Ndip, and one of his own sisters was mother of Nykint and Mɜra, prominent men in Mandembo clan. Kuri has extended his partnerships out

[1] By 1969 he seemed definitely to be retired; but if he lives, pigs will certainly be given to him when the Kawelka make returns for the moka of January 1965, perhaps in 1972.

M

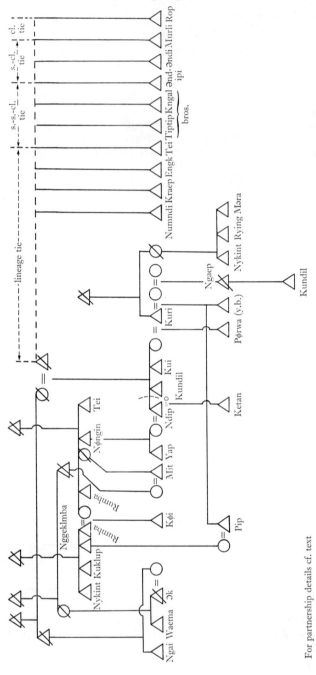

Case 6

For partnership details cf. text

from his immediate set of wife's brothers to nine men, including one major big-man, Ɂndipi, and two minor, Murli and Rop. Four of these nine partners belong to the same small lineage as Kuri's immediate wife's brothers. There are 14 men in this group, so that Kuri and his son Pørwa between them gave to half of these. Of the others, four take little part in moka, two were young in 1965, and the other lives away from the local nexus of moka relations at the Gumant river (where some of the Kawelka have migrated).[1]

Kuri's son Pørwa gave to Tiptip, his associate and classificatory cross-cousin; and his grandson Kundil gave to Tiptip's elder brother, Kngal. Ngai, a Ndikmbo man who has come to belong to Kuri's settlement via a kinship link with Kuri's Membo wife, made a partnership with Membo Waema (no. 2 in the diagram). Ngai is looked on as a 'helper' of Kuri, but this does not debar him from owning and disposing of pigs in his own right. Pɪp (no. 19), Kuri's other adult son, concentrated his gifts on his father-in-law.

Kuri gave generously to Nykint, his big-man sister's son, but did not extend partnerships to other men of Nykint's clan as he did to his wife's clan. Clearly, he was heavily committed to his wife's people. In fact, these partnerships which he maintains with his affines are an important nucleus for the alliance between Kitepi and Membo clans as a whole: an alliance which relates to the fact that these two clans were not 'root men of war' to each other but only allies of Oklembo and Mandembo clans respectively.

Another reason for Kuri's apparent choice of confining himself to Nykint as a partner, apart from the fact that Nykint is himself a major big-man and required a large gift, was that partnerships with other men of Nykint's clan-section were already pre-empted by a number of other Kitepi men of Kolkal sub-clan. Partnership sets are limited by the size of other similar sets. It is clear, however, that big-men expand their sets by using both their own classificatory and other men's immediate kin and affinal links, and that the shape of their sets thus comes to be different from that for ordinary men. For example, the big-man status of Kuri has given his set a different shape from that which formed between Kolkal men and men of Nykint's clan-section. In the latter case a number of men on both the donor and the recipient sides have paired off as partners; in the former a single eminent man and his sons have contracted partnerships with a whole body of related men on the recipient side. Closer examination

[1] Men living at the Gumant have been gradually establishing ties in their new local setting, and some, but not all, have progressively given up their moka partnerships at Mbukl. For example, Rying, who is elder brother of Nykint and Mɘra, quarrelled with his brothers over the disposal of some pigs and withdrew to live at the Gumant with his father-in-law. Big-men, such as Nykint and Ongka, maintain *dual* residence, at both Mbukl and the Gumant, but concentrate their moka activities at Mbukl. By 1969 the Kawelka were in conflict with men of the Ndika tribe over the use of land in the Gumant area, and there was some question whether they would all remain at the Gumant or not.

of Kuri's and his son Pørwa's partnerships indicates also that Kuri maintained partnerships with big-men on the whole, leaving his sons to give mostly to ordinary men. It is a question whether this situation will change when the return moka is made, for Kuri is now very old. Table 21 (*c*) gives an account of his and Pørwa's partnerships in 1965 with Membo men.

To sum up these cases: the extension of partnership ties is determined by the status of participants, the incidence of close links between them, and their opportunities for taking over partnership positions not used by others. Classificatory kin and affinal links can be invoked as a reason for striking up optative exchanges, or the partners may describe themselves simply as 'friends'. Sets of brothers and of fathers and sons to some extent establish clusterings of partnerships through affinal ties: within these clusterings, which represent a duplication of ties between small clan-segments, men differentiate themselves by pairing off with separate individual partners. Big-men predictably extend their partnerships more widely than others, but the latent competition between them and between them and other men, is not regularly made overt. Occasionally a man chooses to give to a distant or indirectly related big-man rather than to a close kinsman or affine. If it is an affine who is ignored in this way, the reason is likely to be that he is of low status and to give to him would be a poor investment. If a man's wife's father is an ordinary man or big-man and belongs to the recipient group there is a clear expectation that he will make an adequate gift to him. Otherwise the father may influence his daughter to leave her husband, or he may invoke the ghosts of his relatives to send sickness to his daughter's children. Similar sanctions support the position of a mother's brother, as I have mentioned before. The sanctions are less strong in the case of brothers-in-law and cross or matrilateral parallel cousins. Often, these are involved elsewhere and a man can negotiate with them not to give to them on a specific occasion.

Although I cannot illustrate precisely how priorities are determined between partners falling into different categories, it is possible, from the twenty-one cases in which marriage ties were not used in the 1965 moka at Mbukl, to specify circumstances in which affines are unlikely to exchange with each other.

There are two broadly different types of case here: those cases in which one or both of the affines is disengaged from moka-making as a whole, and those in which the affines are drawn apart by their separate commitments in a specific moka-occasion, although they may be partners on other occasions.

Counting pigs and shells

From the series of twenty-one cases we can extract features which help to explain why marriage ties were not used.

1. Either or both of an immediate affinal pair may be men of low status. (A low-status man may on occasion give to a man of high status, if he participates at all. But this may be a bad investment too, for the big-man is likely not to waste resources on a generous return to him. In general, low-status and high-status men do not contract egalitarian moka partnerships.)

2. They may be old men, retired from moka activity and without vigorous adult sons or lineage mates.

3. They may have become baptised members of the Lutheran Church. Many baptised Christians are old men or men of low status as well, but in any case it is regarded as Lutheran Mission policy that Christians should not make moka.[1]

4. They may be men who are fully involved in other partnership sets.

5. They may have had definite disagreements (*a*), or the married pair may be estranged (*b*); although the latter does not necessarily mean that brothers-in-law curtail exchange relations, it does mean that the wife no longer raises pigs for her husband, which reduces his production capacity; and in some cases estranged women go back to live with their brothers, which makes it unlikely that harmonious relations between her brothers and her husband will continue.

6. One party may fail, not deliberately but by miscalculation or temporary inability, to provide initiatory gifts.

7. One or both of the men may live away from the main body of men in their clan, and may have become involved in partnerships separate from those which operate between their clan and its local allies.

8. The wife may belong by patrifiliation to an allied clan but in fact have been brought up by someone of her husband's clan and subsequently married to him. In this case she is unlikely to have close paternal kin who could be her husband's exchange partners in the allied clan, since she was probably an orphan or her kinsfolk have scattered to join other clans.

9. (Similar to 8). The wife's immediate father and brothers may be dead, for whatever reason. (Lineage kin of hers may take up the relationship, but this is a matter for their choice.)

---

[1] The issue is discussed, for the case of the Enga, in a Lutheran Mission (Missouri Synod) publication, by Kleinig (Lutheran Mission n.d. – the paper was written in 1955). I am uncertain whether European missionaries from Kotna ever suggested an actual ban on moka-making; but disapproving remarks they may have made are likely to have been taken as *tok bokis* implying such a ban. One of the early Missionaries, Jaesche, is said by some big-men to have made moka with them in the past.

10. The affine's sub-group as a whole may be disengaged from the moka. (This need not prevent an individual man from taking part.)

11. Either affine may be young and/or away at wage-labour or at school. His mother and/or wife may look after pigs for him but he may send word that he does not want these to be disposed of in his absence.

Usually more than one of these reasons is involved, as Table 22 indicates. (I do not know details in three of the twenty-one cases.) From Table 22 it appears that in most cases there were reasons on both sides, and the

TABLE 22 *Reasons for the non-use of marriage ties in a moka prestation*

Case no.	Reasons on Kawelka side	Reasons on Tipuka side
1	—	2, 8
2	2, 3, 7	11
3	1, 7	?
4	7, 9	?
5	1, 3	2
6	9	2, 7
7	9	7
8	1, 7, 5*b*	—
9	1, 3	4
10	1, 3	1
11	1, 3	4, 11
12	7	4
13	2, 5*b*	4, 9
14	—	11
15	4	4
16	4	11
17	1	4, 11
18	4, 7	4

reasons effectively precluded the likelihood of the marriage tie being used as a vehicle for partnerships between immediate affines on other occasions as well as the one in question.

As a final point, it should be emphasised that this prestation involved not just two clans but four, and all were intermarried. This situation provided a wider potential ambit of choice for men in finding exchange partners, and also a greater likelihood of multiple commitments, than a moka involving only a pair of clans or two clans not closely intermarried. Men may choose to give to all their close relatives or to only some, depending on circumstances as we have seen. Unused links are then often taken up by big-men, and these also attract gifts from unrelated partners who might otherwise have confined themselves to their kin and affines.

Counting pigs and shells

SUMMARY

In prestations between ex-major enemies big-men are clearly important as chief donors and recipients. They act as guarantors between their groups. The pigs they receive they distribute at once to supporters, unless they can pass them on in a further prestation within a few weeks of receiving them. In the more elaborate prestations between ex-minor enemy groups there is greater participation by adult men of ordinary status as well as by big-men, but major big-men are still financially pre-eminent; whereas minor big-men often do no better than ambitious young men or established older men who are not recognised as big-men at all. All men tend to distribute their gifts between affines, kin, and unrelated partners, but major big-men contract the most relationships with the latter category.

The largest gifts tend to be made to immediate affines, especially to fathers-in-law, and particularly when one or both partners is a big-man. Clusters of partnerships form round particular marriages, and within these men partly duplicate each other's exchanges and partly differentiate themselves. Major big-men extend their partnership sets more widely than others. In some cases, however, marriage ties are not used as a focus for exchange relationships, either because the affines are for some reason disengaged from moka-making or because their commitments lead them into separate partnerships on a particular occasion.

In the next chapter we shall see how dissatisfactions arise out of the complicated process of choosing whom to give to and whom not to give to in a moka, and how big-men struggle with each other to set alternative dates for a prestation, in accordance with their differential states of preparedness for it.

8

DISPUTES AND STRUGGLES PRECIPITATED
BY MOKA OCCASIONS

'If the Kiap had not come there would have been a different way of paying
back debts among us. But only a madman would start fighting among us
now. You must give pigs to your partners, so that they can feel good and
take them away.'

Kape, a big-man of Tipuka Kengeke clan

Almost every moka-occasion is preceded by struggles between big-men
of the donor group, who set rival times for the prestation, and some are
followed by a crop of complaints from the recipients. In fact disputes with
defaulting partners are often the inevitable aftermath of the struggle by
which a moka's timing is decided. Those who are ready may be able to
push the moka through; but those who are not are unable to give satis-
factorily to their partners, and disputes result.

Some men attempt to make a court-situation out of their moka debts, but
the time for making these complaints is limited to the actual period of
hand-over, for the only effective sanction that a recipient can publicly
bring to bear is that of shaming his partner. He must make his complaints
loudly on the ceremonial ground at the time of the final ceremony. This
does not mean that he will obtain more pigs or that his clansmen will rally
to his help, for they are likely to be busy with their own problems; but
other men hear the complaint and note the apparent failure of the donor to
settle with his partner. Until the final ceremony, as I have mentioned
earlier, recipients are uncertain of the total number of gifts, and they
maintain an air of anxious apprehension, while the donors hurry about
dunning their own debtors and using the fact that the moka is due to take
place soon as a lever for obtaining pigs and shells from as many sources as
possible.

Formal complaints are sometimes accompanied by threats of violence
or actual fighting with fists and sticks, but it is important to notice that they
are usually confined to the ceremonial ground. A recipient big-man may
talk quietly at his donor's preliminary 'showing' held at the donor's settlement but erupt into angry recriminations on the day of the public gift.

Listeners, rather than supporting him and causing a confrontation, are likely to restrain him if the enactment of his rage carries him too far. Moreover, the stance adopted by aggrieved partners is sometimes more political than personal. On one occasion I noticed how a man who made a biting, hostile speech against his maternal kin for not making gifts to his group in time for them to be fed into a further prestation afterwards sat down and talked in a friendly and confidential fashion with the big-man who had been his major target for public attack. The institution of the formal speech allows participants to express more than one aspect of their feelings: in their speeches they act at least partly as representatives of other men in their group, while at the same time they can give vent to personally-felt animus; in private discussion they maintain the ethic of good behaviour and friendliness which is considered appropriate between moka partners.

I shall look first at some individual cases of defaulting, and then at struggles between big-men to arrange the timing for a prestation.

DISPUTES BETWEEN INDIVIDUAL PARTNERS

Table 23 shows the relationships between partners in twenty-seven instances of complaints which arose from the Kitepi–Oklembo gift to Kawelka clans in January 1965. The aggrieved party in each case was the recipient. Although there are eleven complaints made by an ordinary-man recipient against a donor of the same status, men of different status also appear as disputants; moreover, since more ordinary men than big-men were involved in the moka, it would seem that the figures do not indicate a tendency for ordinary men to default proportionally more often on men of their own status.

The number of cases is limited, and it would be unsafe to draw any strong conclusions from them. However, it is interesting that the cases where an ordinary man complains against a big-man are quite few. Given that men of ordinary status are able and expected to complain if big-men let them down, the implication is that big-men do not particularly choose to default on men of lower status than themselves. Although it is very important for a big-man to retain other big-men as his allies, it is also important for him to give adequately to the whole range of his partners at a public moka, since an upset partner of whatever status other than a rubbish-man can do harm to his reputation by voicing grievances.

The second part of the table shows a preponderance of cases involving unrelated partners; but it is clear also that complaints can occur throughout the whole range of relationships. For example, there can be defaulting between immediate affines, the category to which, overall, men tend to give most generously. The cases here all involve brothers-in-law, not father-in-law and son-in-law, and this seems significant, given the expectation that a father has a degree of influence over his daughter even after she is married and may suggest she leave her husband if he fails to pay up his moka debts. A brother has less clear authority and influence over his sister, and hence the relationship between brothers-in-law is easier and less unequal than the father-in-law/son-in-law relationship.

TABLE 23   *Relationships between partners in twenty-seven instances of defaulting*

(*a*) Relative status

Status of donor	Status of recipient	No. of cases
Ordinary man	Ordinary man	11
Ordinary man	Big-man	5 ⎫ 8
Big-man	Ordinary man	3 ⎭
Minor big-man	Minor big-man	5 ⎫
Retired big-man	Minor big-man	1 ⎬ 8
Major big-man	Major big-man	2 ⎭
		27

(*b*) Relationships

	No. of cases
Unrelated	12
Immediate affines	5
Classificatory affines	2
Immediate kin	4
Classificatory kin	4
	27

The cases involving these brothers-in-law show a number of points. One case indicates that already in 1965 there was some uncertainty about the position of pearl shells in the exchange system. In this case a man simply declined to continue exchanging pearl shells with his affine, on the grounds that these were now becoming old-fashioned. By 1969 this viewpoint was common, at least among younger men, and one (Kawelka) informant assured me that the Kawelka would not give pearl shells back to the Tipuka in return for those they received in 1965. Nor would debts in shells be converted into debts in pigs. This proposed abandonment of pearl shells as a medium for ceremonial exchange was to parallel the previous abandonment of nassa and cowrie shells. In about 1962 Kawelka men gave large numbers of these shells to Tipuka partners, but no return for them was made in 1965. The Kawelka did not complain. 'The shells are with the Tipuka. We have given up these rubbish things. It is finished,'

I was told. A Kawelka refusal to return pearl shells to the Tipuka in 1971–2 would thus neatly square the debt-situation.

Another case indicates that men may cut off partnerships with a sister's husband who is growing old, and transfer their gifts to the sister's sons. In this way sons succeed to their father's partnerships, but he does not necessarily himself hand them over to the sons. The sister's husband in the case commented 'They could see how old I am and that is why they did not give to me'. The cut-off point has to come a few years before a man's expected death, since there is such a long period of delay before moka gifts are reciprocated.

Finally the cases indicate clearly that immediate affines may maintain a bargaining attitude towards each other. In one case a Tipuka man gave his sister's husband eight pearl shells, but the latter wanted two more, to cover an extra small pig he had given earlier. When the two shells were not forthcoming, he removed his pig. His partner then removed four shells from the set of eight he had given. The dispute was taken no further.

In most cases of defaulting or dispute about what is a fair exchange of valuables little can be done to settle the dispute amicably on the spot.

A man defaults on a partner only if he is unable to meet his commitments, and other men of his group are unlikely to come to his help when they are under pressure also. The plaintiff can thus do little more than relieve his feelings by shouting or by mounting a physical attack. Major and minor big-men do not hesitate to brawl and cast abuse at each other if they are angry. Feelings can rise in debates prior to a moka also, for a big-man who is short of pigs will try to hold up the event, and men of the recipient group who are not his immediate partners are likely to taunt him with being a procrastinator and a rubbish-man. Such an insult often leads to a fight. Resort to physical fighting, however, can be an implicit admission that a big-man has temporarily lost financial control over events and has to divert attention from his shortcomings.

Before the Kitepi–Oklembo moka to the Kawelka in 1965, one leading big-man of Oklembo was particularly hard-pressed. Before the final gift to the Kawelka, his clan was required to give live pigs in moka to men of Eltimbo clan (cf. previous chapter). On 2 January they had still not done so, and the Eltimbo, becoming restless, decided to go across to their Oklembo neighbours and demand to know how things stood. At the time the big-man was in his men's house urging his clan-section mates to wait until they could raise enough money to buy a steer for presentation in the main moka, as their pair-clansmen, the Kitepi, had already done. This was part of a move to play for time in which he could raise more pigs, and to hold the moka up it was necessary to delay the gift to the Eltimbo. An Eltimbo man came to the men's house, and, standing outside, he interrupted the conference by striking up a speech of personal invective. The big-man came out of his house and the two buffeted each other with their fists. When the Eltimbo man threatened to use his spear, he was restrained by a group-mate, who eventually pulled the two apart. If the big-man had been speared, not only would the moka have been delayed for longer but Eltimbo would have been obliged to pay compensation for the wound, and the matter would probably have been taken to an Administration court also: hence the restraining action by the Eltimbo group-mate. The big-man and his opponent were not related nor were they direct exchange partners. That the big-man was seriously embarrassed at this moka is shown by the fact that he later gave only a single pig to one of his most important exchange partners, Ongka, when he had already taken three pigs as initiatory gifts.

A typical context in which frustrated partners may show violence is the occasion when a big-man divides out his pigs to recipients, in the preliminary stage of 'showing' before the concerted *kng ndi* is held (cf. Chapter 6, pp. 115–8, *Events leading up to a moka*). On these occasions a number of partners, including men from groups other than the one to which his group is planning to make its main prestation, come to view the pigs and remind the big-man that he has a debt to them which he should meet sometime, preferably on the spot. This he may be unable to do, given that he is concentrating on meeting the demands of a particular section of his total network of partnerships. A clever big-man may be able to effect his division in private, away from covetous eyes, but this is more difficult if he has a large number of partners to satisfy. If he gives to each secretly he may create more jealousy still, whereas if he makes his division publicly he can claim that everyone is able to see how he apportions his resources. In addition, interested spectators are likely to turn up and act as a restraint on irate recipients-to-be.

Big-men react to the strain of these occasions differently. A further complication they may have to face is the attitude of their wives to the disposal of pigs which they have raised. A wife feels that her husband should give pigs to her own relatives, but the husband may wish to do otherwise in order to spread the scope of his partnerships. Kot, at his division early in January 1965, was majestic and unruffled even when an angry wife, whose pigs were not being allocated as she wished, ran at him with a heavy lump of wood and then rolled screaming on the ground in combat with a co-wife of whom she was jealous. Ongka, at his divisions,

always put on an air of desperate management, appearing to talk so fast
that neither his wife nor his partners could think rapidly enough to make
effective demurrals to his decisions; but in fact his success was based on
careful consultation with his wives as well as his recipient partners. By
contrast, Ruk, a clan-mate of Kot, was severely harassed at the division he
made before the 1965 moka to the Kawelka. He and Kot were distributing
a large number of pigs each, owing to their status within the small Eltimbo
clan, and news of this fact attracted a host of creditors. Ruk received the
highest number of pigs in the Oklembo gift to Eltimbo on 3 January 1965
(34, compared to 21 received by Kot), and on 7 January he prepared for
his distribution. Crowds of men filtered in from the nearby road to watch
as he brought out his pigs to root at stakes in his sweet-potato garden.
Numerous creditors were present. Ruk was given some support by Kot,
and by Kuri and Nditing. The latter two stormed in and told idle spectators to leave and allow Ruk to discuss affairs with his partners in peace.
All agreed to what the major big-men said, and a few left.[1]

Ruk's main difficulty was that he was due to settle some internal debts
with Kot before distributing to his other partners. In order to satisfy the
important claims of Kot it was clear that Ruk would have to default on
some of the peripheral partners who had turned up.

Figure 11 shows where some of Ruk's obligations lay. Three of his
creditors were group-mates, three were matrilateral kinsmen, six were
affines or kin of affines, and eight were unrelated moka partners. To eleven
men Ruk owed only a single pig each. One man, however, had given six
pigs as initiatory gifts in August 1964 and now wanted ten in return. Kot
also required eight. Ruk had got no further than apportioning Kot's pigs
and four to other Eltimbo men when a dispute flared up between him and
an old Eltimbo man, Parka. Parka had for years lived away from his group-
mates in Oklembo territory, and this fact was brought against him in the
ensuing altercation. Parka truculently seized a pig, and when Ruk challenged him he began to shout out that Ruk owed him three pigs. Kot tried to
quieten him, saying 'My brother, don't speak like that, it's all wrong',
but Parka, a much older man, took no notice. Both Ruk and Parka now
raised pig-stakes to fight, but were at once parted by four intercessors – a
clansman, a neighbour, a recipient partner, and the big-man Ongka, who
took charge of the debate. He sharply asked Parka:

Did you help to obtain wives for Ruk and his brothers? No. Well, then, go away.
Let go of your stick. If he gives you just a single pig later, it will be enough.

---

[1] There were still about seventy men present when Ruk began his distribution.

You can look after it and it will grow big. It was I who helped to give bridewealth here, and I'm prepared to say you simply don't exist. You can't fight this man to get his pigs. You old man, you come here and talk now and I let you be. But when I came to give help with bridewealth payments you weren't to be seen.

Thus Ongka reminded Parka that as he had not helped his clansmen in the past they were unlikely to be generous to him now. The question of his

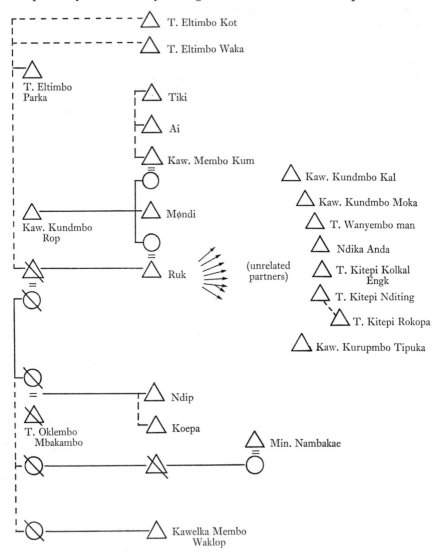

Fig. 11   Creditors of T. Eltimbo Ruk at his distribution, 7 Jan. 1965

precise debts was left unsettled. The mixture of moral homily and self-aggrandisement in Ongka's speech is an example of the means a decisive big-man uses to handle situations of conflict.

Parka was quelled but not appeased. An old spectator of Kengeke clan now took the rope of a pig which Ruk indicated he was willing to offer and handed it to Parka (thus keeping Ruk himself out of direct contact with him) but Parka adamantly refused it, and his case was left unsettled. There was no suggestion that the case should be heard as a court by a Local Government Councillor, since disputes between exchange partners are not considered matters for others to deliver judgement on. The spectators now at last agreed that Ruk should be allowed to distribute his pigs without 'dying of shame in his heart', and they moved off to witness another conflict which was developing on a nearby ceremonial ground. Ruk finished his division, and although there were hard words between him and his other partners there was no more open fighting. Parka's action was definitely regarded as reprehensible.

Kot later gave one of the eight pigs he had received from Ruk to Ongka. The two men are neighbours, their ceremonial grounds meeting at a point half-way between their settlements. It seems clear that Ongka stepped in during the dispute as much to help Kot as to disentangle Ruk from his embarrassing situation.

THE FAILURE OF MOKA PRESTATIONS ON A GROUP SCALE

Disappointment with gifts received can be quite general among the recipients of a prestation. Relationships between locally-allied groups continually fluctuate between friendliness, marked by mutual aid, and hostility, marked by court disputes and recriminating speeches at moka festivals. Part of the reason for this situation is that individual partners bring a keen economic reckoning into their transactions. Recipients are quick to assert that donors are 'rubbish', in order to spur them on before a moka or to shame them after it if they default. Donor groups may overstrain their resources by attempting too large a prestation, and thus they weaken their position in the network of local ties between groups. Further, they weaken the position of their immediate allies within the network. I shall consider one case where this happened in detail: the pig and shell moka given by Minembi Yelipimbo clan in December 1964.

There were two reasons why it was likely that this prestation would be difficult to complete successfully. First, in it different sets of Yelipi men were giving to recipients in a number of groups. The demands of these recipients made divergent pulls on the donors. For example, Yelipi men of a single sub-clan were committed to two different main sets of extra-clan partners. Competition for supporters occurred between factions led by big-men in the sub-clan, and donors who tried to help in too many directions found their resources unequal to their commitments.

Second, the prestation was involved with the moka chain which was discussed in Chapter 7. The Yelipi were due to help T. Oklembo clan

TABLE 24 *The Minembi Yelipi moka, December 1964*

(*a*) Segments involved

Donor-segment	Recipients	Links	Type of gift
1. Tipukmbo sub-clan: followers of Rangk	Kawelka Ngglammbo	Rangk's mother was of Nggl.	Gift to maternal kin. Live pigs; shells
2. Tipukmbo sub-clan: followers of Kambila and some others	(*a*) T. Oklembo (*b*) M. Mimke	Kambila's affines	War compensation. Pigs and shells
3. Tipukmbo: Ekit	K. Membo	Ekit's affines	Pigs
4. Rokmbo sub-clan: Ruin and others	A Kope man	Classific. MB of Ruin	Pigs
5. Rokmbo: Pəra	K. Kundmbo Ndamba	F-in-law of Pəra	Pigs
6. Nambakaembo sub-clan: Nggoimba and others	A Kope man	Immediate MB of Nggoimba	Pigs

(*b*) Balance sheets

1. With T. Oklembo (excluding shells and initiatory gifts of pigs for shells)

Yelipi man	Received as initiatory gift	From	In Dec. 1964 gave	To
Ruri	2	Mek	5	Mek
			4	Køu
Wøya 1	2 large	Ruk	2 small	Ruk
Owa	4	Pun	4	Pun
Nggoimba	4	Rokla	2	Rokla
			1	Pana
Wøya 2 (of Rokmbo)	5	Rokla	7	Rokla
Kambila	1	Køu	(returned by Ruri)	
Yei	1 large	Nøpil	2	Ui (Nøpil's F)
Wømb	1	Ui	2	Ui
Məra	1	Nøring	1	Nøring
Ekit	2	Ui	2	Ui
	23		32	

Table 24 *contd.*

2. With K. Ngglammbo – pigs

Kawelka man	originally gave	to Yelipi partner	who returned in Dec. 1964
Ongka	8 pigs + 1 cassowary	Rangk	4 small pigs
Pundukl Tiki Pena Nøni	8 in 1956	Rangk and sons	4
Tiki Nøni	3 in 1962	Rangk and sons	0
Rop	8 in 1956 2 in 1962	Rangk and sons	4
Kaep Ndoa Ruk	4	Rangk and sons	4
Koepa	5 in 1956 2 in 1962	Rangk and sons	3
	40 + 1 cassowary		19

3. With Minembi Mimke – pigs

Mimke

Pun — gave 4 to meet an earlier debt and 4 in addition, 2 to Kui, 2 to Pørwa. Kui returned 6, but Pørwa only 2.

Woi — gave 3 to Maep + 1 which was exchanged directly, and 4 to Kelpa. Maep returned 3, Kelpa 4.

Kona — gave 2 to Wøya no. 3 and 1 to Røi, who returned 4 and 3 respectively.

Ui — previous gifts unrecorded, but he was satisfied with 6 from Ndoa, his son-in-law, and 3 from Kaukla.

Nggoimba — gave 2 to Ekit, none returned, 2 to Køpi, 1 returned, 4 to Kambila, none returned.

Nøkin — gave 3 to Rangk, 2 returned, 1 to Yei, 2 returned, 1 to Ruin, 3 returned, 1 to Køpi, none returned.

Kum — gave 2 to Rumint, 2 returned, 2 to Wapra and Nui, no return.

Kont — gave 2 to Kewa, 3 returned, 2 to Nggoimba, 1 returned, 1 to Wøya no. 1, none returned.

Rumba — gave 2 to Ekit, 2 returned, 1 to Ketepa, 2 returned, 3 to El, 8 returned.

Balance for 9 recipients (there were perhaps others): gave 46, received 48.

with their gifts to the Kawelka. A time-limit was thus implicitly placed on the preparations of the Yelipi, and this was exploited by one of their big-men in opposition to a big-man of a different sub-clan from his own.

The Yelipi numbered fifty-six adult men at the time of their gift, but some of these were living partly away from the clan territory and participated less effectively than they might otherwise have done. In earlier years

N

they had been scattered after a defeat by the Minembi Engambo and had been granted a new territory as refugees by matrilateral kinsmen of Tipuka Kengeke clan. They re-settled in the new territory in response to a call from one of their big-men; but they do not seem as yet to have re-established their strength and unity as a clan.

How widely the Yelipi were attempting to spread their gifts can be seen from Table 24. Prestations 4, 5, and 6 involved only a few men on each side, but 1, 2, and 3 involved larger sets of donors and recipients. Further, the chief donors in these larger prestations were all men of a single sub-clan, Tipukmbo, and the big-men who were to some extent competing for supporters within it are close lineage kinsmen. The division within Tipukmbo was played on by a minor big-man of Rokmbo sub-clan which was in a much easier situation.

The major split within Tipukmbo occurred between Rangk and his father's brother Kambila. The two men live in separate settlements, with their sons and other kinsmen who have joined them. I was told: 'There is a stream between the two and they make moka separately.' Kambila is very old and had been sick, but in 1964 he was still unwilling to allow Rangk to be pre-eminent as the clan leader. It was Kambila who obtained a new territory for the Yelipi and called them together after their military defeat and dispersal. Rangk is a managerial type, a fast talker and planner with a number of adult sons as his supporters. Ekit had no support-group behind him at all, after Rangk and Kambila had taken theirs. Of the others in Tipukmbo sub-clan, Røi and El were in 1964 two men of some importance. El is not a powerful speaker: but he has a strong set of exchange partners and he concentrated on giving to these separately from the other Yelipi men, thus making a reasonable success of his moka. Røi is an excellent orator, but in this moka he committed himself both to Kambila, his neighbour, and to Rangk, and let the latter down. Within Rokmbo sub-clan, Wøya is an emphatic orator, and it was he who led a movement to hold the moka before Rangk was prepared for it. Ruin is quieter, but has a higher reputation as a big-man. Like El, he avoided conflict and concentrated on satisfying a small number of partners.

The Yelipi were preparing for their prestation throughout 1964, yet they received only a single helping moka, from M. Kimbo clan, who are not their traditional allies.[1] The gift was small: seven Yelipi men received a total of 27 pigs, in return for eight they had presented earlier as initiatory gifts. The pigs were rapidly redistributed to meet debts among the Yelipi themselves.

[1] They are, in fact, allies of the Yelipi's enemies, M. Engambo.

With Tipuka Oklembo clan the situation was more complicated. The Yelipi were attempting from early 1964 onwards (cf. Fig. 12) to shunt gifts of pigs back and forth between the Oklembo and the M. Mimke, while at the same time raising sets of pearl shells to give to both.

The Oklembo, in turn, depended directly on the Yelipi for help with the moka within the chain sequence to which they were committed. The shells the Yelipi raised were sufficient: partners are much more willing to give away a shell or two and so help make up a set of eight or ten than they are to part with a pig, which is much more valuable. Hence the Yelipi were able to obtain shells from diverse sources and put these together to make a prestation. Raising pigs was a more severe problem: the ones they received from the Oklembo as initiatory gifts the Yelipi passed straight on to Mimke men as advance moka gifts. Had they invested the pigs elsewhere, using them as initiatory gifts to pull in a larger number of pigs from some further group later, they could then perhaps have satisfied the Oklembo. Instead they gave them to a group to whom they owed pigs already, and who would make no return for them. In the end they produced only 30–40 pigs for the Oklembo, although the latter probably expected and needed about 60–70.

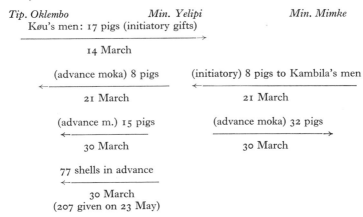

Fig. 12   Relations between Oklembo, Yelipi, and Mimke, March 1964

The Oklembo had expected more Yelipi to join in as donors, but this was made impossible by the Yelipi's multiple commitments (cf. balance sheets, Table 24 (*b*)).

What was crucial to the failure of the Yelipi was that in 1964 they had little leeway for creating new financial arrangements, given the commitments of other Minembi groups to the moka chain sequence. A brief review of the situation of groups around them will show this.

179

The Rope of Moka

Minembi Papeke are the pair-clansmen of the Yelipi and supported them at the final dance for their moka. But the two clans fought in the past, and relations between them are still strained. In 1964 the Papeke gave moka to three Tipuka clans and to a segment of Kawelka Kundmbo clan; one Papeke sub-clan also gave over 100 pigs in an internal prestation to another. They did not help the Yelipi. *Minembi Engambo* are old enemies of Yelipi and have never exchanged war-compensation payments with them. In 1964 they gave to Tipuka Kitepi and M. Papeke. *Tipuka Kengeke* are close allies of the Yelipi, but in 1964 they were heavily committed to the moka chain sequence, and gave only a few items to help Yelipi Rangk with his moka plans. *Kawelka Kundmbo* clansmen were occasional allies of Yelipi in the past, and in 1964 younger men among the Kundmbo organised a prestation in moka style of over \$A600 and quantities of cooked food, including rice and tinned meat. This, however, did not help the Yelipi greatly with their moka, for much of the money was soon lost in card-games. Finally, *Minembi Kimbo*, as we have seen, gave the Yelipi only a little help.

The Yelipi were thus caught. Other groups were enemies and/or fully occupied in other transactions; or else they were due to be *recipients* of moka from the Yelipi themselves.

A full account of events leading up to the Yelipi moka would show that public discussions were held two or three times each month from March 1964 onwards. I take up the description from the point where conflict became acute.

Throughout the year the Yelipi were waiting for their 'helping gift' from M. Kimbo. This was finally made in mid-November and enabled men of the Rokmbo sub-clan to complete their preparations by 22 November. They handed over their pigs in advance to their recipient partners, and turned to castigate the Tipukmbo, who had much heavier commitments and were not yet ready. Yei, who was at that time Local Government Councillor for the Yelipi clan, pointed out that soon the new year (1965) would be starting, and he was afraid that it would bring with it new Government work (on road-building, etc.), so that the moka must be completed before this. An attempt was made to mark out pig-stakes for the gift to T. Oklembo, but it was delayed by excited speeches from Rokmbo men and curtailed by a heavy fall of rain.[1] On 24 November Tipukmbo Ruri, a leading partner of T. Oklembo men, turned up, and there was a more coherent effort to mark out stakes on the ceremonial ground. T. Oklembo

[1] It is usually rainy in the Hagen area between October and April.

men arrived, and there was a spirited exchange of accusations, Yelipi men accusing each other of tardiness as well as contriving to defend themselves as a whole against the Oklembo.

Kawelka Nggl. Ongka now began to put heavy pressure on his partner Rangk, arguing that Rangk was his true sister's son and ought to give to him properly and on time.

The actual immediate mother's brother of Rangk is a 'little man', a supporter of Ongka's and Ongka, as leader of his clan-section, knew that it was up to himself to persuade Rangk to give to them. He knew also that if the gift to him were delayed, it would mean a delay in the moka chain sequence also, and for that reason he tried to hurry Rangk on. On 25 November the Ngglammbo examined the shells they were due to receive, at Rangk's ceremonial ground, and Ongka declared that they were enough to meet debts only, there were no extra shells given for moka. He was worried also that the Yelipi had made no firm promises as to how many pigs they would give. Rain again interrupted the ceremony of handing over the shells, but as soon as the shower was over Ongka made a tremendous fuss, demanding that the Yelipi 'show the stakes' for the pigs they would give. Rangk then forced his clansmen to admit their inadequacies; in particular he insisted that Røi should come and say how many pigs he had to give. Røi arrived, rather shaken, and had to admit that he could not meet his debts. It is possible that Rangk knew Røi was supporting Kambila rather than himself and so deliberately humiliated him. At any rate, the failures of others to some extent drew attention away from his own troubles. At 3.45 p.m. heavy rain fell again. Rain during a moka ceremony is regarded as a sign of ancestral displeasure; Rangk excused himself by saying that rain had fallen only when his clan-mates had come to the ceremonial ground, not when he was there by himself, so clearly the ancestors were angry with the others, not with him personally. This process of elaborate internal bickering among donors is in fact deliberately pursued, in order to make recipients think that the donors are really trying to do their best; but, as in this case, it may get out of hand.

One of the events the Yelipi were waiting for was the completion of the internal moka within Papeke clan, for the latter were to dance at the Yelipi's festival after their own was finished. It took place on 2 December and on the same day the debate was reopened among the Yelipi. By now Kambila's section of Tipukmbo sub-clan were almost ready for the moka. Supported by Kambila's sons, Rokmbo Wøya suddenly appeared as a direct opponent of Rangk, and more men of Tipukmbo went over to his side. Rangk curtly insisted: 'It's dark. I'm not giving till later. Go home.'

Ongka, Rangk's chief recipient, was torn between his anxiety that the moka should take place as soon as possible and his fear that if it were held prematurely Rangk would default on him. He hung his head, indicating that he was upset, but said nothing. Finally, only Rangk, Ekit, and Røi, the three men who stood to lose most by an early completion, were left holding out against the majority opinion that the moka should take place forthwith. Although no formal decision-making process had occurred and no full consensus had been achieved, the Rokmbo sub-clansmen felt that they had won, and they went off chanting their victory. Rangk finally acquiesced.

On 3 December the Yelipi's pigs were brought to the ceremonial ground and displayed. The affair was a fiasco. Backbiting broke out almost at once, both between donors and recipients and among the Yelipi themselves. The main argument centred this time around Ekit. All his creditors had appeared, and his wife's brother, a big-man of Kawelka Membo clan, was pushing their claims forcefully. Ongka tried to calm the wife's brother, but he would not listen; Yei was reduced to trying to push creditors away from the pigs while Ekit attempted a division of them. Ekit's wife supported her brother. Yelipi Røi had retired from the fray into the position of official orator, and he marched up and down the lines of pigs delivering a non-stop speech in *el-ɪk* style.[1] Big-men among the recipients jumped on to the tree at the head of the ceremonial ground and shouted him down. Rain threatened, and by 5 o'clock most of the shivering disputants were on their way home.

On 4 December the Yelipi cooked pigs to distribute to visitors who had brought them decorations. On the 5th they danced and formally handed over their pigs and shells.

Such an occasion is meant to be a ceremonial demonstration of the donor clan's strength and well-being. But at this dance the Kawelka recipients refused to bring to the stakes pigs they had received in advance, and in embarrassment the Yelipi tried to remove some of the stakes and throw them away. Ongka opposed this move, and explained loudly to visiting big-men of other clans how badly he was being treated. He threatened that the Yelipi gift was so poor he would not make returns for it later. He would simply cook the pigs he received and eat them, rather than re-investing them. Nevertheless he brought to the stakes the pigs Rangk had given him in advance, and remarked privately to me later that only unimportant men who became angry too easily would refuse this courtesy to a donor.

[1] I.e. in measured phrases, each ending in o – o – o.

Disputes and struggles

When Rangk came to make his speech as a leading donor, Ongka cut him short. 'You have given your pigs and shells', he announced, 'and now you dance. But you have not given us extra pigs to cook, you have not given us cassowaries or numbers of tubes of decorating oil. You are making your talk out of nothing. This is the last time you will make moka, you will give now and then go home and stay there. You came down to me at Mbukl and I gave properly to you according to the standards that men go by. But you don't understand these things and you can't even meet your debts now.'

This extended example has shown us that when a big-man fails financially he cannot hold up an event which a majority of his clansmen want to push through. There is no stable hierarchy of relations between big-men in a given clan, and rivals may exploit situations to discomfit even a prominent leader. He loses prestige and has painfully to work himself back into a position where his credit stands high. But the cost of embarrassing him may be that the clan as a whole becomes for a while a byword for defaulting in its moka relations. The situation is not necessarily permanent, however, for the clan may manage its affairs better next time. In 1969 I was told that Rangk was still a major big-man among the Yelipi, although it was now known that 'sometimes he gives well, sometimes he gives badly'.

Conflict over the timing of a prestation seems to occur at two different levels. At one level there is the presentation of apparently objective arguments: 'the moka must be finished by such and such a time because other groups are waiting on this moka to make theirs and new government work will soon begin also.' But the periods of waiting could in fact be extended. What seems to be the real catalyst of conflict is personal ambition. Big-men are rivals, attempting to gain temporary advantages over each other, and they use the 'objective' factors I have mentioned as weapons in their battle. To some participants the 'objective' reasons may be the really compelling ones; while to others, particularly those directly engaged in the struggle of wills, it is possible that they are no more than idioms which they employ to pursue their own ends.

CONFLICT IN THE LAST STAGES OF THE MOKA CHAIN
SEQUENCE, 1964–5

Conflict over the timing of a prestation does not always result in the moka being a fiasco; but it does always imply that big-men are struggling against each other, and that one or more of them is likely to 'lose', as the final example in this chapter will show. The example is the T. Kitepi–Oklembo moka to K. Membo–Mandembo, which I have examined from other points of view in the two previous chapters. It was held soon after the Yelipi moka, and was directly influenced by the latter.

By the end of September 1964 it seemed that the Kitepi clansmen were almost ready to make their moka. But there were internal shufflings of goods within the wider Anmbilika tribe-section (which includes Kitepi) which had first to take place, and it was over the timing of these that conflict emerged. The T. Oklembo clan, relying on their expected gift from M. Yelipi, had agreed both to give shells to their pair-clansmen, the Kitepi, and live pigs to Eltimbo clansmen *before* the main moka to the Kawelka should take place. In turn, the Eltimbo were to give pigs to the Kitepi, also in advance of the main moka. The clear result of this arrangement was that the Oklembo were most hard-pressed, while the Kitepi were most favoured. The Yelipi moka was not completed till 5 December, and it had been agreed earlier that the whole moka season must be over by mid-January in order to give men time to 'find money' with which to pay their Council taxes[1] shortly thereafter. There were also rumours that work on a big new road to go down to Madang on the northern coast would begin in the new year, and then there would be no time for making moka. On the other hand, the Yelipi gift to the Oklembo was insufficient, and they needed time to obtain pigs from other sources before furthering the moka sequence. Predictably, conflict began between Kitepi and Oklembo clans. By 25 December Kitepi big-men were busy showing gifts on their own private ceremonial grounds and there were rumours that Kitepi men would give the moka by themselves leaving the Oklembo behind. This was a rather empty threat, for the Kitepi were dependent on the Oklembo for shells and ultimately, via the Eltimbo, for pigs as well. The threat was part of the usual campaign for haste. Another factor was that both clans were raising money to buy full-grown steers which they would present as impressive 'extra' gifts to their Kawelka allies.

Kitepi Pørwa, a commanding young big-man who combines modernism with an interest in traditional inter-clan politics,[2] was the major proponent of a quick finish to the moka. He announced that he would have to be off in a week's time on Local Government business, so the moka must be over by then. He did not hesitate to label the Oklembo 'rubbish men'. Goaded by this, on 29 December the Oklembo men travelled several

[1] This is a Local Government Council head-tax, for which, in 1965, men paid $4 each and women 50 cents. In 1969 it was $10 each for men and $1 for women and unmarried girls and youths.

[2] Since 1966 he has been President of Dei Local Government Council. In 1964 he was its Vice-President. In 1968 he stood as a candidate in Mul-Dei constituency in the House of Assembly elections and came second in the polls.

miles over to territory of the M. Papeke to ask for pigs, but came back empty-handed and disgusted. They did not receive their 'helping gift' from the Papeke until 1 January 1965. When they finally brought the pigs back to Mbukl, enthusiasm was raised again and the Tipuka marked several more stakes as promises of moka pigs which they would give away. But there were still further preliminary stages to be completed. It was not till 4 January that the Oklembo 'showed' pigs to the Eltimbo (they had completed their gift of shells to the Kitepi late in December). A total of 112 pigs was displayed, destined for only ten recipients, of whom Kot, Ruk, and an older big-man, Rumba, were to receive as many as seventy. The final transfer occurred on 5 January.

Kot and Ruk now wanted two days in which to take stock of their numerous gifts and to decide on their division. By now, however, people from other areas were arriving with decorations for Tipuka men to wear at the final dance, and they were placing a strain on household resources. Pørwa threatened to jail the Eltimbo, but their chief recipients, men of Kitepi Kolkal sub-clan, remained polite. Kot clearly aimed at making his own moka in style, for he was not short of pigs and is a man of major big-man status. Pørwa, using threats of sanctions from the Administration-introduced political system, was attempting to excise this stage. He demanded that Kot, as a man 'inside his Councillorship', hand over the pigs without ceremony. This was precisely what Kot wished to avoid. His clan, the Eltimbo, are few and scattered, and their continuing corporate existence, as well as his own prestige, depends on their participation as a group in moka ceremonies. Ruk and Kot delayed allocating their pigs to recipients until 7 January; and on the same day the pigs were formally transferred on the Eltimbo ceremonial ground.

A coalition now developed between Pørwa and another young big-man, Wai. Together, they adamantly declared that they would finish by the next Saturday. The still struggling Oklembo were displeased, and even Pørwa's father, the old major big-man Kuri, told him that he, too, was not ready and Pørwa must make moka without him. Pørwa replied that he had a brief from the Administration to finish the moka quickly, and no-one seemed to be in a position to check this assertion. Two relatively uninvolved big-men now interrogated the leaders of each donor and recipient group in turn, asking if they were ready, but several wavered, and, as in the case of the Yelipi moka, no full decision was apparently taken. Nevertheless, the last preparations were completed two days later, and the prestation finally took place on 10 January. Although it was not accounted an overall failure, at least one big-man, who had been heavily dependent on the Yelipi and had not received from them, was seriously discomfited at it.

In this case the young big-man who was the chief instigator of a speedy completion of the moka was not simply motivated by particular rivalries with older big-men but was rather trying to introduce sanctions from a new, European-introduced institution, in order to establish an ascendancy over a number of segmentary groups involved in the moka chain sequence. His tactics were thus partly new ones, rather outside the usual range of means whereby big-men achieve and maintain their status.

9

MOKA AND THE STATUS OF BIG-MAN

Big-men have appeared frequently in my discussion of the moka so far. It is clear that they are prominent organisers and financiers of ceremonial prestations and that from time to time they emerge as instigators of inter-personal as well as inter-group competition. In this and the final chapter I shall examine the position and importance of big-men further. In this chapter I consider 'big-manship' as a status which is aimed at by ambitious men and is marked out by custom in numerous ways. Within every clan there is rough agreement as to who can and who currently cannot lay claim to this status,[1] and in the second part of the chapter I shall discuss patterns of status-differentiation within a number of clans.

CULTURAL MARKERS OF THE STATUS OF BIG-MAN

There is a proliferation of terms describing attributes and actions of big-men. The most general term, which one hears most often, is *wuə nyim*. This is the term which I translate as 'big-man'. Both 'rich man' and 'chief' are inappropriate as translations here, the first because it is not the fact of wealth but its deployment which is important and the second because the big-man occupies no definite office of headship over specific numbers of subjects (cf. Strauss 1962: Ch. 26).

As Table 25 shows, the terms for 'big-man' employ concepts of size and physical well-being as well as referring directly to the financial status and power to speak and propose plans which big-men are supposed to have. It is notable also that the greatest spread of terms occurs at the top and the bottom of the social hierarchy, and that rubbish-men, who are at the bottom, are often described by symbols which make them the opposites of major big-men, who are at the top.[2] Thus major big-men have strong heads, while those of rubbish-men are soft; they are like strong forest trees while rubbish-men are like humble, weak ones; they know how to speak

---

[1] Important complications are noted by Bulmer 1960b: 323 ff. In particular, he points out that there is greater consensus as to who the most important big-men are than about those who have lesser claims to eminence.

[2] These symbolic themes are explored in more detail in *Self-Decoration in Mount Hagen*.

whereas rubbish-men do not. And big-men in general 'make grease' – which carries connotations of both health and wealth – whereas rubbish-men are dry, like ashes.[1]

TABLE 25   *Terms for big-men and others*

A. General terms applying to both major and minor big-men

1. *wuə nyim*	big-man
2. *wuə mel pei*	a man who has valuables
3. *ukl mbø iti wuə*	a man who does things, i.e. gives moka, makes speeches
4. *wuə kopong iti*	a man who makes wealth (literally 'grease') to be there
5. *kng kokla iti wuə*	a man who gives away pigs and shells

B. Terms for major big-men

1. *wuə peng ombɪl*	a man who has a strong head. (Cf. *ɪk peng ombɪl*, 'a weighty, leading pronouncement')
2. *wuə peng mund*	a man whose head-dress is large and round
3. *wuə peng ile*	a man who is at the head
4. *moka peng ile mumuk ropa amboklpa nɪtɪm wuə*	a man at the head of the moka who gathers and holds the talk
5. *rumɪnt mum wuə*	a man like the centre post of a men's house[a]
6. *wuə nde kraep nggøklamb*	a man like the tall forest beech tree
7. *wuə køng aorom*	a man who is large and healthy (literally 'whose skin swells' i.e. with 'grease' or fat underneath)
8. *wuə ou, wuə nyim ou, wuə nyim pukli*	an important big-man
9. *ɪk-nga paklmonge wuə*	a leading orator
10. *ɪk nɪmba etɪm wuə*	a man who knows how to speak
11. *ngge ropa nɪtɪm wuə*	a man whose words initiate plans

C. Terms for minor big-men

1. *wuə nyim kel*	less important big-man (literally 'little big-man')

D. Terms for ordinary men

1. *wuə mandung* or *mana-mɪl*	a man who is below (while big-men are above, *okla*)[b]
2. *wuə manda*	a man who is sufficient (but not more than this)
3. *wuə akele*	a man who is behind (i.e. in support, while a big-man is *koemb ile wuə*,[c] 'a man in front')

E. Terms for men of low status

1. Many of the terms are derogatory. Rubbish-men are supposed to be soft (*rimb rimb*), not to understand matters (*ɪk pɪlpa kungndi nøngndi*), to be incapable of making persuasive talk that 'sticks' (*ɪk rømb nøni*), and to be men who are dry, i.e. without wealth (*wuə køp*, opposite of *kopong iti*). They are also described as *wuə korpa kik*, 'rubbish-ash-men', and as *kim omong wuə* 'men who fetch greens' (for big-men, who cook them along with pigs). They are said always to be bending down to enter new doorways, i.e. to be incapable of staying in one place and always to be moving from one big-man's settlement to another. They are *kng kongon wuə*, 'pig-work-men', men who look after pigs for big-men; *nde mboi wuə*, 'little trees' (by contrast with the

---

[1] When a man wishes to tell an exchange partner that he cannot pay a debt at the moment, he explains that he is 'down to the bone' i.e. has no grease (= wealth) left (*ombɪl nde nor*, 'I am bone-wood').

forest beech, to which big-men are likened); *nulya pəlya wuə*, 'little, newly-planted sections of sugar-cane'; and *ık ruk wuə*, 'men whose talk is inside', i.e. is heard only inside the clan, not when political speeches are made to other groups.

2. There is also a set of terms which are applied in general to men of low status. The 'meanings' of these terms can best be shown in tabular form.

Term	Small man	Bachelor	Servant of big-man	Helper of big-man	Does not make moka much	Has recently failed in moka
1. *Wangen*	—	+	*	*	+	—
2. *Etamb*	+	*	*	*	+	—
3. *Kintmant*	—	*	+	+	+	—
4. *Korpa*	—	*	*	*	+	*
5. *Eta*	—	—	*	*	*	—

— = no particular likelihood;   + yes;   * = possibly

1. *Wangen.* This is applied to any bachelor above the usual age for a first marriage. (It can also be applied to a married or once married man who has no children. It is not a regular term for widowers as such.)

2. *Etamb.* All men who are short can be described as *etamb*, and there is a tendency to symbolise low status by describing unimportant men as small or short. *Etamb* can thus be applied to helpers of big-men even if they are not physically small. (Cf. Bowers 1965: 32.)

3. *Kintmant.* This definitely implies a position of subordination to a big-man. None of the other four terms listed implies this so specifically.

4. *Korpa.* This is the most common term for rubbish-man (as *wuə nyim* is for big-man). It can apply to men in categories 1, 2, 3, and 5 as a general, rather derogatory cover term. It can also be used as an insult to any man, including a big-man, who has defaulted on his partner in a particular moka transaction.

5. *Eta.* An *eta* is a refugee, in the past a refugee of war. An affine who comes to live in uxorilocal residence is also described by this term if he is not a man of high status. The term expresses the position of a man who has no claims in his own right to the land he is living on and using. Such men may or may not be specifically taken in by big-men.

F. Status symbols

Big men traditionally wear a number of status symbols recording their participation in moka.

1. *koa mak* or *omak.* This is the standard symbol worn throughout the Melpa and Temboka areas. Each slat in the tally records that its wearer has given away a set of eight or ten shells in moka.

2. *køi kundıl.* This is an assemblage of packed teasels formed into a cone and lined on the outside with cassowary feathers secured to a frame. The *kundıl* was traditionally worn to mark that a man had given a set of shells in moka to a partner at a public ceremony. A single man might thus wear several *kundıl*. (Vicedom 1: 138.)

3. *moka ka:n.* This is a four-sided column of carefully interwoven pandanus strips. It should be worn only by a man who is a prominent donor and organiser at a public moka. (Vicedom 1: 140.)

4. *korpel.* This is a rounded pack of rushes, its ends decorated in red and yellow with ochre paint. It was traditionally carried by big-men at festivals as a sign that they would be the next to make moka.

5. *wənya elyıp.* This belongs to Aua, Kambia, Ialibu, parts of Køwul (and to the Wiru speakers of Pangia). In Kambia it is constructed on a base of teasels, with a light frame of bamboo strips. The assemblage is netted with fibre string, then covered with a bark-cloth hood, which can be coloured red with ochre, or nowadays with

a piece of trade-cloth. The formal criterion for wearing it is 'to have cooked eight pigs' at a festival; but whether this criterion is rigidly applied seems doubtful.

6. *pøya*. Hageners say that in the Aua area men who own a number of shells or pigs place leaves of the *pøya* tree in their rear-coverings or wear a bracelet on a bamboo frame at their elbows.

---

[a] The house-post supports the roof, and men gather round it while it remains in the centre. At its foot are buried magical substances which are supposed to draw wealth to the men's house. In representation of the *rumnt* symbol men place their fingers together in an arch. The point of the arch is the major big-man and his fingers are the minor big-men of his group who 'surround and help him' (*wør kup ile moromen*).

[b] Ceremonial grounds are also regarded as places which are *okla*, high up, and public moka gifts made on them are said to be made *okla* by contrast with gifts made *mana*, i.e. 'low-down, privately'. Big-men have a special association with ceremonial grounds and public activity.

[c] He is supposed to go in front of his clansmen just as ancestral ghosts are thought to do in helping their descendants to be successful in moka and (previously) in warfare.

One set of terms seems particularly to focus on the big-man's head as a symbol of his abilities. Traditional funeral customs emphasise this point also, for after the death of a big-man care was traditionally taken to ensure the preservation of his head and its emplacement high on a pole as an ancestor-shrine. The term *peng mumuk* indicates that the head is thought of as a 'concentration of power' (Strauss 1962: Ch. 26). Symbolically, the big-man, as 'head' of his clan, concentrates and holds together the strength of the clan. The meaning of *peng mumuk* is made most evident at two stages in the performance of the Male Spirit cult.[1] First, when the cult performers eat a special communal meal of steamed sweet-potatoes in one of the cult-houses and are blessed by an officiating ritual expert, their action is called *peng mumuk* and is said to ensure their health. Second, at a later stage the participants enter an inner enclosure, take hold of a strong forest-creeper rope, and together dance round one of the central cult symbols, the *porembl*. This is a set of upright sprigs placed beside the pit where cult-pigs are slaughtered. The symbolism of dancing with the creeper is that the men will be as strong as the creeper rope is and united as it unites them. Their penes will be as erect as the *porembl* is, and they will 'make grease' (i.e. be healthy) just as the pigs cooked in the pit do. The dance is called *peng mumuk iti*.[2]

If the major big-man is seen as holding together his group and ensuring

[1] No Northern Melpa groups perform this cult, but the concepts and values which it reveals seem to be shared by Melpa and Temboka speakers in general.

[2] The same cult features a spirit-house with a very tall central pole or *rumnt*, and one big-man who was planning to hold a cult performance emphasised to me how high and straight the central pole would be in the spirit-house which he would build. This is interesting, given (1) the phallic symbolism in the *peng mumuk* dance, (2) the term for a big-man, *rumnt mum(uk) wuə*, 'central pole holding-together man'.

its strength and unity, it is not surprising that his death causes a crisis among his clansmen, and that his head, as the particular symbol of his strength and the strength of his clan, was traditionally made the focus of a shrine.

After a man's death he is taken into a men's house and watched over by his close group-mates. Traditionally, they flexed his legs and arms for burial in a reclining position. They remove his front apron and cordyline-leaf rear-covering and at this time cook a small pig as a first sacrifice to his ghost. They tell the ghost to seek out the enemies who have killed the man by poison and to take revenge. Taking a type of creeper, they join one end to a finger of the corpse and the other to that of a living man. Men hold the creeper in turn until one of them shakes, and this is taken as a sign that the dead man's ghost is entering him and will begin to whistle in his neck. The men ask the ghost to come back and help them. This ritual is especially likely to be performed if it is a big-man who has died.

Next day, again if it is a big-man who is involved, his corpse may be placed on a high platform, dressed in new clothing and placed beside the special tree at the ceremonial ground where he made moka during his lifetime. Closely-related mourners stay beside the platform. Visitors bring large quantities of food and firewood for the close mourners. Less closely related clansmen of the dead man greet visitors ceremonially, with twirling axes, and lead them to a sitting-place, while the chief mourners remain crying. Putting a big-man's body on a platform advertises to the ancestors that their descendants are upset with them for allowing him to die, and is supposed to make the ancestors pity the living. It also indicates that revenge will be taken for his death and that many pigs will be cooked at a later stage to make returns for gifts of vegetables and wood which visitors bring. Close kin plaster themselves with ashes, others with white and orange clay. New mourners tear their hair as they enter the ceremonial ground. Wigs are not worn. After a day the actual body is removed and buried, but the big-man's personal decorations are left on the platform for a while and mourners may continue to come for a week. At the end of this time there is a small cooking of pigs (or nowadays rice and meat, purchased with cash), and visitors disperse. Traditionally it was at this time that the dead man's widow(s) would don the net-bags to provide a lodging-place for his ghost and necklaces of *coix lacryma – jobi* seeds to mark her widowhood. A ritual expert removed the net-bags after her husband's death was avenged. At this time also some of the dead man's decorations may be divided among his lineage mates as reminders to avenge him. The rest of his shell-decorations and feathers were in the past broken over his body, as his kin were said to be 'sorry' for him and did not want others to gain his possessions;

only his own decorations were thrown in the grave, for otherwise, it was thought, his spirit would take off the soul of the owner of the extra items deposited there.[1]

After some weeks or months the chief mourners hold a final pig-cooking. Visitors who brought food earlier, and those who assisted in bringing the body home or reporting the death if the man died away from home, and in burying the corpse, are all rewarded fully. Special death-payments to maternal kin may have been paid earlier or may be given at this stage. This cooking marks the establishment of the dead man's ghost in the cemetery. It is called *peng ndi kng kotimin*, from the fact that his human-hair wig (*peng ndi*) is now hung beside his grave, perhaps with one of his aprons and his *omak* tally sticks.

In between the initial and the final cooking of pigs the corpse's head was exhumed and prepared for placement in its shrine. For ordinary men who had died, a small 'ghost men's house' was built and their heads were placed in these to receive domestic sacrifices and prayers from their close kin. The house was built either in a cemetery-place or behind the house of living men within the settlement.[2] Only for a big-man was a higher structure called *peng manga*, 'head house', erected. This consisted of a long pole, at the top of which was a platform with a conical roof made of tough tree-bark. The big-man's skull was placed on this platform, and subsequently living big-men of his own small group would sacrifice to him. The skull was decorated with Cyatheaceae ferns and white-backed Lauraceae leaves (in Melpa, *nøng* and *mara*).

An alternative method (mentioned to me by only one informant) was to place the skull on a top shelf of the shrine, the arms on the next and the leg-bones on a third. Men came to sacrifice at this shrine only when they had avenged the big-man's death. They are supposed to have eaten cooked pig-liver mixed with red ochre, while informing the dead man's ghost that now they were eating the liver of his enemies. Later they gathered the bones and placed them in the crook of a tree, and set the house on fire. This would seem to be making an end of the relationship with the ghost; and it is probable that for an important big-man the former method, of setting up a permanent 'head house', was followed.

---

[1] This was done for a fine young woman or youth as well as a big-man. It was given up in *c*. 1954–6, owing to Lutheran Mission teaching. The Kuma (Reay 1959: 97) had a similar custom. Reay points out that Kuma sons had to destroy some of their dead father's wealth in order to avoid suspicion 'of causing his death by witchcraft' (*ibid.*).

[2] In the Nebilyer Valley a man's head was placed in the *ndangakl manga*, similar to a 'ghost men's house'. Sacrifices to the spirits of close ancestors, siblings, children, etc., who could bring good luck to men, were made separately at small shrines called *kil køi manga*.

Moka and the status of big-man

Nowadays, as a result of Mission influence, 'head houses' are no longer constructed. But the ghosts of big-men are still thought to be active as guardians of clan morality and to foray out to kill rival big-men in enemy clans who spoke harsh words to them while they were alive. And a big-man's death still provokes a crisis of feeling among his clansmen. Funeral songs invariably emphasise how weak and helpless the survivors feel without their big-man to guide them and answer back to their enemies and rivals. The clansmen try to re-establish their confidence by planning revenge, protesting to their ancestors, and later distributing large quantities of pork to indicate to surrounding groups that they are still strong and have resources.

At the occasion of funeral speeches made for a big-man it becomes clear that his death precipitates not only considerable grief among his clansmen but an objective crisis in his group's gift-exchange ties with other groups, for many of these ties may to a considerable extent have depended on his personal partnerships and policies. Moreover the death revives old suspicions of poisoning activity between the bereaved group and its neighbours. I shall consider the death of one big-man in more detail in order to illustrate these points.

Rying was a big-man of Numering section in the Minembi Engambo clan. He moved down from his own clan-territory to the land of his mother's people, the Andakapkae tribe in the Baiyer Valley, where, along with his brother Rokopa, he exploited his kinsmen's excellent pig-pastures. He became sick and was taken to Kotna Mission hospital, where he died. A struggle developed over his body. His brother tried to take it down to the Andakapkae; mission supporters, of a rival sub-clan, wanted to secure it for Christian burial; and so Rying's own sub-clansmen decided to place him on a platform, thus determining that he would be buried within their own territory and in full traditional style.

The Andakapkae, Rying's maternal kin, were upset. Rying had been promising to make moka to them and had received their initiatory gifts. They were planning to kill pigs at a celebration of a religious cult shortly and had been hoping that Rying and his sub-clansmen would help them with pigs for this occasion. But placing Rying on the platform meant that a large *peng ndi* cooking would have to be held for him and there would be no spare pigs for the Andakapkae. At the funeral the Andakapkae tried the further tactic of demanding gifts of compensation due to maternal kinsmen. Nøring, Rying's lineage-mate, met this demand with three points of his own, all of which indicated the gap which Rying had left in the local network of exchange partnerships. He pointed out that his own maternal kin were of another tribe and he had just made moka to them, so he had nothing left for further gifts. Second, his brother was dead and he was too upset to think about making moka. Third, 'Now Rying has died', he said, 'and his debts have died with him. The talk of fathers and brothers and sons goes together. Now Rying has died and only Rokopa and I are left and we cannot give to all of you by ourselves.' The Andakapkae then threatened in retaliation to remove Rying's widow and children and Rokopa as well down to their area. They hinted that their ancestors had actually killed Rying because of his and his group-mates' debts to them.

This crisis between the clansmen and the maternal kin of the dead big-man was the point of maximum tension in the Engambo's relations with their neighbours, but it was mirrored by suspicions between the Engambo and two other clans, Minembi Mimke and Kawelka Kundmbo. The Mimke had been granted land as refugees by the Engambo and owed them moka gifts. They were disputing with the Engambo the right to cultivate a piece of bush-fallow ground, and Rying had forbidden them to do so. Nøring spoke hard words about the Mimke's debts and hinted that they had poisoned Rying out of spite. With Kawelka Kundmbo, relations were more complicated. Ndamba, a Kundmbo major big-man, has a sister's son of Rying's sub-clan, but he also has a daughter married to a man of Kawelka Kurupmbo, traditional enemies of the M. Engambo. Ndamba is thus related to both of a pair of traditional enemy groups, and he was suspected of being an intermediary in sending poison from the Kurupmbo to Rying via his sister's son. He was quick to protest his innocence, however, and to point out that he was in the middle of making preparations to give pig-moka to the Engambo and did not want to see his partnerships disrupted by suspicion.[1]

Within Numering section of the Engambo clan itself there was a split between one sub-clan, which had become Christian, and the others, which had insisted on putting Rying on his platform. There were hints that the Christians had poisoned Rying. In reply the Christians suggested that God had killed Rying for not confessing to a theft he had committed. He and Rokopa were supposed to have stolen and eaten a pig belonging to a young man of their own set of sub-clans within Engambo clan. The owner heard rumours and challenged the two to lick the tribal divination-stone as a test of their innocence. He had not pushed his challenge through, and Rying had not confessed to the theft. While Christians suggested God had punished him, others thought the tribal divination-stone might have been responsible.

Most of these suggestions were made only obliquely. The official version, presented and agreed to openly by all, was that Rying's father's ghost had killed him. Nøring protested to the ancestors that Rying's father had in life been a rubbish-man, and now that his son had become a big-man he had become jealous and had killed him. This suggestion formally absolved the living from responsibility and directed aggression towards the ancestors. It was clearly a piece of diplomacy; but, as clearly, it was not seriously considered the true version.

This example shows, then, that the death of a big-man may provoke a reassessment of his group's relations with its neighbours. The problem

[1] Still further groups maintained their own private versions of how the death was caused, which were not revealed to their neighbours of other clans.

of continuity in moka relations can become acute when a big-man dies: there may be no-one who is willing or able to take on his specific exchange partnerships; and other moka arrangements, which are disturbed by suspicions of poisoning, have to be reaffirmed.

RELATIVE STATUS WITHIN THE CLAN: THE PARTNERSHIPS OF INDIVIDUALS OVER TIME

The Hageners' view of a big-man is that he makes moka, marries many wives, and lays out his own ceremonial ground. What conditions help or hinder a man in achieving this status? I shall start with an account of how boys enter the moka system.

Young men rarely become active in the formal moka system until they are married. But from an early age they are used to establishing casual partnerships between themselves for the exchange of minor objects. Younger boys exchange small pieces of food; older ones bows and arrows and nowadays marbles; and young adolescents money and feather and fur decorations. The exchanges may be immediate but are more often delayed; the period of delay is indeterminate, depending on when the partner who is in credit sees something the other has and which he would like. The 'equivalences' established are only rough and the objects employed are heterogeneous. Where they can be counted, as in the case of marbles, a principle of increment may be introduced, one boy giving four, say, and later receiving eight back. (Girls make similar exchanges with beads, net-bags, and decorations; but they do not regularly go on to participate as independent exchange partners in the moka system proper.) These friendly casual exchanges are part of a boy's preparation for the sterner and more standardised world of moka prestations; they are known collectively as *rok-moka*, 'tobacco moka', from the fact that tobacco may be one of the items employed in them.

The father of a boy and his more closely-related clan-segment mates provide bridewealth and may choose a bride for a boy; but she may instead be a girl who comes of her own choice to the boy's settlement, perhaps after he has courted her at nocturnal singing sessions. A big-man tries to endow his older sons with a wife or two wives each before he dies, but he does not invariably link himself only to other big-men via the marriages of his children, for if he did so he might find that the demands of his affines on him were too great. It is partly for this reason that boys and girls can exercise a certain range of choice in deciding whom they shall marry; although any marriage arrangement can be jeopardised if the bridewealth offered by the groom's people is regarded as insufficient by the bride's kin.

(Almost all bridewealth discussions resolve themselves into demands for more pigs by the bride's side.)

Young men regularly enter into moka as a continuation of bridewealth exchanges, and also as a continuation of payments which their father makes on their behalf to their maternal kin. The maternal kin are likely to make returns for these payments, and moka exchanges may result from this. A young man thus enters the moka through exchanges with his own and his father's wife's people.

Before the discovery of the Highlands by Europeans and the influx of European-introduced shells, the only way in which a boy could obtain valuables would be through an initial gift by a kinsman or affine. During the 1940s and 1950s young men could earn shells in wage-labour on plantations, but money has replaced shells as the currency for wages now, and they must depend again on initial gifts by senior kinsmen. Boys also depend on their fathers for young breeding sows with which to start raising litters. If a boy's father dies while he is young, his mother may look after a number of pigs for him, or he may be helped by an elder married sister or brother. Widows have a say in the disposal of their husband's pigs, and this helps to safeguard the position of younger sons of polygynists.

For his own bridewealth a boy is again largely dependent on his father. Men say that a boy's immediate father will always be 'sorry' for him and try to raise his bridewealth. If the father dies before his son is grown up, the lineage fathers are less likely to be 'sorry' in this way. They will raise bridewealth for a boy if he shows some ability, but otherwise they may not. Bachelors of 25 or so whose fathers are dead are in fact in danger of being passed over altogether. However, if a boy's mother survives the father and lives to see her son grow up, she helps to ensure that either her own kin, her ex-husband's kin, or her new husband, if she has remarried, provide bridewealth for him.

Commonly, a boy receives a breeding-sow long before he is adolescent, and he gives piglets away in directions suggested by his father and elder brothers. Big-men are not necessarily generous to their sons, except in the matter of obtaining wives for them. Nor does the son enter into the full range of his father's partnerships on the father's death: there is only limited continuity, based on the 'affinal-maternal complex' (Reay 1959: 61).

A few examples suggest that boys first obtain shells and pigs mainly from their in-group kin. In 18 of 23 cases boys first obtained valuables from their father or senior sub-clansmen or incorporating[1] kinsmen (who

---

[1] I.e. kinsmen who had taken the boys into their groups.

might be on the maternal side); in the other five cases they were helped by their mother or sister (after their father's death) or by non-incorporating extra-clan kin or affines. In the same cases (plus two further cases) the boys first made moka to the following categories of persons:

MB, MZH, cross-cousin	7 cases
Affine	6 cases
Clansman	6 cases
F's cross-cousin (or this man's son)	2 cases
F's unrelated partner	1 case
Aid to F for a death-compensation	3 cases
	25

From beginnings such as these – most of them anchored in kin and affinal relationships – young men can build up as many partnerships as they can manage. However, analysis of accounts of men's moka gifts over periods of some years from the time when they begin making moka as young men suggests that the majority of gifts are made to immediate kin or affines. It is only in group-moka between locally allied clans that there is a wide extension of gifts to unrelated partners, facilitated by the group tie, within which such partnerships can be pursued with relative financial security. Partnerships with unrelated men may be activated only at these times of group-moka, while exchanges with kin (including clansmen) and affines may be pursued more frequently. To illustrate this point, and to show how one big-man has managed his partnerships, probably over a period of 25 years, I shall give some material on the moka-history of Roltɪnga, a big-man of Kawelka Kundmbo clan (cf. Fig. 13).

Roltɪnga's father was killed in warfare when Roltɪnga himself was very young. He has no surviving brothers and his father's surviving brother is a rubbish-man. His mother helped him to raise bridewealth, and his entry into moka-making was facilitated by a sub-clansman of his father and his father's mother's brother. None of his sons is adult yet, but two of his sisters, separated from their husbands, live in his settlement with their two grown-up sons and the sons help Roltɪnga in his moka activities.

Roltɪnga's main partnerships are with (1) men of his elder daughter's husband's sub-clan, pursued despite the fact that the husband himself neglects the daughter and prefers a co-wife; (2) his major big-man neighbour, Ai, who is also his co-clansman and his wife's sister's husband; (3) his wife's clansmen, pursued in co-operation with Ai.

In his total list of moka partners over his life-time Roltɪnga named eighteen clansmen, his two co-resident sisters' sons, fifteen affines, and two cognatic kinsmen not living with him. Of the clansmen, one lives at his settlement and is

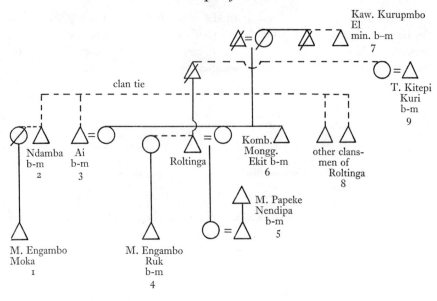

(Men marked 1–9 are Roltinga's moka-partners)

2. Framework

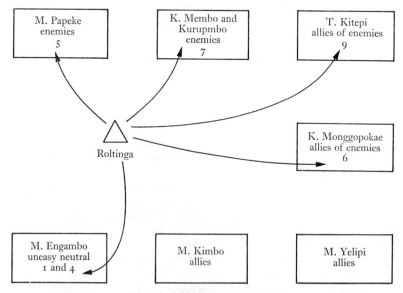

Fig. 13   Roltinga's exchange ties

his adjutant in moka, four others are also in his sub-clan, seven of the other sub-clan within his clan-section, and the other six are distributed through the sub-clans of the other clan-section in his clan. He thus has twelve partners in his own section and six in the other. The partnerships help to give him support and standing in his clan, and he can call on them when he needs gifts to make moka to his extra-clan partners. In his extra-clan activities he co-operates with two other big-men: Ai and Ndamba. Ndamba is perhaps the pre-eminent big-man in the clan and belongs to the same clan-section as Rolt*ı*nga. The two give pig-moka to their 'sisters' sons' in Minembi Engambo clan and to their affines in Minembi Papeke clan. (Rolt*ı*nga has given 136 shells in sets of eight to six different partners in Papeke.) With Ai he has given moka to his wife's kin (93 shells and eight pigs to three different men). He has not, however, co-operated with Mør, the other significant big-man in his clan, for Mør's partnerships are with Minembi Kimbo clansmen, and one of Rolt*ı*nga's co-resident sisters was married to a Kimbo big-man: disputes over the custody of her children and the return of bridewealth paid for her have embittered Rolt*ı*nga's relationships with Kimbo men and precluded moka partnerships with them.

The factors in Rolt*ı*nga's success, despite the early death of his father, have thus been: (1) he was helped by his mother and by other kinsfolk to raise bridewealth and begin making moka; (2) he has attracted to his settlement two married sisters, whose sons now help him, and a sub-clansman who is his close supporter in moka; (3) he has built solid partnerships with a number of men of his clan, which give him a measure of financial security, and (4) he has successfully co-operated with two other important big-men of his clan. He appears not to have challenged them as rivals (they are both older than he) but to have used them as his allies.

Finally, we may consider how Rolt*ı*nga's main partnerships relate to the broader alliances of his clan. Figure 13 indicates that there are two clans, allied to the Kundmbo clan, with which Rolt*ı*nga has no special links. By contrast he has several links with clans which were enemies in the past. By and large, his main partners are big-men, but he has extended his investments also to other men in their clan-segments.

Ndamba, as well as matching Rolt*ı*nga's partnerships with men of Papeke, Membo, Kurupmbo, Kitepi, Engambo and Monggopokae clans, *also* has strongly maintained links with Kimbo and Yelipi clans. The greater spread of his ties results from the fact that he has more married sons and daughters than Rolt*ı*nga, and reflects his overall pre-eminence. Ai similarly mirrors Rolt*ı*nga's ties but in addition has strong links with Kimbo men, as has Mør. Mør also has partnerships with men of the Kope tribe (as has Ndamba). Each big-man, of course, has separate individual partners in these various groups. The reduplication of their partnerships in particular directions, however, strongly influences the building of new alliances between groups; while a certain amount of differentiation of interests between them helps to avoid financial over-crowding.

I shall follow this account of relations between big-men within Kawelka Kundmbo clan with a more comprehensive statement of status-differentiation in this clan and others.

STATUS-RANKING WITHIN A NUMBER OF CLANS

Even over a period of a few years there are changes in the composition of a clan: a few men may leave or join it, others may change their residence

TABLE 26 *Status-ranking in a number of clans*

(a) Kawelka Kundmbo clan			
Status	Agnates[a]	Non-Agnates	Total
1. Major big-men	2	2	4
Minor big-men	1	—	1
Adjutants of big-men[b]	1	1	2
2. Ordinary men (married)	35	12	47
	39	15	54
3. Widowers, not re-married	3	—	3
4. Divorced men, not re-married, and now attached to big-men	1	2	3
5. Younger men who have never been married:			
(1) attached to big-men	1	—	1
(2) living with close kin	2	3	5
(3) working on local plantations	2	1	3
(4) Christianised and living in the 'house-line'[c]	1	1	2
6. Older *wangen* men who have never been married:			
(1) living as *kintmant* of big-men	1	—	1
(2) living as *etamb* of big-men	1	—	1
(3) living with minor big-man brother	1	—	1
	13	7	20
Final totals	52	22	74

[a] I use here a rather unorthodox definition of agnate: a person whose father's father was accepted as a member of the clan group. The reason for using this rather than a literal definition of agnate is that above the level of grandfathers of living men the character of genealogies often changes: they became adjusted genealogical charters rather than literal records of relationships. I have discussed this at greater length in *Descent and Group-structure among the Mbowamb* (1965). (Cf. p. 27, footnote 1.)

[b] This is not a well-defined status; however, such men may be on the way to becoming minor big-men.

[c] Baptised Christians build family houses together in a 'house-line' near their church and are supposed to live there.

(b) Kawelka Ngglammbo clan-section

Status	Agnates	Non-Agnates	Total
1. Major big-men	1	—	1
Minor big-men	2	—	2
Retired big-men	1	—	1
2. Ordinary men (married)			
(1) resident in clan or pair-clan's territory	10	—	10
(2) resident elsewhere	4	—	4
3. Widowers, not re-married	1	—	1
4. Divorced men, not re-married	—	—	—
5. Younger *wangen* men	4	3	7
6. Older *wangen* men	—	—	—
7. Married men of low status	2	2	4
	25	5	30

NOTE: Three of the men in categories 5 and 7 were attached to Ongka, the major big-man of this clan-section. At one stage Ongka had six *etamb* or *wangen* men as his helpers, but by the end of 1965 one had left, another had married, and a third had begun to change his allegiance back to his patrifilial clansmen.

(c) Kawelka Membo clan-group (summary)

Status	Agnates	Non-Agnates	Total
Major big-men	2	1	3
Minor big-men	7	4	11
Married ordinary men	28	26	54
Men of lower status, rubbish-men, bachelors	12	20	32
	49	51	100

(d) Minembi Yelipi clan-group (summary)

Status	Agnates	Non-Agnates	Total
Major big-men	2	—	2
Minor big-men	6	1	7
Married ordinary men	35	4	39
Men of lower status *et al.*	6	2	8
	49	7	56

(e) Overall percentages

Clan	Big-men %	Ordinary men %	Men of lower status, etc. %
Kaw. Kundmbo	7	66	27
Ngglammbo	13	47	40
Membo	14	54	32
Min. Yelipi	16	69	15
Overall	13	59	28

The Rope of Moka

from one settlement to another within the clan-territory, the supporters of a major big-man may change, and one or two men may become newly regarded as minor big-men. The position of major big-men, however, seems to remain fairly stable. The figures which I give in Table 26 relate to 1964–5, the period during which most of the moka ceremonies I have been discussing were held.

Each clan shows some features particular to it. For example, Membo clan has expanded territorially over the past 40–50 years and has taken in a relatively high percentage of non-agnatic immigrants. Some of these are big-men but a majority, in 1964–5, were of low status (cf. Table 26 (c)). Ngglammbo clan-section has no non-agnates of high or ordinary status; its five non-agnates are all of low status, and many of them are men who are attached to Ongka, the clan-section leader (cf. Table 26 (b)+note). Kundmbo clan has only a small percentage of big-men: this is because it is dominated by four major big-men and few minor big-men have emerged to emulate them.

The percentages of men of lower status are quite considerable, although not too much weight should be placed on the figures, for they are not based on any systematic survey of opinion or any clear multiple common measures of status, but only on estimates by a number of persons I knew well in each clan and on my own impressions. Not all of these men of lower status were without wives, but most were, and this provides us with one reliable measure, for a man without a wife is considerably handicapped in running his affairs: he cannot raise children, and if he keeps pigs he must depend on someone else's wife to help him make gardens and feed them. The most common solution is for him to attach himself to a big-man, one of whose wives can look after him in return for help with daily tasks.

By contrast, big-men do tend to be polygynists. Figures from Kawelka Kundmbo clan indicate this point (Table 27). The clan is not noted for its polygynists, but the figures show clearly the distinction between at least major big-men and others. Polygyny is not entirely the prerogative of big-men, as part (c) of the table shows. Many ordinary men are ambitious to obtain at least a second wife, and it is every big-man's ideal ambition to make eight or ten marriages. A few manage to make fifteen or twenty, but some of these are likely to be with inherited widows or divorcées who came to a man without bridewealth having to be paid for them. It is difficult to retain large numbers of wives for long, owing to co-wife jealousy and the problems of dealing fairly with each wife in terms of garden land, exchange partnerships, and favours. Co-wives deliberately

202

TABLE 27   *Marriages of men of Kawelka Kundmbo clan*

(*a*) Current wives of married men at end of 1965

	3 wives	2 wives	1 wife
Major big-men	3	1	—
Minor big-men	—	—	1
Adjutants of big-men	—	—	2
Married ordinary men	—	4	40
	3	5	43

Total: 51

(*b*) Numbers of marriages made by men of the clan group, up to the end of 1965

	Big-men		Adjutants	Ordinary men and others who have been married
	Major	Minor		
6 marriages	1	—	—	—
4 marriages	1	1	—	1
3 marriages	1	—	—	—
2 marriages	1	—	1	9
1 marriage	—	—	1	41
	4	1	2	51

Total: 58

NOTE: the ordinary man who had been married four times but was in 1965 without a current wife had a big-man as his sponsor, but seemed to be temperamentally incapable of retaining a marital partner.

(*c*) Total number of wives of men at any one time

	Big-men		Adjutants	Ordinary men and others
	Major	Minor		
3 wives	3	—	—	—
2 wives	1	—	—	7
1 wife	—	1	2	44
	4	1	2	51

Total: 58

compete for their husband's attention, and the one who loses may become dissatisfied and run away.

In Kundmbo and Ngglammbo groups more than a quarter of the clansmen were currently without wives. Only the older ones among these must inevitably continue to be of low status till they die (an older bachelor finds it hard to obtain a wife and is likely to remain unmarried). The younger bachelor men were roughly between twenty and thirty years old. Each had been neglected at least slightly by his kin, either temporarily because of quarrels with his father, or more permanently owing to the loss of his parents. For example, Kundmbo Mak, whose father was an uxorilocally resident man of the Kope tribe, was about 30 in 1964. He lived with an ordinary man, while his nearest kinsman, Mek, had gone to join the settlement of a major big-man, Rolt*ɪ*nga. Mak is slightly built and mild. He was away at plantation-work in earlier years and collected some pearl shells, and he rears pigs by himself; but no-one has felt a strong enough duty to help him raise a complete bridewealth.

Other young *wangen* are men whose parents died when they were young, or who are the youngest in a set of sons and whose brothers are being dilatory in helping them. In Kundmbo clan 17 per cent of the agnatic male adult members and 22 per cent of the non-agnates have never been married. If we consider *first generation* non-agnates within the whole Kawelka tribe, we see that the tendency for these to be *wangen* men is more striking. But agnates, also, who lose their fathers and do not have energetic or helpful lineage seniors, are likely to be neglected.[1] Some of these men nowadays go away to work elsewhere at wage-labour (one I knew was in 1969 trying to raise help to obtain a bride but few of his clan-mates were willing, as the proposed bride was reputed to be subject to fits of madness); some become helpers and a few servants of big-men; others simply live with their ordinary-man agnates, who share land-claims with them and whose wives help to feed them.

Although many bachelors are men whose upbringing has been disturbed by the loss of one or more parents, it is possible for men with ability, as we have seen in the case of Rolt*ɪ*nga, to overcome such handicaps. But do we find that in fact *most* big-men are the sons of big-men before them, even though a few may 'make good' from less fortunate beginnings? Before discussing this problem I must take up the question of Vicedom's earlier analysis of stratification in Hagen.

Vicedom (1943-8) gives an interesting picture of stratification in Hagen about the time when Europeans were entering the Highlands. He himself arrived in Hagen in 1934 and stayed there till 1939, so his observations cover the early

---

[1] Sometimes there are complicating factors which must be considered as overriding the question of whether a man is an agnate or not. Thus men who are dumb, crippled, mentally deficient, temperamentally incapable of living with a wife, or who do not have complete genitals are unlikely to marry, or, if they do so, to retain their wives for long.

period of contact with Europeans. He presents first his account of the indigenous system of stratification, and then observes how this has been modified by the presence of Europeans. He divides the population into a number of status categories, ranked from top to bottom. At the top are the *wuə nuim* (= *nyim*) amongst whom the *pukl wuə* ('root-man') is the most influential. These are equivalent to my 'big-men' and 'major big-men'. Next are the *wuə ketl* (= *kel*, 'small'). These Vicedom describes as a kind of middle-class: they are independent of the *nuim*, although they may sometimes work for him and help him with his enterprises, and they make their own contributions to clan and tribal festivals. Below these are the *wuə noumə* (= literally 'nothing' men), whom Vicedom describes separately from but later merges with the *wuə korpa* (= rubbish-men). Vicedom speaks of these as men who do not have independent means. If they need valuables they must ask the *nuim* for help. They thus become indebted to the *nuim* and Vicedom looks on them as *kentəmənt* (= *kintmant*) of the important men, their servants. *Wuə korpa*, 'worthless men', or 'poor men', are even more firmly in this situation. They are usually slovenly and dirty, do not have pigs of their own, and can be seen at festivals trying to obtain pieces of pork from the rich. They also do the greatest part of the work for the rich. The lowest category of all are the *wuə wangen*. Vicedom notes that the term literally means 'bachelor', and adds 'Whoever remains a bachelor becomes a slave' (p. 48). Slaves have to work for a particular wife of a *nuim*, who may not look after them well. They may have only a rough shelter to live in. They work as swineherds. Their 'masters', however, may refer to them affectionately, see that they have food, and occasionally give them pork.

Vicedom presents these terms – *nuim, ketl, wangen*, etc. – as referring to clear social strata within the population, whose members also have differential access to the means of production and power. The picture is close to that of a class society. The strata are at least partly defined by economic criteria: at the top are the rich and at the bottom those with no valuable property at all. Further, Vicedom argues that the *nuim* are drawn only from certain families. Rich men ensure that their sons are endowed with wives, land, pigs, and valuables, so that they inherit their father's status, although they may not all become as eminent leaders as their father: the sons are rivals, and one is likely to outdo the others. On the other hand Vicedom notes that 'slaves may be born from any social class' (p. 48). This observation sharply modifies the picture of inherited social status, and suggests that some *wangen* men, at least, must be those who, whatever their birth-status, are incapable of obtaining or retaining a wife or of managing their own affairs.[1] Two questions which Vicedom does not explicitly analyse here are the extent to which marriage alliances are contained within the boundaries of social classes, and the extent to which, if slaves can be born from any class, *nuim* can also be born from lower classes and make their way up. He implies,

---

[1] On page 73 of vol. 2 Vicedom himself notes the case of two brothers who differed sharply in status: one was a big-man with eight wives, while the other remained an unmarried rubbish-man until his brother took pity on him and paid bridewealth to obtain a wife for him.

however, in his later discussion of European influence on the system, that the latter (traditionally) could not happen.

The *nuim* maintain their position, according to Vicedom, in a number of ways. The basis of their power lies in their polygyny, which gives them wives as workers and strong external contacts; in their employment of the poor as their workers; in their performance on behalf of the clan at inter-clan debates and festivals; and in their relative monopoly over the moka system. Vicedom suggests that, although the *nuim*'s power is curtailed in many ways, he must be a man who can ruthlessly pursue his own ends: 'if he cannot obtain something by reasonable methods he will try to force his way by violence.' Another way in which he can increase his influence is to induct outsiders into the clan, either as individuals or as whole groups of refugees to whom he offers land and pigs in return for labour and help in moka. These are the *eta*. They are not like the *nuim*'s personal bondsmen and slaves, but they may have to work for many years before they can recover their former independence and wealth.

Vicedom's account of stratification may be a little over-rigid. In particular his choice of the term 'slave' for the *wuə wangen* may be too dramatic. The *wangen* were not actually possessed *in toto* by the *nuim*. There was no question of them having rights of life and death over their *wangen*, for example. The term 'bondsman', like 'slave', also implies a degree of coercion and rigidity in the relationship between big-men and their supporters which is hard to demonstrate from actual cases.

Earlier (vol. 2, p. 23) Vicedom gives some figures on the population of the Ndika tribe. He counted 3,395 persons in the tribe, of whom 824 were mono-gamous men, 187 polygynists with 496 wives between them (= 2.65 wives each), 54 widowers, and 171 widows. In addition there were 181 men whom Vicedom describes as slaves, 'men who do not obtain wives' (p. 23). If we omit the widowers, whose status cannot be inferred directly from their marital situation, we can suggest that the monogamists (about 70 per cent) represent the proportion of ordinary men in the tribe, polygynists the big-men (about 15 per cent) and the bachelors, of course, men of low status (also about 15 per cent). This equation of status-categories with marital situation can only be a rough one. Widowers are left out; not all polygynists are, or were even in Vicedom's time, effective big-men; and we do not know whether those Vicedom lists as slaves were really all men past the ordinary age of marriage who had little prospect of marrying and were working for big-men as their servants. Nor do the marriage categories here make exactly the same discriminations as Vicedom makes in his account of status-categories, for they do not enable us to distinguish between the supposed middle class, the *wuə kel*, and the more subservient *wuə noumə*, who may have been married men. Again, Vicedom's figure for 'slaves' corresponds closely to the figure for the proportion of bachelors to married men in the Kawelka tribe in 1965.[1] Certainly not all of these Kawelka bachelors were actually the servants of big-men. My enquiries suggest that 'servants' (*kintmant*) have always been fewer than the total number of bachelors (nor are *kintmant* men actually always

---

[1] This point is made in Strathern, A. M. 1968a.

bachelors), and that big-men have always obtained help from a wide range of connections.

Despite these reservations, it is clear that the arrival and actions of Europeans *could* have transformed a structure such as Vicedom describes into one more like that which I observed in 1964.[1]

Vicedom notes that Europeans provided a market for crops and labour, as well as stopping warfare. They paid for services with cowries and other types of valuable shells. These actions all had definite effects. 'Poor men', who previously had to work for the *nuim* in order to obtain financial help, and were usually repaid with pigs rather than shells, could now obtain shells independently and could enter the moka system. With luck and effort they could become, as Vicedom says, *nouveaux riches*. Vicedom states that these men were not accepted as clan leaders, since they lacked the right family connections. Lack of such connections would not be a serious drawback nowadays, so this feeling must have disappeared with the rise of newly wealthy and energetic families.

A crucial point here is that poor men must have had independent claims to land if they were able to grow crops and market them to Europeans. The *nuim* did not control all land claims within the clan.

One effect of the stoppage of warfare would be to give refugees and servants of big-men more freedom of manoeuvre. Servants could now more easily switch from one big-man to another or to working for a European. Refugees could return where they came from, provided that their original territory had not been taken over. Possibly the presence of European authority also curtailed that of the *nuim* over their dependants, to some extent. *Nuim* would thus be deprived of much of their labour-force. To attract dependants they would have to become more generous. At the same time, with the end of warfare and the greater mobility of 'little men', the big-men might well become more afraid that 'servants' of dubious loyalty were likely to poison them in return for pay from enemy clans. This would discourage them from taking in too many men as their *kintmant*. To maintain their position, then, they would have to increase the size of their networks of exchange partnerships so as to be able to finance large festival occasions despite their loss in production capacity. This could in turn help to explain the elaboration of the moka system as it existed in the 1960s.

Such an interpretation certainly helps to make sense of the pronouncements I was given by Central Melpa big-men whom I questioned on the subject of *kintmant wuə*. While some agreed they kept these, others argued that the dangers of poisoning were too great, or that 'little men' would not come to them, or that if they did they would not stay long but went elsewhere. Few claimed to have

---

[1] At one point Vicedom draws back from his description and notes that it is given in the categories of a Western European observer, and that to the Mbowamb (Hageners) themselves the class distinctions within the clan did not destroy its unity; also that the distinctions were not obtrusive in everyday life. He was clearly aware of the economic and political value of the *nuim* to the clan, and that each *nuim* was influenced by the fact of his own clan-membership.

The passages I use from Vicedom's account are: vol. 2, pp. 45–61, and 149–52. See also *ibid.* pp. 173–7, 216–19, and 452–78.

had more than two *kintmant wuə*, and some insisted that they had kept none, but done everything by their own efforts and with help from their clan 'brothers'.

Nowadays *kintmant* are a useful, but not essential, adjunct to big-men's activities. Major big-men are quite likely to have one or two men who are more or less in the position of being their 'servants'. The term should, however, not be interpreted as meaning that these men work for the big-men all the time in return for a definite wage. They are a part of the big-man's household and settlement. They may be married and have a household of their own. In Kawelka Kundmbo clan, two of the four important big-men have *kintmant wuə*. One of these 'servants' is described by his clan-mates as slow-witted, and they give this as their reason for not obtaining a wife for him. Another is quick-witted enough, but has a speech defect and is apparently deaf. His clansmen communicate with him by a series of signs and treat him with affectionate good humour. He has his own land claims. The third seems to have no physical defects, but lost his father early in life, and being quiet and unassertive has never obtained a wife. He has alternated in residence between the settlements of the two big-men, Ndamba and Roltɪnga. Although these three men are of low status, and are dependent on big-men for care and food, it would be thoroughly inappropriate to describe them as the big-men's slaves or bondsmen. It is much more the case that big-men have taken on their care in return for a certain amount of help in garden-work. Possibly their position is strengthened by the fact that all have belonged to and lived with their clan since childhood, and so are not cut off from other close kinsmen. Men without kin, or men who have had to flee from their own clansmen, are less likely to enjoy a secure position.

Vicedom's rather elaborate set of status-categories can be collapsed into three broad categories, within which, of course, finer distinctions can be made: big-men, ordinary men, and men of low status. If the structure has changed since Europeans came to Hagen, it has changed most markedly in the relationship of big-men to men of low status. Big-men do gather men of lesser status than themselves around them as supporters, but one cannot nowadays speak of a substantial class of poor people who hang about at pig feasts and are employed as the main workers for big-men. If a large class of such people existed before, they have either risen in status since the 1930s or else have been absorbed into the larger economic system introduced by Europeans. Perhaps class-stratification will emerge again more strongly if a few men gain control over profit-making productive enterprises and employ others to work as labourers for them in the same way as European businessmen do.

I now return to my own sample material on patterns of succession to big-man status.

SUCCESSION TO THE STATUS OF BIG-MAN

Hageners say:

> The sons of a big-man may emulate him. We watch them as they grow up, and see if they are going to be big-men or not. Promising boys are those who speak well, learn quickly to make exchanges and to ask for things, and whose

eyes are like a pig's, taking in everything around them. Boys spend their time playing and have no sense, and we don't judge between them till they are older. It may turn out to be any one or none of a big-man's sons who themselves become big-men. We decide by the skill they show in moka and in speaking.

What are the empirical patterns? Table 28, based on data on ninety-seven big-men in 1964–5 in fourteen clans of the Minembi, Tipuka, and Kawelka tribes, gives some information on this matter.

TABLE 28: *The antecedents of current big-men*

(*a*) Status of fathers of big-men

	Father was big-man	Father was not a big-man	Totals
Current major big-men	27	9	36
Current minor big-men	31	30	61
	58	39	97

(*b*) Clustering of big-men within lineages (88 cases)

	Minor big-men		Major big-men	
	(*a*) Whose fathers were big-men	(*b*) Whose fathers were not big-men	(*a*) Whose fathers were big-men	(*b*) Whose fathers were not big-men
Immediate bros. big-men	4	6	9	2
Imm. bros. and FBS big-men	4	—	2	—
FB or FBS big-men, where no imm. bros. or imm. bros. are not	6	8	4	3
Some imm. bros. big-men, others not	6	—	—	—
Bros. and FBS all ordinary men	5	9	4	2
No imm. bros., and lineage bros. ord. men	1	7	4	2
	26	30	23	9

(*c*) Situation of sons of 81 current big-men[a]

	Current major big-men	Current minor big-men
With one or more sons who are big-men	3	1
With one or more sons who are promising	1	2
With ordinary men sons	7	15
With no sons or sons not yet grown up	18	34
	29	52

[a] I do not know the situation for all 97 of the men in part (*a*) of the table.

P

Part (*a*) of the table suggests that major big-men have a 3 : 1 chance of being the sons of big-men; for minor big-men the chances are almost equal (1 : 1). Hageners do not invariably claim that a major big-man's father was also a big-man, so the pattern is not simply produced by courtesy assignments. On the other hand it is difficult to be sure whether a man's father was a major or a minor big-man, so I have not attempted to tabulate this variable. The status of father's fathers is even more hazily remembered, although they are sometimes 'semi-mythologically' (cf. below) described as big-men.

From the second part of the table we may surmise that there are certain clusterings of big-men within particular lineages of a clan. For a current big-man whose father was a big-man the chances are > 2 : 1 that there are or have been other big-men in his small lineage. These may be immediate brothers or close lineage brothers: less often, both some of the immediate and some of the lineage brothers are (or were, if they are now dead) big-men: the six examples of this situation are all, in fact, men of a single lineage. A similar concentration of big-men is found also in a few other lineages, notably in that of T. Kitepi Kuri, one of the major big-men whose activities I have discussed in earlier chapters. Twelve out of eighteen major big-men among those for whom I have details are said to be descended from fathers and fathers' fathers who were big-men.

How do we explain these apparent tendencies to the clustering of big-men in certain lineages? We could perhaps argue that assertions about the immediate lineal ancestors of a current major big-man are retrospective charters designed to bolster his prestige and that of his clan. But a major big-man does not require to be bolstered in this way; nor is he the incumbent of any office for which there is a rule of succession to which the facts have to be fitted. Occasionally men over-generously ascribed big-men status to the deceased father of a current big-man, but my impression is that this is done more often for a current minor big-man than for a major one.

It is true, however, that the situation becomes more 'mythical' at the level of the fathers' fathers of living men or beyond. The supposed founding ancestors are often placed at this level or one generation above it, and founding fathers do tend to be spoken of *en bloc* as big-men, especially in conversation with outsiders: this is perhaps why I met with the assertion most often when I was taking genealogies away from the Northern Melpa area, near to Hagen township and in the Nebilyer Valley, where I was known less well. Hence a man whose father *in fact* was a big-man may be *represented* as the grandson of a big-man as well, if the grandfather is accounted a lineage founder. Meggitt (1965: 59) has argued for the Mae-Enga, western neighbours of the Hageners, that it *is* in fact the big-men who become the founders of distinct patrilineages and hence are remembered in genealogies, while other men are not. Some of the Hagen lineages would appear to fit this argument; but there are others for which neither dead nor living members are asserted to be or to have been big-men. It is possible that the Mae patrilineage has more definite functions and requires more definite leadership by a big-man than does its perhaps slightly more shadowy Hagen counterpart. Small lineage sets are often named and established simply for internal distributions of meat within the clan: they do not always 'emerge' under the leadership of a big-man (cf. Chapter 2).

In some cases, then, the attribution of big-man status to a founding ancestor may be purely conventional; but in cases where it is accompanied by a further clustering of big-men within the same lineage it is more plausible. We may, then, accept the twelve cases of 'succession' over three generations as probably genuine. But the succession here is not one which is simply a result of patterns of inheritance of wealth. Big-men rarely have a large stock of shells at their death which is not already promised to partners or has to be paid to maternal kin. A big-man divides out his gardens to his various sons and other junior members of his settlement as they grow up and marry; it may be that big-men hold more garden claims than others, but success in the moka system is not based entirely on production criteria (Strathern A. J. 1969*b*). Some of his wives may be inherited, but not by his sons, and others run away at his death. Most of his pigs are killed at the funeral feasts. Transmission *inter vivos* is much more important than *post-mortem* inheritance, and it is true that a big-man can start his sons off well. But a good start does not guarantee success, for a son must be a good manager and speaker on his own account if he is to become a big-man. Nor do fathers ever elaborately teach or train their sons to become big-men; it is a matter of emulation and personal ability. What we can perhaps suggest is that a big-man stimulates others[1] of his lineage to engage vigorously in moka and in return he helps them to obtain wives, and so they may become big-men also, although they may not become as important as he is. In particular, a son may learn to emulate his father provided the father is not too old when the son becomes a young adult. If the son is fairly experienced by the time his father dies, he may be able to take up some of the more important exchange partnerships in which his father was involved and thus effectively to 'step into his

---

[1] Cf. Reay 1959: 97: 'Memory of their father's wealth is a strong incentive' [to his sons].

shoes'. From Table 28 (*c*) on p. 209, it is clear that there are a few cases in the clans around Mbukl where the sons of a major big-man are likely to succeed him: two outstanding cases are Kitepi Kuri and Nditing, whose sons Pørwa and Wai are already prominent and were forceful participators

TABLE 29   *Sibling position of big-men*

(*a*) Cases where only one brother in a set is a big-man

Big-man is	Major big-man	Minor big-man	Total
Eldest brother	6	15	21
Middle brother	1	7	8
Youngest brother	4	3	7
	11	25	36

(*b*) Cases where more than 1 brother is or was a big-man (not all are still living)

All:

All of 6 brothers	1 case	= 6 men
All of 4 who are so far adult	1 case	= 4 men
All of 3	3 cases	= 9 men
Both of 2	4 cases	= 8 men

More than one brother but not all:

Eb+yb	2 cases	= 4 men
Eb+middle b	3 cases	= 6 men
Middle b+yb	1 case	= 2 men
		39

Full total: 75

(*c*) Combining the material

Only elder brother is a big-man	21 cases
The big-man is an only son	17 cases
All of a pair or larger set are big-men	9 cases
Middle brother is only big-man in set	8 cases
Only youngest brother is big-man	7 cases
Combinations of brothers but not all in a set	6 cases

in the 1965 moka at Mbukl. The table, of course, includes major big-men of widely varying ages, from perhaps 35–70, and some of them have sons who are not yet grown up. Major big-men certainly do place value on the idea that at least one of their sons should take their place – the Melpa phrase is *kokl ile mukli*, 'to be in the place where the father's house was before'. One old major big-man, K. Membo ∂ndipi, has spent years with his hair matted and unkempt in sorrow at the early death of an eldest son who had shown himself fit to become a big-man.

Moka and the status of big-man

It is clear that the eldest son is the one most likely to overlap in adulthood with his father and thus to be endowed by the father with a second wife. Is he also most likely to become a big-man?

In 17 of 92 cases (out of the 97 in Table 28 (*a*) on p. 209) the big-men were in fact only sons, or the only sons who survived to adulthood out of a number originally born. This may have given them some advantage, for it would enable their fathers more easily to concentrate on obtaining wives for them. Table 29 shows the pattern for the other 75 big-men. The largest single number of cases is in fact provided by eldest brothers, so it would appear that they do have the best chance of succeeding, although I cannot show that in each of these cases the eldest brother *was* actually helped by his father. Overall, there are more than twice as many cases in which only one brother has become a big-man as cases in which some or all have done so. This may depend to some extent on the particular stages of domestic development reached by the families of the brothers in the sets considered.

We have seen, then, that a number of factors in the family situation of men are probably important ancillary influences on their success in life. But it must be stressed that a young man, even if given a good impetus by his father, may fail; while another, receiving no such help, may, it seems, succeed by his own drive and intelligence. To that extent Hagen society resembles a 'meritocracy'. The factors which explain this aspect of the situation are: the possibility of obtaining help from extra-clan kin, the capacity of pigs to reproduce rapidly, the absence of patterns of entrenched inheritance of wealth on the part of an élite, the ease of entering the moka system, and the opportunities it provides for the manipulation of credit and the wide-scale organisation of exchange partnerships with men outside one's own clan as well as within it.

10

THE MOKA SYSTEM AND THE BEHAVIOUR
OF BIG-MEN

Extractive devices for accumulating political funds are underdeveloped, and
collection of goods for a climactic give-away would have to be gradual . . .
The dilemma is resolvable by monetary manipulations: by converting wealth
into tokens and by calculated deployment of money in loans and exchange
so that a time will come when a massive call on goods can be made and the
whole pile of stuff, given away, converted into status.

Sahlins 1965c: 186

EMERGENCE OF THE MOKA: MAUSSIAN THEORY

The moka has many parallels, both in Melanesia and elsewhere. Each of
these systems of ceremonial exchange has its particular features; but all
are crucial institutions by which relations of equality or inequality are
established between groups and individuals. At the beginning of this book
I suggested that to understand the moka we must constantly focus on
processes of competition. The two main arenas of competition are relations
between allied, ex-enemy groups and relations between individual big-men.
Big-men struggle to obtain and increase their influence and eminence
within their clan and outside it: the result is that a few men gain and preserve a superior status for several years of their life – these are the major
big-men – while others gain lesser prestige and may or may not maintain
it for long – the minor big-men and others. The whole system can thus
be seen as a mechanism creating status-divisions within the society. But
this mechanism (and the big-men who emerge through it) has to be placed
into the context of group relations also. It can be seen as emergent from
the twin aims of living peaceably with other groups and also competing
with them for dominance. Here the most apposite formulation we can offer
is in Maussian terms: the moka is a system of total prestations, involving
economic, religious, aesthetic, and political components. The prestations
are made between groups which are in an unstable state of alliance with
each other: the only way they can maintain their alliance is by continuing
positive, ceremonial exchanges of valuables. This is literally the way in
which they 'come to terms' with each other. That there is some process

of coming to terms, some adjustment of interests between the parties, is important. It is this process which underlies the form of the gift, which Mauss (1954: 1) describes as follows: '... prestations which are in theory voluntary, disinterested and spontaneous, but are in fact obligatory and interested. The form usually taken is that of the gift generously offered; but the accompanying behaviour is formal pretence and social deception, while the transaction itself is based on obligation and economic self-interest.'

In this passage Mauss sets up a number of oppositions, in a dialectical manner, between the social appearance and the social reality of those gifts which are prestations – in theory they are voluntary, in reality obligatory; in theory they are disinterested and offered in generosity, in fact they are based on economic self-interest. These propositions may not be fully universal, but they do point out that the gift may not be what it seems to be or is said to be, and in particular that it may be prompted by self-interest rather than by generosity. Re-formulating the propositions, as Mauss himself implicitly does later in his book, gifts may be supposedly 'freely' given, but in fact they always imply some kind of reciprocity, that is they are always made to ensure that some return benefit will flow to the giver. In that sense they are always motivated by self-interest. Further, where there is some potential opposition between the parties to a gift, the gift may both express and mediate this opposition. It expresses the opposition in two ways: first, because it is a result of demands for value on the part of the recipients: the gift must be up to the required mark; second, because it may exceed the demand for value and represent a move to demonstrate the superiority of the donor over the recipient or a challenge to him to make at least an equivalent return later. It mediates the opposition in so far as it secures objective benefits for both parties, with which, if the mediation is successful, they are both satisfied. This in turn implies that the recipient in a given bout of exchanges is happy to receive a large gift, even if it is made to him in an aggressive spirit. If he is not happy, this probably means that he feels he will be unable to make returns for it and so will have to admit the donor's superiority.

These latter considerations apply to a system in which reciprocative transactions prevail and the relationship between partners is relatively egalitarian. Where there is an accepted hierarchical relationship between the parties the meaning of the gift changes accordingly. It can express either the superiority or the inferiority of the donor, but in either case the relationship is in theory stable, insulated from the effects of the gift itself. On the other hand, here again the theoretical situation may not hold. There may, for example, be a transactional relationship between a leader and his followers, such that the size of their mutual prestations affects the success of their relationship even if it does not at once alter the formal status difference between them. To the extent that this transactional aspect of their relationship comes to the fore, we can say that hypotheses such as Sahlins's, on the limits to which big-men can extract support from their followers, become potentially applicable.

Mauss's insistence that the gifts he calls prestations are motivated by 'economic self-interest' fits neatly with a theory that in their transactions men try to maximise value (Barth 1966). To what extent can a transactional theory of this kind be applied to the Hagen moka?

THE MOKA SYSTEM

One of the most striking features of the moka is the basic rule that to make moka one must give more than one has received. It is strictly the increment that entitles a man to say he has made moka; if he returns only the equivalent of what he was given initially, he is said to be 'simply returning his debts'. The calculation of what he was given initially is done in two ways. First, the initiatory gifts are set against his moka gifts: the latter should exceed the former. Second, a further comparison may be made with a previous moka-occasion, if the two partners have been exchanging over a period of years. The size of the moka gift on the previous occasion may be compared with the size of the present one. Ideally the present one should be larger; but in practice it is sufficient if it exceeds the initiatory gifts which have been made for it.

Since the moka gift is explicitly supposed to exceed the initiatory gift, we are obviously not dealing with a simple situation in which the partners exchange material things which they agree to be of equivalent value. They are not both maximising, or adjusting, material utilities in that sense. In what sense, then, can self-interest be involved?

Sahlins, in his essay on 'Exchange value and the diplomacy of primitive trade' (Sahlins 1965*b*: 105–6), has sketched a theory of how rates of exchange are established in trading deals between persons of different local groups. Trade does not necessarily make friends, but it is important, if the trade is to continue, not to make enemies, as can happen if one or the other side feels that he has not been given adequate measure in an exchange. One of the best ways to insure against ill-feeling is to give not just adequate measure but good measure. Sahlins suggests a model of how transactions might proceed on this basis, each partner, when it comes to his turn, doing more than making an equivalent return for his debt, and thus making sure that the relationship continues. Any given exchange is thus unlikely to represent a mutual handing-over of exact equivalents: each exchange is unbalanced, although it proceeds on an understanding of what *would* constitute an exchange of equivalents, since in order to know that one has given more than one received last time one must at least be able to calculate whether one has given the equivalent of what was received.

The theory does not explain how equivalences are established, but how actual transactions are conducted. Sahlins accepts (*ibid.* p. 107) that supply and demand and labour-value may be involved in people's estimations of the equivalence of goods. His theory is thus not a theory of value but a theory of exchanges. Establishing the relative value of items may depend on the degree to which the items can be standardised for purposes of measurement and accounting. Here, I am not concerned to discuss how equivalences are created between disparate trading items, but simply to note that in the case of ceremonial exchange it is sometimes the same types of good which move against each other: pigs for pigs, etc. – and this clearly facilitates measurement of equivalences. Where shells move against pigs we may find that a simple rule of equivalence is established: 1 shell token = 1 pig. It can be seen that a rule of this kind conceals bargaining possibilities, because neither shells nor pigs are entirely standardised. Keeping to the rule of equivalence, men could ask for a better shell in return for their pig, for example, or could offer a smaller pig. It is not unless the supply or demand situation changes markedly that the overall rule of equivalence needs to be changed.

Sahlins's model of trading exchanges applies well to the formal shape of moka transactions. In his model extra items are given in order to 'keep the peace' between the parties involved and to maintain their relationship. Thus the giver of the extra items *does* receive a return for his apparent generosity: he places the recipient in his debt and thus maintains the peace between them. If exchanges in any given bout are unequal, what is being maximised on one side is not material, but political value.

For Sahlins's model to be applied fully to the moka system we must add to it an element which he seems to underplay, but which is hinted at by Mauss. Sahlins implies that diplomacy requires generosity. In the moka system this apparent diplomacy cloaks the fact of competitiveness. Partners make large gifts to each other in order to 'win' and to gain prestige. The value of the increment in a moka gift to its donor is thus not only that it 'keeps the peace' between him and his partner, but that it gives him prestige and some claim of at least temporary superiority. Clearly, the moka gift is thus an excellent vehicle for some kind of political competition between groups and between individual big-men.

There are two complexities in the moka system which modify the generalisations I have attempted so far.

The first is that moka can be made to anyone, a political ally or enemy or a comparative stranger, or also to a group-mate; and the second is that it may be made either in private or publicly and either in concert by a number of men or by a single man. I have so far argued for a single 'meaning' of moka gifts, and have suggested that the meaning is political or at least is concerned with the acquisition of prestige. But the meaning is hardly likely to be exactly the same in all the possible contexts which I have mentioned.

In order to handle this difficulty it is necessary in fact to agree that political competition may not be present in all instances when moka gifts are made: for example, when a man makes a moka transaction with a clansman, perhaps even a man who is co-resident with him in his settlement. For private moka, made between pairs of men, we must argue that there are special functions, namely, consolidation of support and the spread of investment interests. These partnerships may be mobilised from time to time by a man in furtherance of some specifically political end: he may call on a partner to make moka to him just when he needs goods in order to make an important gift to men of an allied group. Moreover, these private partnerships do bring him a certain amount of general prestige and esteem among those who know that he is conducting them. Finally, they may have the function of supporting his marriage or securing the absence of mystical attacks on the health of his children by their maternal ghosts. Private partnerships may also be built up into partnerships between whole groups through the innovating actions of big-men. Individual big-men may begin exchanging because they are related as kin and affines; later they may involve others, on the basis of a relationship of past enmity and the need to make compensation payments between their groups as a whole. New transactions between whole groups can be traced, as I have suggested in Chapters 7 and 8, both to the aim of general expansion of the exchange system and, more specifically, to the financial need to organise transactions which will feed into chain sequences of large prestations between allied groups. The prominence of big-men in this process of expansion and in the organisation of moka sequences is clear. They are major planners, and guarantors of good faith, between groups which were formerly traditional enemies. They take on this task because it enhances, if they are successful, their total degree of control over the networks of exchange.

The basic moka transaction, then, in which A gives x to B and B should return $x+y$ items, must be looked at from a number of different perspectives. First, as Sahlins says, it may be employed for diplomatic ends, either between two groups, say, or between a pair of affines. Where two groups are involved, it helps to 'keep the peace' between them. This is pointed up sharply by the fact that moka transactions are often embedded in war-compensation and reparation payments between allied and ex-minor enemy groups, or nowadays also between ex-traditional enemies. Second, the transaction is prestige-conferring. Moreover it lends itself well to the alternate acquisition of prestige by partners, since in theory moka gifts are continued indefinitely and their direction is regularly reversed: A gives x items to B who later returns $x+y$, and later again B gives x to A in return for (at least) $x+y$. Third, the moka gift can be employed in certain contexts, for example between allied groups at particular structural levels, as a more definite instrument of competition. The aim is to 'win' over an ally by making a massive prestation to him. Less directly, it can be an instrument for competition between big-men of the same clan: by means of gifts they attract supporters within their clan and partners outside it and aim at outshining each other, either in major group-prestations or in moka which they hold by themselves at their own ceremonial grounds. The acquisition of wives, by means of exchanges of the same types of valuable as are used in moka, is another crucial part of this process of competition. Finally, many moka partnerships can be looked on simply as means of investment-making. The initiatory gift in moka can be regarded as an investment of capital or an interest-bearing loan, and the rate of interest is high. Properly managed investments of this kind help men in their competition for prestige. It should be remembered, however, that in theory the recipient of a moka should later reverse the sequence of gifts, thus bringing accounts closer to a state of equilibrium; although the reversal does not always occur in practice. One guarantee of reversal is to make one's gifts part of an ideologically-bolstered sequence of gifts between groups which are corporately in competition with each other. It is the problem of managing investments through networks of exchange partnerships that gives rise to the development of definite sequences of prestations which cycle through a number of groups. While the particular forms of these sequences may become complicated, the general principle behind them is clear: they are an attempt to organise the flow of gifts such that men's exchange partnerships are activated in a particular, defined way, and the dominant networks of exchange between local communities do not interfere with each other. Instead, groups actually finance each other for the prestations they make, and to that extent they have a co-operative interest in each other's affairs which helps to increase what I have called regional integration between them. Somewhat paradoxically, it is the existence of radiating personal networks of exchange partnerships which makes it advantageous to organise chain sequences between groups, for personal networks become hard to manage and one man's network may interfere with another's. Chain sequences ensure at least some limitation on the extent of networks activated for a particular moka, and they add group-pressures to those that the individual can bring to bear on his partners.

The use of extra-clan networks, whether in the form of group chain sequences or not, is of great significance for the analysis of competitive processes in the moka system, and I shall consider this point further in the next section.

COMPETITION AND THE USE OF NETWORKS

The moka system reveals a situation which is common in New Guinea Highlands societies. There are well-defined social groups, in relations of opposition to, and alliance, with each other, and it is possible to analyse the political system of the society at least partly in terms of these groups and their interrelations. But crossing over all the boundaries of opposition there are networks of exchange ties between individuals, developed to a high degree of organisation. Whenever a group holds a festival, the importance of these individual ties is demonstrated, as well as the solidarity of the group. Pig-festivals, in which each man distributes to his own set of recipients, show this situation strikingly.

The value placed on these networks is twofold. In one sense they enable the individual to serve his group. When he gathers pigs, shells, and dancing decorations from his network of extra-clan partners, he uses these to take part in what is a display by the whole clan to its neighbours. What he is helping to maximise is clan prestige. But not all moka prestations are organised on a clan basis – some public moka are made by single outstanding individuals. Moreover, even in clan prestations, there is latent competition between individual participants on the donor side. In this sense, each competitor is using his network of contractual ties as a means of surpassing the others; those who lack such a network do less well. Clearly, for big-men it is important both to have large networks and to manage them well.

It is important that these networks are built out of reciprocative partnerships. Each man has a number of partners and he can bring pressure to bear on them. But he cannot bring pressure to bear so effectively and directly on *their* partners in turn. He exerts pressure only through his immediate partner. Chain sequences, as I have argued, are a means of overcoming this limitation of control.

How does the existence of networks affect the parameters of competition between individuals and groups? In the first chapter of the book I argued that the use of networks increases the possibilities for rivalry between individual big-men. Networks set the big-man free, to some extent, from his 'segmentary enclavement'. A big-man need not depend entirely on a limited quantum of physical resources and a limited number of helpers for mounting his prestations. Here I want to argue further that while networks thus set the big-man free, they also tend to make political relations unstable.

I have often suggested that big-men and groups are in competition. Their aim is to 'win' over each other. But there is no finality in such 'wins'. Indeterminacy is assured both by the fact that there is no hierarchy of defined officers within the clan for which big-men could compete, and by the fact that a recipient group always has the possibility of investing a large gift it has received and recovering enough resources to 'strike back' at its rival. This 'investability' of resources is significant. Making the fundamental stuff by which prestige is gained something which is 'free floating' in the sense that it can be obtained through a multiplicity of contractual exchange partnerships means that access to prestige is made relatively open. Without a proliferation of networks facilitating investment the power situation between groups and individuals might be more rigidly defined.

That this is so can be seen if we consider the situations of big-men within their clans and of groups in relation to each other. Clans are segmented and each big-man belongs to a particular segment. If we stipulated that his basis for power lay only with his own segment and only with the productive resources directly controlled by his segment, it is clear that his segmentary enclavement would be rigid. A small segment could not produce an important big-man. Only if he were able to recruit more men to his segment and/ or obtain more basic productive resources, for example land, at the expense of neighbouring segments, could a big-man increase his power. Transactions through exchange networks obviate the necessity for moves of this

kind and make potentially more equal the positions of big-men in segments of different size. (It may still be the case that a big-man does attract
supporters into his segment, for these may give him a different kind of
service from that which he obtains from his exchange partners; but his
need for directly productive services is partly diminished.)

Similar considerations explain why a relatively small group can hold its
own in moka, provided it has within it some capable big-men who can
take on themselves a heavy load of exchange partnerships. There are
limits, of course: it was clear in 1964–5 that the struggle of the big-men
Kot and Ruk to maintain the corporate importance of the Eltimbo in
moka sequences between the Tipuka and the Kawelka was becoming an
unequal one. Their numerous partnerships were a strain to manage; and
Pørwa, the Kitepi politician, used the fact that the Eltimbo are few and
are incorporated within his own clan for purposes of Local Government
Council representation, to demand that they relinquish their independence
as a moka-making unit.

THE MOKA AND SCHISMOGENESIS

Given that the competition between groups and individuals in the moka is
relatively egalitarian and that the competition continues indefinitely over
time, we can suggest that the pattern of relationships between allied clans
comes to resemble that which Bateson (1958: 177) describes as 'symmetrical schismogenesis'. Bateson instances reciprocal boasting activity
between groups as an example of this process. The boasting leads to further
boasting, in a continuous progression, neither side gaining a once-and-for-
all advantage over the other.

Bateson raises an important question in relation to such processes of
progressive change. He points out that they may reach a stage where they
are at the limits of cultural tolerance and at this stage some means may be
employed to relieve 'schismogenic strain' (*ibid.* 194). Alternatively, the
processes may never reach the limit of tolerance but be held under control
in a condition which Bateson refers to (p. 190) as 'dynamic equilibrium'.
The latter phrase, slightly altered, applies well to the inter-group situation
which is brought about by moka ties.

Instead of 'dynamic equilibrium' I see schismogenesis between Hagen
clan groups as resulting in 'alternating disequilibrium'. That is, if we take
two clan groups which are in exchange relations with each other over
time, at any given stage the side which has most recently given moka is
the one which has gained prestige and temporarily demonstrated superiority over the other. But at the next bout of exchanges the position will be

reversed, and the other side will be 'on top'. The two sides are thus always 'unequal' at any given time but are 'equal' in a longer perspective of time, since the system provides in theory for an equal number of 'wins' on both sides. In practice the results may not be like this, but for reasons that I have outlined in the previous section, competition is open enough for this to be the prevalent pattern.

In Bateson's terminology, the symmetrical schismogenesis reduces itself to a relationship of alternating complementary schismogenesis. Clan *A* admits that clan *B* is superior in one bout; in the next bout it is the other way round. In this way the schismogenesis between them is controlled.

EXTRACTION AND DESPOTISM

In the section immediately above I have argued that there is a mechanism, built into the rules of the moka system, which controls the competition between groups. What factors control the competition between individuals? I have already suggested that the answer has partly to do with the existence of extensive exchange networks, and will review the question again in relation to the hypotheses of Sahlins and Salisbury which are referred to in Chapter 1.

Sahlins (1963) suggested that big-men in some Melanesian systems may go through phases in which they become 'over-extractive'. Their aim is to gain renown, and they can do this only by making gifts to the external world outside their own support-group. Their demands on the support-group may eventually become so heavy that they can no longer be tolerated.

Two facts of the moka exchange system obviate this process. The first I mentioned earlier: since a big-man can rely on partnerships with men outside his own clan-segment, he need not ever become 'over-extractive'. Instead he must learn to manage his partnership network, and if he fails it is because of faults which have developed within this, perhaps through competition with another big-man, perhaps because the 'load' of exchanges within a local area is becoming too great. This does not mean that he does not *also* make use of men of his own clan-segment as a partial support group. For example, he may distribute to them pigs which he has received in moka, and he can require returns for these later. But – and this is the second point – his relations with these supporters, as with all his other partners, are transactional. They depend on general rates of exchange which apply in all social relationships. The only parameter in terms of which the rates are 'easier' within one's group is that a group-mate may not demand return for a gift so rapidly as an outside partner. The degree to which a big-man can become extractive thus seems to depend partly on the cultural definition of transactions.

Sahlins cites as a type-case of his over-extractive big-men, the *mumi* among the Siuai of Bougainville in the Solomon Islands (Oliver 1955). On the other hand, in the Siuai case, just as in Hagen, big-men are supposed to raise the pigs and shells they require for a prestation by calling in their debts or by asking for loans, on a basis of balanced reciprocity. But the Siuai big-man, it seems, obtains valuables by putting direct pressure on the adherents who frequent his club-house, and the adherents do not make prestations on their own account (cf., e.g., *ibid*. p. 430). The leader–follower relationship thus seems to be different from the relationship Hagen big-men have to their clansmen. Siuai followers are more likely to feel that their leader is making excessive demands on them because they constitute most of the immediate nodes in the networks which he operates.

Second, to Salisbury's hypothesis. This is more difficult to discuss, first because it employs as a key concept a word which may be understood differently by different people. Salisbury (1964) suggested that although the indigenous ideology in Highlands societies was one of egalitarian competition for leadership, before European contact leadership was in practice characterised by the serial *despotism* of powerful big-men. These prevented other aspiring big-men from reaching the top.

Such a hypothesis is hard to evaluate, both because of its use of the strongly emotive term 'despotism', and because it is restricted to the period before European contact, when *ipso facto* there were no anthropologists about to study leadership. We are dependent on descriptive accounts after the fact.

The prime example of a despot whom Salisbury instances in his article is Kavagl, the Chimbu big-man who was patron of Fr. Schäfer, a Catholic Missionary. Kavagl was an example of the 'violent man' who is known as a character throughout the Highlands. Elsewhere (Read 1959) such violent men do not become pre-eminent leaders, although they may indeed exercise a kind of despotism for a while. The context in which such a violent man could be of some value to his group was, of course, warfare; and once warfare is removed the value of the violent man correspondingly drops. (Watson has given a long and careful analysis of stories about the doings of Matoto, a Tairora despot of pre-contact times.)[1] We may

---

[1] Watson 1967. Matoto died just before 1930, killed in an ambush. This was after the first white man had entered his area but before the establishment of European administration over it. Watson points out that Matoto thus died with his reputation for strength 'unsullied by either declining years or the indignities and loss of initiative that might have come with the introduction of the pax britannica' (*ibid*. 61).

hypothesise that as long as the violent man appears to be of greater value to his group-mates than the internal cost of his violence, he will be tolerated; as soon as the balance swings, toleration will turn to discontent. This may explain why writers in post-contact times (e.g. Read 1959, Westermann 1968, Strathern A. J. 1966) have all reported that the true political leader is not simply a man of violence but a manager of exchanges who has some understanding of diplomacy and restraint.

But what evidence there is for Hagen suggests that the big-man has *always* been separated as a type from the violent man. Even in warfare, the skills of the manager and his financial resources were needed as well as the aggressiveness of the warrior, for the outcome of battles depended to a great extent on the marshalling of allies on either side, and allies had to be persuaded and paid. Moreover, from time to time it was advantageous to organise peace, and this, too, could be done only with the aid of oratorical skill and exchanges of wealth (cf. Chapter 4).

It is true, however, that there are and have been in the past times when big-men have at least attempted to act autocratically.

First, it does appear that in the past they had a more monopolistic control over moka exchanges than they have now, owing to their relative command of the limited trade-routes by which shell valuables entered the Hagen area. This must have given them a high prestige-rating in their communities and enabled them to exercise control over war-compensation payments and bridewealth payments also (although both of these could be made largely in pigs, which were open to all to rear). That they had such control does not necessarily mean, however, that they acted as despots. As I have argued elsewhere (Strathern A. J. 1966), the basis for this monopoly was removed when Europeans brought in thousands of shells and flooded the population as a whole with these.

Second, there are cases where major big-men have behaved arbitrarily in disputes.

For example, Kawelka Kurupmbo Mel was a major big-man, praised by his group-mates as 'father of his clan', and exceptionally generous with hospitality to guests and passers-by. Once a pig of his ruined a garden of a minor big-man within his own group. The minor big-man, Rumba, told him to tie up his pig properly, and also demanded a pig in compensation. Mel replied that the garden's fence had been rotten and refused to pay any compensation. Rumba warned Mel that he would shoot the erring pig if it entered his garden again. The pig was duly shot, and now Mel told Rumba to eat it himself and pay a pig in replacement for it. The two argued for a day, shouldering the pig and dumping it alternately in front of each other. Eventually Rumba cooked and ate it, and refused to replace it with another, although he paid Mel a pearl shell for it.

225

The informant (from the same group as the two disputants) commented: 'Rumba was not afraid of Mel, for they were both equals, on their own territory together.'

This case points up the limitations on the extent to which even a major big-man can force his will on a clan-member. Supporters do not take his side. The dispute is left to its immediate protagonists. Another case shows a big-man becoming enraged with a group-mate but later making peace.

The major big-man Ongka (of Kawelka Ngglammbo group) once fought with his sub-clansman Pena. When Pena's eldest daughter was married, he gave no share of the bridewealth to Ongka. Later, when the second daughter came to be married, Ongka demanded two pigs and five shells, an excessive request. Pena offered him one small pig only. The cooked meat brought by the groom's kin was to have been presented at Ongka's ceremonial ground, but now Ongka forbade this. Pena asked 'Why, did you make this ceremonial ground by yourself? No, we all made it together.' Enraged, Ongka broke up with his axe all the vegetable food which had been prepared for the marriage celebration; and in retaliation Pena cut down a new sapling which Ongka had planted on the sacred mound at the head of his ceremonial ground. Pena then held the distribution of bridewealth items without Ongka. Later he fell sick, and this was interpreted as a sign that the group *mi* or divination-object was now automatically killing him, not for quarrelling with a big-man, but for cutting down a sacred tree. Ongka, in fact, gave him a leg of pork to patch up their quarrel; but Pena later died. He agreed before his death that Ongka should take the bridewealth for another of his daughters.

Like the previous case this one shows that while the big-man may be demanding, the ordinary man or minor big-man may be stubborn. In this case, however, the two patched up their quarrel, perhaps in an attempt to forestall the death of Pena from 'frustration' (*popokl*) at the quarrel between himself and his group-mate.

Third, while not attempting to dominate or 'extract from' his group-mates, a major big-man may sometimes decide to 'go it alone' and hold a moka by himself, without waiting for his clansmen to complete their own preparations and give to their partners along with him. In doing so he is acting 'autonomously', if not 'autocratically'. Few big-men seem to manage prestations of this kind. In 1964–5 I saw only one example, provided by Ongka, who regards making moka by himself as his special ability. On the occasion[1] he was praised by visiting big-men. However, when soon afterwards he wished to arrange a funeral distribution, his clan-section mates refused to help him with contributions of pigs, as they were upset with him for giving his prestation before they were ready to join him. He was

[1] An account is given in Strathern A. J. 1969*b*: 59.

saved by generous contributions from his affines, but made a point also of apologising to his clan-section mates. He emphasised that he himself was not upset with his clan-section for withholding support, and put a cordyline leaf, divination-object of his tribe, on his head to mark this. If he were not speaking the truth, the divination-object would kill him. In this way he showed that he realised his 'brothers' were right in refusing him support and that his disposition was good towards them. Later in the same day they were asking his advice on moka plans again and he had recovered his position as clan-section leader.[1]

Big-men vary in the degree to which they enter into conflict, and afterwards seek reconciliation, with their group-mates. However, Ongka's actions in this last case indicate that he valued his relationship to his clan-mates. This is because, although he was able to finance himself and make moka with the aid of his extra-clan network, as a political leader in relations between his clan and others he is anchored to his clan-mates. They are his followers, if not his financial supporters or partners. He makes prestations of advice to them and speaks for them at public meetings. In return they make prestations of verbal support for his plans. This nexus of prestations can in fact operate separately from the nexus of material prestations, although it is also useful for big-men and their followers to help each other in exchanges. That is why Ongka's relationship to his clan-section mates is important and why, if he wishes to retain them as followers, he cannot afford to become too autocratic.

SOCIAL CHANGE

The moka system has clearly not remained static over the years since Europeans first entered the Highlands with their quantities of valuable shells and their powerful technological resources. The two most striking initial influences on the system as I have argued in Chapters 5 and 9, were the abolition of warfare and the inflation of shell currency. Together these circumstances made possible an expansion in the exchange relations between groups in Hagen, just as Salisbury (1962) has recorded for the Siane of the Eastern Highlands. Since then the most significant social changes have been the spread of Mission activity, the establishment of Local Government Councils, and the development of first a market for labour and then cash-cropping, both of coffee and of vegetables. I shall look at each of these influences briefly in turn.

---

[1] He is now (1969) Local Government Councillor for both his own (Mandembo) and Membo clan.

227

Mission influence on the moka has been negative. Baptised Christians are not supposed to make moka, but to devote themselves to religion and business. Many cultural practices associated with the moka seem to have been banned either directly or indirectly by decision of the Missions, because of the association of the practices with beliefs in magic and in ancestral ghosts.

With the introduction of Local Government Councils some of the big-men, younger and older, have been elected as councillors, and must now maintain a double role of leadership; they have to organise government work on roads and rest-houses and encourage cash-cropping, while on other occasions taking the lead in moka plans. Some councillors reject moka and decide on an entirely 'modern' role; others, usually older big-men, pursue both, and are sometimes caught in unhappy situations, having to postpone a moka because of local government concerns. Local government certainly means that there is potentially less time for moka-making; moreover, councillors are at times expected to support cash-cropping as a new way of life, involving changes in important social values, and to persuade their clansmen to take it up.

The labour market, provided by local plantations or by schemes for the transport of Highlanders to the coast, enabled some energetic men in the 1940s and 1950s to amass shells which they brought home and used to launch their moka career. It also provided an outlet for boys and men with few social prospects at home to leave their own milieu and find subsistence elsewhere. Nowadays contract labour on the coast is less popular; people prefer to work for piece-money at local plantations when they need money to spend in the numerous trade-stores, which have sprung up all along the Administration roads, and in Hagen township. This allows them to spend some of their time on traditional pursuits as well. More money probably enters the economic system through the sale of coffee grown by Hageners themselves and sold to a variety of companies. Some of the money is invested in bridewealth and moka exchanges; some in lorries and trucks, purchased usually through men of a group clubbing their money together. Near to Hagen township people are less often to be seen in traditiona dress, more often in shirts, shorts, and perhaps shoes or boots; and they drive or ride in cars from place to place at least as much as they walk.

It is apparent, then, that the market, through its introduction of cash and the uses to which cash can be put, is creating considerable changes in Hagen society. In part, however, cash is channelled back into the tradi-tional system of prestige, either in standard moka prestations or in the form of parties at which prestations of food and drink are made on a large

scale. As population grows and cash-crop planting continues (with diversi-
fication into tea owing to the fact that New Guinea has reached the limit
of its quota for the sale of coffee on the international market), problems of
land ownership and use are likely to emerge. The question then will be:
what kind of life are the Hageners to lead? Are they likely to give up the
value they place on moka with pigs and money as willingly as they say
they will soon give up shell-moka? Will they be able to find some means of
combining moka with participation in a market-based cash economy? At
present moka relations seem on the one hand to be expanding, linking more
and more groups together, and on the other hand to be compressed into
shorter periods of preparation, owing to the demands of other activities.
Whether the system can survive such pressure remains to be seen. Much
will depend on whether younger big-men decide to combine prestige-
seeking through ceremonial exchange with application to cash-cropping
activities: whether to extend the rope of moka in new directions or to
untwist it altogether.

APPENDICES

APPENDIX I
Populations of some Hagen tribes in the early 1960s

1. South Wahgi groups (Kuli Local Government Council)

Tribe	Population
Kuli	2901
Kope	918
Mingga	843
Andakelkam	647
Koukla	538
Rungøi	451
Ronye	432+176 Yemi
Onombe	356
Dongai[a]	334
Maninga	298
Worəki	116

2. Central Melpa (Hagen L.G.C.)[b]

Tribe	Population
Ndika	6,749
Refugee groups with Ndika:	
Kungunaka	755
Penambe	678
Elti	445
Palka	314
Mokei	6,199
Semi-incorporated with Mokei:	
Epilkae[c]	153
Yamka	2,281
Kukilika	1,155
Kendika	992[d]
Mimka-Ruruka[e]	470[d]
Keme	266
Tea[f]	213

[a] This looks suspiciously like a variant spelling of Rungøi. Unfortunately I did not resolve this problem.

[b] Some of these groups may now be in the more recently-formed Nebilyer Council.

[c] These migrated from the Baiyer River area to join the Mokei (cf. Dei Council figures, where the Epilkae appear also). There is still movement back and forth between their two settlement areas.

[d] Northern Nebilyer Valley; probably Temboka speakers.

[e] A tribe-pair.

[f] Uncertain identification. There is a Tea group paired with the Ndena in the Southern Nebilyer, but I am not sure if the group named here is an offshoot from the Southern Nebilyer group or not. The Administration spelling may be misleading.

Appendices

3. Western Melpa (Mul L.G.C.)

Tribe	Population
Kumndi	5,414
Refugee groups with Kumndi:	
Mokei	346
Kungunaka	329
Kenaplka	169
Pøndi	47
Kope	26
Nengka	3,677
Mundika	1,218
Rəmndi	1,196
Mile	836
Klalka	335 (associated with Rəmndi)
Milaka	264 (paired with Klalka)

4. Northern Melpa including North Wahgi (Dei L.G.C.)

Tribe	Population
Minembi	2,813
Tipuka	2,419
Ukini g	1,775
Kombukla	1,542
Wəlyi	1,224
Kendipi	1,196
Kawelka	860
Roklaka	744
Kope	711
Kimke	388
Kumngaka	368 (associated with Kendipi)
Nølka	364
Waklpke	348
Prandike	252 (associated with Kendipi)
Klamakae	241
Kiklpukla	130
Andakapkae g	73
Epilkae g	70
Ndilika	68

g Not in Dei Council. The Ukini live next to Kyaka Enga groups at the western end of the Baiyer Valley.

APPENDIX 2

The size of exogamous units

Gross population densities in three parts of the Hagen area in the early 1960s were:

		Population	Area sq. m.	Density per sq. m.
Western Melpa	(Mul)	14,033	52·3	268·31
Central Melpa	(Hagen)	31,279	264·8	118·1
Northern Melpa	(Dei)	14,323	211·2	67·81

231

These figures could scarcely be made meaningful without closer examination of different types of land available to each clan and tribe; but at a gross level densities do seem to be much higher in the Mul Council area, and it is also this area which provides a good many examples of large, high-level exogamous units, within the Kumndi, Nengka, and Mundika tribes. If population density is higher and the population is fairly evenly distributed, it will be easier to maintain large exogamous units, since brides and affinal exchange partners will still be obtainable within reasonable distances. Large tribes also take in fragments of smaller ones as refugees and these partly incorporated groups, interspersed with the segments of the host tribe, can provide a further source of brides and affines. Conditions of this kind seem to be met among the Kumndi and Nengka tribes in Mul, as well as among the Central Melpa Ndika, and they may help to explain why we do find large exogamous groups in these tribes. A neighbouring tribe of the Nengka, Mundika, may have found it important to maintain itself as a single exogamous unit in order to keep its military unity in the face of similarly large units among the Nengka and Kumndi.

By contrast, where density is lower and the population is similarly scattered fairly evenly there may be a more rapid development of feelings of 'separatism' between segments of a tribe, and this could be expressed by setting up relations of intermarriage between them. Tentatively, I would propose such a situation for some of the Dei Council groups.

My argument here must depend on the tribes with large high-level exogamous units also showing a higher population density than others; and this I cannot demonstrate, although the figures from Mul Council, which is dominated by the large Kumndi tribe, suggest that it is so.

APPENDIX 3

Terminology for groups used by Vicedom and Strauss

Vicedom (1943–8 vol. 2: *passim*) identified five levels of group structure: 1. the *Gross Stamm*, a set of tribes linked by an origin myth. This = my Great Tribe. 2. The *Stamm*, Melpa *mbo tenda* = my Tribe. Vicedom says this is the exogamous unit and is important also in warfare. 3. The *Gross-Sippe* or *Klan*, cf. vol. 2: 25. The account of this level is not entirely clear. Vicedom instances the Ndika Milakamb group, which I would call a clan-section or possibly a clan. 4. The *Sippe*, Melpa *andakang*. This corresponds to my 'clan'. It is possible, however, that Vicedom sometimes uses the word when referring to activities of clan-sections and sub-clans. 5. The *Kleine Sippe* = any segment within the *Sippe*.

Strauss (1962: 74 ff.) bases his paradigm on the large Ndika tribe, and he allows for the maximum number of segment-levels likely to be found in a given tribe. His scheme is: 1. The *Mi-Gruppe*, Melpa *mbo tenda*. This is the tribe, which he regards as the original exogamous group. It may contain more recently-developed exogamous groups of level 2. 2. The *Ableger Mi-Gruppe*, Melpa *mbo kat* = major section of a tribe. 3. The *Feld Abteil Gruppe*, Melpa *pana ru*, = the clan. Strauss points out that this is conceived of as a territorial group,

Appendices

hence its name 'field-ditch (or boundary) group'. 4. The *Alt Vater Penis Gruppe*, Melpa *anda noimb*. This must roughly correspond to my 'clan-section'. Strauss suggests that the term for it brings 'the concept of patrilineal descent sharply to mind' (p. 77). I found the term applied most often to what are in fact much lower-level units, the lineages. 5. The *Männerhaus-Gemeinschaft*, Melpa *rapa* = the sub-clan, whose men meet in a single house for discussions on moka. Strauss reports that the men in each *rapa* of Ndika Opramb group considered themselves descendants of the men who originally lived in a single men's house and so founded the segment.

Below these five levels Strauss isolates three lineage levels (in smaller tribes, only one such level is likely to be present, and in my own paradigm I allow for only one). Strauss's three lineage levels are: 1. *Anda Kangêm* = 'Grandfather and son'. This, he points out, is the term which Vicedom says applies to the clan. Both are right here, for the term can in fact be used in reference either to a clan group or to a lineage. 2. *Önginödl* = 'brothers'. I did not find this term applied tightly to a single identifiable lineage level. 3. *Tepam-Kangemadl* = 'father and sons'. This seems, in Strauss's usage, to be simply the set of a father and his immediate sons. I found it applied also to shallow lineages, whose apical founders were sometimes two generations above living fathers.

As a general point, we may note that both Vicedom and Strauss tend to apply Melpa terms to single levels of structure; whereas in fact some of the terms, e.g. *mbo tenda*, = 'one root', can be applied to almost any level of grouping.

APPENDIX 4

Songs and spells for attracting shells

When a men's house, newly built at a ceremonial ground, was consecrated, a ritual expert would lead a song-performance to mark this. I give a translation of an example of this, with notes:

'In the little men's house at Ndan[1] we make the *kuklumb*[2] song-o, the *kuklumb* song-o. I cook the leaves of the *kopiya*[3] tree and fasten them to the central post of the new house. I cook and fasten them. I am on high like the *ndoa*[4] bird, I have a fine bloom on my skin.[5] Let me cook and fasten the leaves. I am on high etc. (repeated). At the small men's house and the large men's house I have arrived. How shall I cook the leaves by myself, I wonder? I shall take the leaves of the *kuklumb* plant that grows on the fringe of cemetery places, the leaves of the *kopiya* tree. I cook and place *kopiya* and *kult*[6] leaves at the base of the post, *kilt*[7] leaves at the base of the post.'

NOTES: 1. Ndan. This is the place where I collected the song, from an old ritual expert, Ambra, and his settlement-mates (cf. Strathern A. J. 1969c). 2. *Kuklumb*. An Araceae plant, with glossy green leaves considered to shine, to be fresh (*kundil*) and to have a good scent, and thus to be able to attract valuables to the men's house. *Kuklumb* is also associated with the ancestors. 3. *Kopiya*. A tree planted on ceremonial grounds in the Nebilyer Valley. It has a multiple red flower, which is held to attract birds and valuables. 4. Ndoa. The Harpyopsis eagle, a strong, carnivorous bird, which finds 'good food' for itself. Just so, the men will find 'food', i.e. valuables and pigs. 5. The men are healthy, flowering, and will attract gifts as flowers attract birds. 6. *Kult.* Probably Melastomataceae *Astronia* sp. (also called *kundumb* in Melpa). Its leaves are smooth and strong, as the men's skin will be if they call upon it. 7. *Kilt.* Rutaceae *Evodiella* sp., a resin-producing tree. The resin is used to make display boards for pearl shells. The tree bears a mass of mauve flowers which attract birds. In the same way, the men who call upon it will attract exchange partners and valuables.

'Bird' imagery is made even more explicit in a spell which the expert traditionally speaks after the song-performance is over. In the version which Ambra gave me he mentioned 38 birds, each one noted for its 'bright' or 'light' plumage or its ability to find 'good food', like the eagle. The first bird mentioned in the spell is a type of bower-bird, which, I was told, 'makes a place for itself with an upright stick and hangs pieces of tree moss on this. We men compare this stick to the central post of our men's house. We take the good customs of this bird to ourselves. We also say that its stick is its *poklambo* and the place it makes is its *moka pena*, at which it dances.'

Another ritual is performed for the first lighting of a fire inside a new men's house. The expert uses a special tinder of wild-dog fur and dry pandanus leaves in his fire-thong, and recites his spell as he operates the thong. Ambra's spell listed 63 place-names in pairs, and envisaged pearl shells leaping from hill-top to hill-top up from the Southern Nebilyer trade routes. If the fire burns brightly, this is taken as an omen that shells will 'come quickly' into the new men's house.

APPENDIX 5

A note on kik kapa payments

Reay (1959: 69), Brown (1961), and Meggitt (1965: 206) have all reported well-developed systems of death payments to matrilateral kin among the Kuma, Chimbu, and Mae-Enga respectively; and we may regard these as partly diagnostic of the important relationship between a man and his mother's clan in many of the New Guinea highlands societies. (Payments to maternal kin seem to be even more important in some of the Papuan Highlands societies, e.g. the Daribi (Wagner 1967) and the Wiru (Strathern A. J. 1968).) Among the Kuma and the Mae, in particular, the maternal kin protest to the agnates of the dead man against their lack of care in allowing him to die: either he was sick and they failed to placate ancestors or remove poison from him, or his agnatic ancestors are to blame for implacably 'claiming' him (i.e. causing his death). The death payments are thus true gifts of compensation to the maternal kin.

Aggression marks the Mae matrilateral mourners, dramatic shows of grief the Kuma. Reay explains for the Kuma that maternal kin are expected to feel strong grief and that the agnates 'feel sorry' for them and hence pay compensation. This fits with the Melpa theory of death payments. For the Mae Meggitt paints a different picture: 'Men of the mother's brother's clan who expect a share in the indemnity assemble daily on a mountain ridge and sing loudly of their right to receive payment ... [At the actual payment] men of the mother's patrilineage who are offered less than their due hurl the smaller objects back and stamp off in a rage.' The greater aggression shown here seems to fit the fact that the Mae 'marry their enemies'. This is not the case for the Kuma or the Hageners.

Cases of *kik kapa* payments actually made or proffered show that in Hagen they are not confined entirely to compensating maternal kin. In one case a big-man of Minembi Papeke clan had died, and a *kik kapa* payment of 10 shells was offered to his close agnates by a big-man of Min. Yelipi clan, Rangk, in order to encourage the agnates to finish their mourning quickly and so be able to join in the dancing at the Yelipi's projected (1964) prestation. Two of the big-man's supporters are close patrilateral cross-cousins of the man who had died, and their relationship was described as the 'road' for this gift. In another case a dead man's maternal kin themselves gave *kik kapa* to his agnates in order to encourage them to complete their mourning, and this payment initiated wider moka relations between them. *Kik kapa* operates also between affines: if a man's wife dies at his own place, he should compensate the wife's clansmen; on the other hand, if she dies at her natal place, her natal kin should compensate the husband.

These examples show (1) that in Hagen *kik kapa* payments can be used as a basis for moka exchanges, and (2) that in the case of a married woman's death the direction of payment depends on where she died. The assumption is perhaps that if, for example, she dies at her natal place, her own ancestral ghosts are responsible for her death; if at her husband's, his are responsible.

APPENDIX 6

The evaluation of pearl shells and their preparation for use in exchanges

Conjectures on the origin of shells

Leahy (Leahy and Crain 1937: 195) reports an early guess of Hageners that shells grew on trees. However, an old Northern Melpa informant gave me a conjecture that fits more closely with Hagen religious ideas. He told me that the *Kewa wamb* (= sky people, sometimes pictured as cannibals, cf. the fact that the Leahys and Taylor were at first thought to be sky people) dropped valuables at the place where the 'legs of the sky' (*mukl timb*) reached the earth, i.e. at the end of the earth; and people there worked shells into shape and sent them along trade routes. Alternatively, he said, people thought that perhaps people in distant places obtained them, like stone axes, from quarries.

Immediate sources

I add here two stories of how shells came to the Nebilyer Valley and Hagen from the south. The first is from an old big-man and ritual expert, Ambra: 'Pearl shells came to us before the White man came. In Aua (the Ialibu area) there is a group called the Muni Pundi. A man of this group first introduced pearl shells to us by sending some to a man of the Kulka tribe, called Pomb Wara.

He gave them to Mbøkwa of the Poiaka tribe. The Poiaka man gave them to Ulka Merua, my father. Merua spread the moka to the Ndika and Elti groups, who spread it in turn to the Mokei and Yamka. The Yamka gave it to the Kukilika, who distributed pearl shells out to other groups.'

In Ambra's view, then, the arrival of pearl shells and the introduction of moka-making were historical events, belonging to the time of his father. It is possible that his view of the time-scale has become foreshortened here.

The second account is more fanciful, and comes from Mbukl in the Northern Melpa area, where less was known about empirical contacts between the Nebilyer and areas to its south. 'We used to speak of a man called Kanggop from Tambul, who appeared in Hagen with numbers of pearl shells hanging from his neck. They say of him that he used to receive pigs and returned a bamboo tube of decorating oil for each backbone, a nassa mat for a stomach, and a pearl shell for each pig leg'. Very generous exchange rates!

The pearl shell esteem complex

Hides (1936) and Leahy (Leahy and Crain 1937) attest the demand for shell valuables of all kinds throughout the Highlands; and Leahy in particular noted that ornaments of shell became fewer in the Eastern Highlands the further one penetrated inland from the coast (1937: 64); in the Western Highlands he noted that shells seemed scarcer in the Enga area, from Walya westwards, than in Hagen (1937: 254).

The relative demand for different types of shell varied, Leahy observed. For example, in Siane the green-snail was most favoured, perhaps as an ornament rather than, or as well as, an item used in formal inter-clan prestations. Brookfield and Brown (1963: 62) note the value of green-snail as an ornament to the Chimbu, and the same may hold for the Siane.

Elsewhere Leahy found that gold-lip pearl shells and bailers were preferred, e.g. among the Bena Bena (1937: 119), and the Enga (1937: 256). Hides (1936: 125) describes how between Mendi and Erave an old man showed him a pearl shell wrapped in bark-cloth dyed with red ochre. 'He held it up with the utmost reverence and looked questioningly ... The expression on his face told us plainly that he was asking if we had such a beautiful thing in our possession.' Meggitt (1956: 163) notes that among the Waka in the past only important men owned as much as a piece of a pearl shell. Hageners similarly told me that only big-men 'held' shells in the past.

When shells were scarce, the larger and better examples were named (cf. Malinowski 1922: 89 on naming of Kula valuables). Some names I recorded were: *Oklmone kep*, 'the beguiler from Oklmone': the man from Oklmone beguiles his partner into giving him a large pig for this shell. *Mbant kint*, 'the shell with hole-marks from Banz' (obtained from an early trade-store at Banz). *Kilua memong*, 'shell from Mt Giluwe, you run to us' (i.e., from the south). *Lkipiri pukl*, 'shell with a smooth and hard skin'. *Klumant parka*, 'the red bird of paradise from the Gumant river', a reference to the shell's admired ruddy colour. *Wøki mbom*, 'shell from the Wahgi with a face as bright as the *mbom*

236

Appendices

flower'. *Kerua Məkapuri*, 'a good hard shell of the Məka river area'. For further names, cf. Vicedom (vol. 1: 118).

Criteria by which pearl shells are judged

These names indicate some of the ways in which pearl shells were evaluated. Both the overall size (which Williams (1940–1 : 139) maintains is the main criterion in Kutubu) and the condition of the shell's 'skin' are taken into account. The best shells are those which are large and ruddy; but a small shell which has the right colour is prized, whereas a large one which is too white is not.

A shell with a deep ruddy colour (*kund*) is called *kin kui*, 'dead shell', that is, it is hardened and tough like seasoned firewood. It may be said of it: *koklpa koklpa moya ronom*, 'it dies, it dies, and lies still'; or *nomba nomba rondokl etim*, 'it stays, it stays, and becomes strong; or *eng nomba rondokl porom*, 'it shines and becomes strong'. A general term for first-quality shells is *kin kekla*. A good red shell is said to make true friends when given away. Such a shell is propped up for display at the head of a row if it forms part of a prestation.

Symmetry of shape is also take into account, although not so much attention is paid to it.

A poor pearl shell is one which is white in places, lacking gold-lip, is small, and has too green an iridescence. Wormholes do not seriously detract from a shell which is otherwise good.

Some shells have a layered appearance, and each layer is called a 'nose' which overlaps with the next. The total effect of this layering is called *wakl up*: each layer carries the next on its back as a mother does her children. Layered shells seem always to have a good gold-lip content.

Less excellent shells are *kin kaklmong*, 'the shell of the nape of the neck' (I am not sure of the reference here); and poor ones are *merima øk*, 'shell added to the handle' (of a better shell, for display). *Kin kekla* are supposed to be reserved for bridewealth and direct exchanges for pigs; *kaklmong* may be used for moka also; and *merima* only for moka. The finest shells thus have a higher unit value, but there is no standardised quantitative value interval (Dalton 1965) between the three grades. Hence they cannot be directly converted into each other. If a man wants to exchange a shell for another shell, he exchanges for one which he considers is an exact equivalent of his own. This transaction marks that men are equals and friends, just as their shells are equivalent.

Preparation of pearl shells for use in exchanges

In the past, as stories indicate, shells entered the Highlands ready-cut, but Europeans brought them uncut, with an encrustation of lime over their skin. This is ground away with sandstone. Smaller grindstones are used to cut out the top-piece (formerly worn by women). In the case of a big shell its lower surface is encased in clay to preserve it and a burning stick or nowadays a piece of glowing iron is applied to shear off its top. Filing off the lime is a time of anxiety. The buyer examines his shell from the back for gold-lip content, but he cannot be sure that it will not be marred by uneven colouring, worm-holes, and hair-like imperfections. In the past a man finding his shell too white at the top would put it away till he had some spare meat to cook as a domestic sacrifice, when he would pray to his family ghosts that the shell would turn out to be yellow further down.

Pearl shells have a resin backing and a handle for display. In the 1930s the backing was small, as it is still in Tambul (cf. Vicedom, vol. 1: 119). Northern Melpa nowadays profess to dislike the Tambul style; they also scorn the Wahgi and Chimbu practice of not mounting the shells at all.

Vicedom's illustration (*ibid.*) shows also the fine handle of plaited fibre which women used to make for the shells (*merima* or *werema*). When pearl shells became too plentiful for the women to produce sufficient numbers of these handles, men turned to using old pieces of sacking, discarded by Europeans, instead. Vicedom speaks of knotted ropes attached to shells, each knot marking a transaction; but I did not see examples of these. Marsupial bones, which he also mentions, are still sometimes added to shells as a decoration.

The current style is to surround the shell completely with a large resin board. Ambra, whose version of how shells come to Hagen I gave earlier, claimed to me that his father was the first to place shells on large boards in this way and to wear the *koa mak* ornament which indicates numbers of moka transactions the wearer has made.

The resin is obtained from the *elua* and *kilt* trees; the first itself oozes resin, I was told, while the second has to be tapped. In Vicedom's time the process of setting a shell in its resin-bed was always carried out in secrecy inside a man's house, in case a visitor should arrive and make an awkward request for the shell. For transport, a neat bark pack was used (Vicedom, vol. 1: 119); this is rare now. In the past Northern Melpa men returning from a journey to the Gumant area with a shell would wrap it carefully in depths of moss, 'silk' produced by a type of insect, and fern leaves. As they passed by people would exclaim excitedly that here was someone with a big pearl shell, and they would clamour to see it.

When a new board is made, heated resin is clapped into the shell's concave back, and moulded round it. Later it sets hard. To help bind the resin in, pandanus leaves are placed in the back. Before a moka, minor repairs in the mounting may have to be made. Men's houses fill with gossiping visitors, while a few heat flat iron rods (previously pointed stones) and apply these to melt and re-shape the resin. A pungent, acrid smoke is given off. For a moka also the boards must be covered with red ochre, obtained for a pearl shell or cash (50 cents up to $4) from manufacturers in the Wahgi and among the Western Melpa Kumndi. Vicedom (*ibid.*) reports that shells were wrapped in cloth and ochre for storage (cf. Hides 1936: 125 again), and that it was said a man would die if his shell were not covered in this way. This custom seems to have been abandoned when shells became more plentiful while ochre remained scarce; but it is still considered very bad form if the ochre has not been applied when shells are displayed in moka. To apply the ochre, men first wash the shell and its board with water and a little pig-grease, and rub it with a pulpy leaf (*menaplka omong*). They then spread the ochre by hand from a bark-cloth bag. Dashes of it fall on the shell and are either wiped off or rubbed in to improve its colour. Vicedom (vol. 1: 117) speaks of a vine used for polishing; nowadays this is done with a hairy leaf (*kotinge*) or European sandpaper (called by the same term).

There are two finishing touches. *Koa mak* sticks are embedded in the resin from the top of the shell to the edge of the board. Second, the top semicircular edge of the shell itself may be picked out with droplets of white juice from the *timb* bush (*Euphorbia plumerioides*). Dots of ochre are placed on these to fix them. A crack may be similarly picked out and worm-holes may be covered by a net-work of raised resin lines.

Preparation of other types of shell

Nassa. The standard backing for a nassa mat is bark-cloth; European cloth or the 'silk-house' of an insect (*mongndamb mokelip*) may be added. To the backing the shell is sewn like a button with fibre thread and a bamboo needle. Hageners say that the raw nassa is an animal with a tail and stomach, which are removed by picking with a flint or nowadays a nail. The same instruments are used to pierce a hole in it for sewing.

Only men were supposed to make the mats. One informant told how he made ten, with shells obtained in exchange for sweet potatoes at a plantation. A small mat took him three days, a medium one five days, to make.

The shells are sewn in symmetrical lines, which form patterns. A diamond-shaped space may be left in the centre. In the past, a large mat might be divided in half at this point when it was used in bridewealth, half going to the bride's group, half being returned to the groom's.

Cowrie. Cowrie ropes are made of plaited fibres, onto which the shells are sewn, a few large ones marking the centre point (where the ropes might be halved, as were nassa mats). Even a short rope is over 12 ft long and has some 285 cowries sewn to it; medium ones have about 350 shells, long ones up to 500. The cowrie shell's 'body' is removed by application of a burning stick and a little water.

Six different sub-types of cowrie are distinguished, and the parts of the shell are named also.

Conus. Vicedom (vol. 1: 106–7) gives a careful account of the adaptation of conus-shell ornaments from the whole shell.

Bailer. As Vicedom (vol. 1: 111) notes, the base of the shell is first removed, (traditionally) with a flint tool. The inward-curving part is also sheared off, separating the *raem noimb* ('penis of the bailer'), which girls occasionally wear as a decoration. The brown colouring on the bailer's surface is scraped off until it remains only in the shell's furrows. Pointed axe-stone fragments, called *ingnggur*, were originally used to bore the holes through which string attachments for the shells are inserted.

Green-snail. Vicedom (vol. 1: 209) has described the manufacture of green-snail pieces from the whole shell.

The whole shell is a long horn, open at the end called its 'head', curving round to a 'navel' at the other, with a 'backbone' running lengthwise. When the shells were bought in stores they had a rough skin, which was compared to tree-moss.

They are ground and polished till they show a rainbow iridescence. Whiter ones are disliked. The best green-snail, I was told, are ones which are like the skin of a shimmering green insect (*nggop nggap kamb*).

APPENDIX 7

Examples of el-ık style

The first speech given here was made by Kawelka Membo Pengk, when Kawelka Membo and Mandembo clans gave pigs as a concerted initiatory gift to their Tipuka allies in August 1964. Pengk's speech was greatly admired for the multiplicity of its veiled figurative references to moka relations between the Kawelka and the Tipuka. He is not a big-man.

Hear me you men, hear me you men, let everyone stop talking. You said you had a young girl in your women's house, a pig in your men's house. 'I have a head-dress of the *kuri* bird wrapped up, I have a pig in my men's house which I shall cook. I have a pig-knife wrapped up, I am making a house for the girls to turn head in.' These are the words you Tipuka spoke. But your head-dress is old now and blackened, do you see? Your bamboo knife is broken, do you see? True, my head and eyes are small, and you can see this is so, but I do as my fathers did before me. As they made moka before me, so I do now; as they made speeches before me, so I do now. My fathers had long combed-out beards, and mine is still short and bristly. But they say if today we see a false dream, tomorrow's will come true, and it is true that I wanted to give moka to you. The people around us may think the moka is not yet, but I have sent a knotted cordyline leaf as a message straight to them that it is on now. Look at the long tail of the *weipø* marsupial I am wearing. If the moka is delayed at Kiling, place of the Minembi Engambo, never mind, for look! I give you my decorated axe and spear as a promise that it will be completed here. Give ripe bananas to your partners, and encourage them to give to you. My mother's people, it is I who say this, be sure then that you will bring back moka from these people and will hold it ready in your hand. When you go to share cooked pork at a bridewealth you must not waste your dance paint by decorating your eyes, nor put on your horned wig; you must not wear Red bird of paradise plumes when you play cards – you must save all your decorations for your moka dance. That is what I have to say, my brothers, making my speech here at the place where men are accustomed to speak. I have pulled the *olka*-wood stakes down, down, down, down, and at Kultke where men used to stand and watch battles, where men stole sweet potatoes from women's net-bags, here I have set up two *olka* stakes, and, do you see, I have thrown down this moka gift to you Tipuka below us.

Some exegesis of the speech seems necessary. The main theme is that the Tipuka have promised to make moka but are delaying: the special houses they have built, the pigs they have gathered, the girls they have collected for courting ceremonies, the head-dresses of the White bird of paradise they have made, and the bamboo knives they have prepared – all these are being wasted, because of the delay. A reason for the delay is that the Minembi Engambo have not yet made their 'helping moka' to the Kitepi clansmen, but the Kitepi, whom he addresses as his mother's people, may be sure that eventually this will be given – Pengk is willing to wager his decorations on that. He himself is not a man up to the standard of his forebears, he says: he does not have the long, combed-out beard which belongs to a mature, vigorous man. But he can speak and make moka. That is why he has brought two *olka* stakes to the ceremonial ground and attached extra gifts of pigs to these. He ends by referring playfully to Kultke, another name for Mbukl (where he made the speech): Mbukl stands high above the valley where the Tipuka live, and men used to watch battles and steal from women at it (there may be a sexual innuendo here). Now he has made moka at it and speaks of himself as flinging the gift down to the Tipuka in the valley.

The second speech was made by a young Kitepi man, Mɪt, when the Kitepi–Oklembo finally gave their moka in January 1965. It makes a claim to 'winning' over the Kawelka by making extra gifts to them.

Mbakla Kawelka men, you spoke and I heard you. I made ready, made ready, and now I have given to you. Where *tizik* tussocks are and grow over our *poklambo* tree, where there are stands of *pit-pit* and spit of spirits, in such a place I live and give to you. I call you my sisters' sons, my cross-cousins. I am your true cross-cousin, living close to you. My sisters' sons, my cross-cousins, you say you see big pigs, big shells, well, now I have given you large pigs on the two *olka* stakes, given you a bicycle too, given you all the food you like to eat. Further, I have given you two steers, and so I win. I have given you all the things which are your food; I give you two steers also and so I win.

NOTES: *tizik* = a type of grass; *poklambo* = the ceremonial tree planted at the head of a dancing ground; *pit-pit* (Melanesian Pidgin) = tall *Miscanthus* cane-grass; spit of spirits = an exudation from the soil which appears in damp parts (Mɪt is saying in all these references that his place is 'bad', not fertile, and yet the Tipuka have managed to make this gift); *olka* stakes = the stakes to which 'extra' pigs are tethered at a moka; bicycle: extra gifts may nowadays include European artefacts; steers: these were bought specially from a local European plantation-owner.

The third speech, by an old minor big-man, shows the opposite technique to boasting, meiosis or self-deprecation. It was made on the same occasion as the second, by Ui, who belongs to Tipuka Oklembo clan:

Man of Pitim, ∂ndipi,
We fought against each other in bad times,
We two fought and the marsupials and birds died,
The fishes and the frogs died.
You gave me pigs, a few small pigs, before;
I acknowledge that, and now
I give to you in return.
My urine is like that of the frog, it is not plenty;

R

I am like the unmarried girl, who holds the child only once:
This time, once only, I give to you,
Give badly to you –
But you must say that I am giving well.
You must put away that side of your mouth with which you eat the big things
And eat with the small side only.
I give badly, my Kitepi brothers,
And yet the fight was mine.
You straighten the ropes of the pigs,
You make the speeches and give them,
You straighten the ropes of the cassowaries,
You line up the long tubes of decorating oil:
So you take me on your shoulders and raise me up.
I, the man who began the fight, am small,
While you want later to eat and so you help me.
Give to the Kawelka the one poor pig you usually do,
The rain will come later, it's not raining yet.
So that we can stay living together,
I give to you Kawelka, give badly here.

NOTES: ∂ndipi = an old Kawelka major big-man; my urine, etc.: these are all figurative ways of saying he cannot give many pigs. The Oklembo, his clan, were hard-pressed in this moka, and it was only the larger gift by the Kitepi that saved Tipuka prestige. And yet, as he points out, the primary obligation to pay the Kawelka for deaths lay with his own clan, for it was the Oklembo who began fights against Kawelka Mandembo clan and later called in Kitepi as their helpers. Thus the Kitepi will 'eat', i.e. receive further ally payments from the Oklembo later. The reference to the rain is made because rain at a moka is a sign of ancestral displeasure: let them complete their gift in good weather, before the rain begins. Ui refers rather poignantly at the end to one of the purposes of making moka: 'so that we can stay living together'.

APPENDIX 8

Ascriptions of big-man status

1. *Kendike* clan

(*a*) = ascriptions by Ant, Kaukla, and Køu
(*b*) = ascriptions by Ongka

(*a*) *Milembo* sub-clan: Ant [acknowledged leader], Mek; Ndip, Møndi, and Tei [all three minor]. *Woumbo* sub-clan: Kaukla. Kur was a big-man before, but he is now dead, and although his two sons show promise neither is quite a big-man yet (1964). *Kombuklambo* sub-clan: there were two big-men, a father and his sons, but both are now dead and there are no successors. *Andakomonembo*: Rying, Nui.

(*b*) Ongka cited only Ant and Mek, two ageing major big-men. His list is an 'outsider's': he mentions only the big-men whom he considers most important. The Kendike informants themselves mention a number of minor big-men as well, including two who are protégés of Ant (Møndi and Tei).

2. *Kitepi* clan

    (*a*) = ascriptions by Tei, with plentiful comments from a brother and also two Wanyembo clansmen who were present.

    (*b*) = ascriptions by Kuri. No-one else was present at this interview.

    (*c*) = ascriptions by Ongka.

(*a*) *Ropkembo* sub-clan. Kuri is the only big-man. Others are 'men at the edges'. Kuri's F Romnde was a big-man and Kuri is his most important successor. A brother, Ore, was also a big-man. [He died in 1965 and was completely inactive in 1964, so I do not list him.] *Rulkembo* sub-clan. The three sons of Wølyi, Kaukla, Mel, and Nditing, all became big-men. The first two are now dead and their surviving sons have joined the Lutheran mission. Nditing remains as a big-man. His eldest son, Wai, is a young big-man. Besides Nditing, there is Nukint, a minor big-man. *Kolkal* sub-clan. Klai was a big-man, and his elder son, Engk, is a big-man also. Tong is 'minor'. *Roklambo* sub-clan. The two sons of a deceased big-man, Kwant, are both big-men also: Parka and Rop. Both are now old and their sons have no speaking ability, and hence are no more than 'men of work'. *Pøndimbo* clan-section. Ok [very old] and three of his sons, Mel, Mara and Ukl, are big-men. In Kitepi clan as a whole, Kuri and Ok are the chief big-men. [I interviewed Mel later and he added Kowa as a minor big-man. He cited Ukl and Tei as minor big-men by comparison with himself and Mara. Mel has thirteen sons by eight different wives, but none seems to be a big-man.]

(*b*) Kuri provided genealogical depth for many of the big-men. He cited himself, his son Pørwa, Engk, Tei, Nøngin, Rumba, Parka, Rop, and Nditing in his own clan-section. In Pøndimbo section, he said, the F of Ok was a major big-man, and Ok and another son Kuri succeeded him. Kuri's son Kowa is 'big', as is Ok's son Tei. Mara and Mel are actually the sons of Ok's brother Mitipa: both are big-men.

(*c*) Ongka described Parka as a previous big-man, now old (Roklambo sub-clan). Now [1964] the big-men are Ok (Pøndimbo), Kuri (Ropkembo) and Nditing (Rulkembo). It is clear that here, as in the first case, Ongka is giving a list of major big-men only and a conservative list at that.

    The ascriptions for the other clans in Table 14 would reveal a similar pattern, with transformations: Tipuka informants give conservative estimates of the big-men in Kawelka clans, while Kawelka informants themselves identify an additional number of men whom they recognise internally as at least minor big-men.

BIBLIOGRAPHY

Barnes, J. A. (1962). 'African Models in the New Guinea Highlands', *Man*, vol. 62, 5–9.

(1967). 'Agnation among the Enga: a review article', *Oceania*, vol. 38, 33–43.

Barrau, J. (1965). 'L'Humide et le sec', *Journal of the Polynesian Society*, vol. 74, no. 3, 329–46.

Barth, F. (1966). *Models of Social Organization*, London: Royal Anthropological Institute, Occasional Paper no. 23.

Bateson, G. (1958). *Naven*, 2nd ed., California: Stanford University Press.

Brookfield, H. C. (1964). 'The Ecology of Highland Settlement', *American Anthropologist* special publication, vol. 66, no. 4, pt. 2, 20–38.

Brookfield, H. C. and Brown, P. (1963). *Struggle for Land*, Oxford, published in association with the Australian National University.

Brown, P. (1961). 'Chimbu Death Payments', *Journal of the Royal Anthropological Institute*, vol. 91, pt. 1, 77–96.

(1964). 'Enemies and Affines', *Ethnology*, vol. 3, 335–56.

(1967). 'The Chimbu Political System', *Anthropological Forum*, vol. 2, no. 1, 36–52.

Bulmer, R. N. H. (1960a). 'Political aspects of the Moka ceremonial exchange system among the Kyaka', *Oceania*, vol. 31, 1–13.

(1960b). *Leadership and Social Structure among the Kyaka*, Ph.D. dissertation, Australian National University.

(1966). Review of Meggitt, *Lineage System of the Mae-Enga*, Man, n.s., vol. 1, 127–9.

Bulmer, R. N. H. and S. (1963). 'Figurines and other Stones of Power among the Kyaka', *Journal of the Polynesian Society*, vol. 71, 192–208.

(1964), 'The Prehistory of the Australian New Guinea Highlands, *American Anthropologist* special publication, vol. 66, no. 4, pt. 2, 39–76.

Chappell, J. M. A. (1966). 'Stone Axe Factories in the Highlands of East New Guinea', *Proceedings of the Prehistoric Society*, vol. 32, no. 5, 96–116.

Chinnery, E. W. P. (1934). 'The Central Ranges of the Mandated Territory of New Guinea', *Geographical Journal*, vol. 84, 388–411.

Commonwealth Scientific and Industrial Research Organization (1958). *Lands of the Goroka – Mt. Hagen area*, Division of Land Research and Regional Survey, Divisional Report no. 58/1, Canberra.

Criper, C. (1968). *The Politics of Exchange*, Ph.D. dissertation, Australian National University.

Dalton, G. (1965). 'Primitive Money', *American Anthropologist*, vol. 67, no. 1, 44–65.

Drucker, P. and Heizer, R. F. (1967). *To Make My Name Good*, Berkeley: University of California Press.

Evans-Pritchard, E. E. (1940). *The Nuer*, Oxford: Clarendon Press.

Bibliography

Finney, B. R. (1969). *New Guinean Entrepreneurs*, New Guinea Research Bulletin no. 27, Australian National University.

Fortes, M. (1945). *The Dynamics of Clanship among the Tallensi*, Oxford: Oxford University Press.

Frazer, J. G. (1922). *The Golden Bough*, Abridged ed., 1 vol., London: Macmillan.

Gitlow, A. L. (1947). *Economics of the Mount Hagen tribes*, Monographs of the American Ethnological Society no. 12, University of Washington Press.

Glasse, R. M. (1959a). 'The Huli Descent System', *Oceania*, vol. 29, 171–84.

(1959b). 'Revenge and Redress among the Huli', *Mankind*, vol. 5, 273–9.

Godelier, M. (1969). 'La "Monnaie de Sel" des Baruya de Nouvelle-Guinée', *L'Homme*, vol. 9, no. 2, 5–37.

Hides, J. G. (1936). *Papuan Wonderland*, Glasgow: Blackie and Son.

Hogbin, H. I. (1958). *Social Change*, London: Watts.

Hughes, I. (n.d.). Some Aspects of Traditional Trade in the New Guinea Central Highlands', unpublished seminar paper, Australian National University.

Kelly, R. C. (1968). 'Demographic Pressure and Descent Group Structure in the New Guinea Highlands', *Oceania*, vol. 39, 36–63.

Kleinig, Revd. I. E. (n.d. – written in 1955). 'Significance of the Tee in the Enga Culture', in a collection of papers published by the Lutheran Mission Press, Wapenamanda, New Guinea.

Langness, L. L. (1964). 'Some Problems in the Conceptualization of Highlands Social Structures', *American Anthropologist* special publication, vol. 66, no. 4, pt. 2, 162–82.

Leahy, M. J. and Crain, M. (1937). *The Land that Time Forgot*, London: Hurst and Blackett.

Lévi-Strauss, C. (1962). *Le Totémisme Aujourd'hui*, Paris: Plon.

Maahs, A. M. (1950). 'Salt-makers of the Wahgi', *Walkabout*, vol. 16, 15–18.

Malinowski, B. C. (1922). *Argonauts of the Western Pacific*, London: Routledge and Kegan Paul.

Marwick, M. G. (1965). *Sorcery in its Social Setting*, Manchester: Manchester University Press.

Mauss, M. (1954). *The Gift*, transl. by I. Cunnison, London: Cohen and West.

Meggitt, M. J. (1956). 'The Valleys of the Upper Wage and Lai Rivers', *Oceania*, vol. 27, 90–135.

(1958). 'The Enga', *Oceania*, vol. 28, 253–330.

(1965). *The Lineage System of the Mae-Enga of New Guinea*, Edinburgh: Oliver and Boyd.

(1967). 'The pattern of leadership among the Mae-Enga of New Guinea', *Anthropological Forum*, vol. 2, no. 1, 20–35.

Meiser, Father L. (1938). 'Beitrag zum Thema: Gerichtswesen bei den Mogä in Neuguinea', *Anthropos*, vol. 33, 663–4.

Oliver, D. L. (1955). *A Solomon Island Society*, Harvard University Press.

Ploeg, A. (1965). *Government in Wanggulam*, Ph.D. dissertation, Australian National University.

Radcliffe-Brown, A. R. (1952). *Structure and Function in Primitive Society*, London: Cohen and West.

Rappaport, R. A. (1967). *Pigs for the Ancestors*, New Haven and London: Yale University Press.

Read, K. E. (1959). 'Leadership and Consensus in a New Guinea Society', *American Anthropologist*, vol. 61, 524–36.

Reay, M. O. (1959). *The Kuma*, Australian National University: Melbourne University Press.

Ross, Father W. (1936). 'Ethnological notes on the Mount Hagen tribes', *Anthropos*, vol. 31, 349–63.

(1969). 'The Catholic Mission in the Western Highlands', in *The History of Melanesia*, 2nd Waigani Seminar, University of Papua and New Guinea, with the Australian National University, Research School of Pacific Studies, 1968, 319–27.

Ryan, D. J. (1961). *Gift Exchange in the Mendi Valley*, Ph.D. dissertation, Sydney University.

Sahlins, M. D. (1963). 'Poor Man, Rich Man, Big Man, Chief', *Comparative Studies in Society and History*, vol. 5, 285–303.

(1965a). 'On the Ideology and Composition of Descent Groups', *Man*, vol. 65, 104–7.

(1965b). 'Exchange Value and the Diplomacy of Primitive Trade', in *Essays in Economic Anthropology*, ed. June Helm, *Proceedings of the 1965 Spring Meeting of the American Ethnological Society*, University of Washington Press, 95–129.

(1965c). 'On the Sociology of Primitive Exchange', in *The Relevance of Models for Social Anthropology*, A.S.A. Monographs 1, London: Tavistock Publications; New York: Frederick A. Praeger, Publishers, 139–236.

Salisbury, R. F. (1956). 'Unilineal Descent Groups in the New Guinea Highlands', *Man*, vol. 56, 2–7.

(1962). *From Stone to Steel*, Melbourne: Cambridge University Press.

(1964). 'Despotism and Australian Administration in the New Guinea Highlands', *American Anthropologist* special publication, vol. 66, no. 4, pt. 2, 225–39.

(1968). 'Anthropology and Economics', in *Anthropology and the Neighbouring Disciplines*, ed. O. van Mering and L. Kasdan.

Scheffler, H. W. (1965). *Choiseul Island Social Structure*, Berkeley and Los Angeles: University of California Press.

Spinks, K. L. (1934). 'Mapping the Purari Plateau, New Guinea', *Geographical Journal*, vol. 84, 412–16.

(1936). 'The Wahgi River Valley of Central New Guinea', *Geographical Journal*, vol. 87, 222–5.

Steadman, L. B. (n.d.). Unpublished seminar paper on the Hewa, Australian National University.

Stopp, K. (1963). 'Medicinal Plants of the Mt. Hagen People', *Economic Botany*, vol. 17, 16–22.

Bibliography

Strathern, A. J. (1965). *Descent and Group Structure among the Mbowamb*, Fellowship dissertation, Trinity College, Cambridge.

(1966). 'Despots and Directors in the New Guinea Highlands', *Man*, n.s., vol. 1 no. 3, 356–67.

(1968). 'Sickness and Frustration', *Mankind*, vol. 6, no. 11, 545–51.

(1969a). 'Descent and Alliance in the New Guinea Highlands: Some Problems of Comparison', *Proceedings of the Royal Anthropological Institute for 1968*, 37–52.

(1969b). 'Finance and Production: Two Strategies in New Guinea Highlands Exchange Systems', *Oceania*, vol. 40, no. 1, 42–67.

(1969c). 'Kor-nga Poklambo or Ui Mbo?', *Archaeology and Physical Anthropology in Oceania*, vol. 4, no. 2, 91–6.

Strathern, A. J. and A. M. (1971). *Self-Decoration in Mount Hagen*, London: Gerald Duckworth.

(in press). 'Melpa Marriage', in *Pigs, Pearl Shells and Women*, ed. M. J. Meggitt and R. M. Glasse, Chicago: Prentice-Hall.

Strathern, A. M. (1965). 'Axe Types and Quarries', *Journal of the Polynesian Society*, vol. 74, no. 2, 182–91.

(1966). 'A note on Linguistic Boundaries and the Axe Quarries', *Proceedings of the Prehistoric Society*, vol. 32, no. 5, 117–21.

(1968a). *Women's Status in the Mount Hagen area*, Ph.D. dissertation, Cambridge University.

(1968b). 'Popokl: the Question of Morality, *Mankind*, vol. 6, no. 11, 553–61.

(in press). 'Stone Axes and Flake Tools: Evaluations from Two New Guinea Highlands Societies', Forthcoming in *Proceedings of the Prehistoric Society*.

Strauss, H. and Tischner, H. (1962). *Die Mi-Kultur der Hagenberg Stämme*, Hamburg.

Vayda, A. P. and Cook, E. A. (1964). 'Structural variability in the Bismarck Mountain Cultures of New Guinea', *Transactions of the New York Academy of Sciences*, series 2, vol. 26, no. 7, 798–803.

Vial, L. G. (1940). 'Stone Axes of Mount Hagen, New Guinea', *Oceania*, vol. 11, 158–63.

Vicedom, G. F. and Tischner, H. (1943–8). *Die Mbowamb*, Hamburg, 3 vols.

Waddell, E. W. (1968). *The Dynamics of a New Guinea Highlands Agricultural System*, Ph.D. dissertation, Australian National University.

Wagner, R. (1967). *The Curse of Souw*, Chicago University Press.

Watson, J. B. (1967). 'Tairora: the Politics of Despotism in a Small Society', *Anthropological Forum*, vol. 2, no. 1, 53–104.

Westermann, T. (1968). *The Mountain People. Social Institutions of the Laiapu Enga*, Lutheran Mission Press, Wapenamanda, New Guinea.

Williams, F. E. (1940–1). *Natives of Lake Kutubu, Papua*, Oceania Monographs, no. 6, Australian National Research Council.

Wurm, S. A. (1964). 'Australian New Guinea Highlands Languages and the Distribution of their Typological Features', *American Anthropologist* special publication, vol. 66, no. 4, pt. 2, 77–97.

INDEX

Abortion 117
Adultery 86
Affiliation processes (non-agnates) 35–6, 86, 154, 165, 173, 199, 200–1, 202, 204
African societies, contrasts and comparisons with New Guinea 27, 53, 86
Aggressiveness 53–4, 65, 75, 215, 225, 235; licensed aggression (*el kaep*) 90
Agriculture 9–10
Ai, K. Kund. 197–9
Alliance 19, 31, 54, 66, 68, 199–200, 222–3; and rivalry 128–9, 175; as defined by Radcliffe-Brown 130; by pairing 19–28, 31, 32, 56 ff.; sanctions between allies 90–1; strength of 56 ff., 145–6
Ambra, Ulka 233–4, 238
Andakapkae tribe 70, 71, 193–4
Ant, T. Kendike 141, 148, 152, 242–3
Araceae 233
Araucaria cunninghamii 29
Aua language 4, 189, 190, 235
Australian Administration xii, 7, 10, 76–7, 101, 107, 110, 172, 180, 185–6, 225, 227–9; appointments of luluai and tultul 108
Autopsies 83

Bachelors 201, 202, 203, 204
Baiyer Valley 70, 74, 193
Banz 236
Barnes J. 36, 53
Barrau J. 37
Barth F. 216
Bateson G. 222–3
Bena Bena 53, 236
Berndt R. 53
Bidder A. 102
Big-men, and networks of exchange partnerships 2–3, 13, 92, 132, 164, 166, 172–5, 193–5, 220–2; and supporters 35, 202, 206, 208, 224, 227; and use of violence 53, 206, 225; as 'despots' 53, 206, 224–6; as directors and negotiators of exchanges 98, 116, 119, 122, 131–2, 167; as leaders in warfare 71, 75–6, 225; as monopolisers of shell valuables in past 108, 133; associated with ceremonial grounds 8, 40 ff.; clustering of in lineages 210–13; competition between 3, 12, 25, 40, 48–9, 176–83, 214, 218 ff., 221–2; contrasted with rubbish-men 187;

co-operation between 48, 199; death of 25, 45, 51, 73, 75, 77, 83, 85, 86, 87, 191–5, 211; distinction between major and minor 44, 138, 140, 148, 152, 167, 200, 202, 210; extent of power 2, 3, ch. 10 *passim*; general importance in New Guinea Highlands 1; high bride-wealth paid by 109; in creating segments 28, 50, 178, 211; in peace-making and dispute-settlement 26, 53, 54, 76 ff.; in the Enga *tee* 114; maintain activities and strength of groups 46, 47, 50, 178, 185; obtain wives for sons 195; polygyny of 77, 78, 196, 202–4, 206; status-markers of 103, 189–90; status-ranking in a number of clans 200–4; succession to position of 210; terms for 187–8; widen scope of exchanges 91 ff., 93, 134, 164, 199–200, 218
Birds, mentioned in spells 233–4
Bowers N. 189
Bridewealth 93, 195, 202, 226, 237; inflation of 109–10; limits placed on by Dei Council 110; use of wealth objects in 105, 107, 109–10, 112
Brookfield H. 9, 20, 105, 236
Brown P. 20, 34, 54, 105, 234, 236
Buk (Mbukl) xii, 23, 45, 46, 47–8, 62, 76, 88, 90, 92, 111, 121, 135, 163, 164, 183, 185, 212, 236
Bulmer R. and S. 27, 35, 54, 81, 95, 105, 111, 112, 137, 140, 146, 187
Bus G. 118

Cannibalism 108, 235
Card-games 1, 180, 240
Cash, introduction of into exchanges 104–5, 107, 110–11, 180, 191, 227–9, 238, 241
Cassowaries 94, 101–5, 107, 108, 111, 135, 189
Castanopsis acuminatissima 29
Cattle, used in moka 101, 135, 171, 184, 241
Celastraceae *Elaeodendron* sp. 120
Cemeteries 8, 39, 192, 233; as mustering places in war 73, 74, 76
Ceremonial grounds 8, 22, ch. 3 *passim*, 117 ff.; as focus for groups 46; as venues for disputes 168, 175, 226; created and used by big-men 42, 51, 190

Index

Change, in decoration of shells 238; in rates of exchange and use of valuables 104, 106 ff., 109, 170; in the moka 121, 227; Vicedom's account of social change 207
Chappell J. 105
Chimbu 20, 34, 54, 224, 234, 236, 238
Chinnery E. 37
Cinnamon 39, 81
Cook E. 18
Cordylines 37, 39, 40, 87, 95, 119, 227, 240
Counting, methods of 116, 120
Courting parties 81, 84, 195
Crops 9
Cult-places 8, 30, 39
Cyatheaceae (*see also* Ferns) 118, 192

Dalton G. 237
Dances 97, 119
Daribi 234
Death (*see also* Big-men), causes recognised 80; in warfare 25, 67, 72, 73; mourning 90–1, 95, 103, 234; of big-men 191–5, 211–12
Death-compensation, alternative to revenge 77; for poisoning 84, 87–8; to maternal kin 90, 192, 193, 234–5; war-payments 47, 55–6, 58, 72, 73, 74, compensation (*wuə peng*) 90, 91, 94–6, 115, 219, reparation (*kui wuə*) 90–1, 94 ff., 135, 219, *wuə ombil* 94, 115, 132, 138
Decorating oil 101–5, 107, 111, 112, 118, 134
Dei Council 231–2
Descent 19–28, 31 ff., 233
Disputes 39, 48–9, 50, 59, 65, 86–7, ch. 8 *passim* (over timing of moka), 225
Divination 30, 83, 87
Divination-stuff (*mi*) 19, 37, 39, 87, 194, 226, 227
Division of labour 8–10, 37, 202
Divorce 200, 201, 202
Drucker P. and Heizer R. 13, 98

Ecology 17; and trade 111
Ekit, M. Yel. 178, 182
El, M. Yel. 178
El-ık 120, 182
El kaep 25, 90
El kləngi 85
El puklwuə–kui wuə relationship (*see also* Warfare) 25
Ellis T. 77
Elti tribe 20, 66–7

Enga area (*see also* Mae–Enga, *Tee*, Raiapu Enga) 73, 105, 112, 118, 137, 165, 236
Engk, T. Kit. 47, 154, 243
Epilkae tribe 70, 71
Erave 236
Evans-Pritchard E. 53, 54, 64, 72
Exchange (*see also* Big-men, Moka), as vehicles for competition 1; bargaining in 217; functions of the gift 10, 214 ff.; in myth 30; made by children 195
Exchange systems (*see also* Moka, *Tee*), as alternatives to warfare 54, 76, 95, 129–30, 227; scope of widened by big-men 91; the *tee* 54, 114
Exogamy, as a political matter 22, 232
Əndipi, K. Membo 154, 155, 163, 212, 241–2

Feathers 97, 102, 107, 111, 120
Ferns (*see also* Cyatheaceae) 119, 192, 238; significance of 118
Finney B. 1
Fortes M. 31
Frazer J. 37

Gahuku-Gama 77
Gawigl language and area 4, 189
Genealogies 23, 32–4, 200, 210
Ghosts (including ancestors) 25, 37, 39, 67, 80, 83, 164, 181, 190, 191, 192–3, 194, 228, 233, 234, 235, 238
Ginger 81, 82
Gitlow A. 7
Glasse R. 36
Godelier M. 105
Groups (*see also* Refugees), idioms of description 32, 34, 232–3; incorporation of immigrants 20; levels defined: great-tribe 19, 31–2; tribe-pair 19–20, 32, 55, 64; tribe 16–7, 20, 22, 55; major section 20–2, 32; clan-pair 22–3, 47, 56 ff., 64, 87; clan 23, 33, 44, 86; clan-section 25, 33, 47; sub-clan 26, 33, 48, 50; sub-sub-clan 26, 33–4, 48; lineage 27, 34, 210–11; pairing of groups 19–28; terminology for 17 ff.; variations in size of 15, 16, 44, 230–2
Gumant River settlement 45, 108, 155, 163, 236, 238

Hagen Sub-District, cultural similarities within 6–7
Hagen, Bernhard 4
Hagen, Kurt von 4
Harding T. 122
Head, symbolism of 190 ff.

Index

Index

Mauss M. 10, 214–16

Meggitt M. 2, 3, 27, 28, 35, 36, 105, 211, 234, 236

Meiser, Fr. L. 83

Mel, K. Kur. 48, 225–6

Melastomataceae *Astronia* sp. 234

Mele, Kendipi 71–2

Melpa areas, Central-Northern differences 41, 96, 107, 118, 134, 189, 190; distinguished 6

Melpa language xii–xiii, 4

Mendi 103, 105, 107, 111, 112, 114, 236

Men's house group, as term for sub-clan 33

Menstruation, beliefs concerning 8, 82

Meritocracy 213

Məra, K. Kur. 154, 155, 161, 163

Minembi tribe 32, 42, 56, 57–9, 62 ff., 68–70, 73, 87, 110; Engambo clan 58, 65, 72, 123, 132, 135, 138, 139, 178, 180, 193, 199, 240–1; Kimbo clan 58, 59, 64–5, 70, 91, 134, 136, 178, 180, 199; Komonkae-Ruprupkae pair 59, 62, 64–5, 91, 122, 133; Mimke-Napakae pair 58, 62, 65, 70, 177, 179, 194; Nambakae clan 58, 62, 70; Papeke clan 57–8, 65, 87, 127, 135, 180, 181, 185, 199, 235; Yelipi clan 48, 57–8, 59, 60, 65, 87, 123, 127, 175–83, 199, 201, 235

Missions 38, 40, 165, 192, 193, 194, 200, 228, 243

Mɪt, T. Kit. 241

Moka, and alliance 130; and equilibrium 219, 222–3; and investment 214, 219, 221; and schismogenesis 222–3; as test for big-men 130–1; as zero-sum game 11, 123, 217; classification of 123, 137; climactic occasions 119–21; decision-making in 182–6; defaulting in 168–9, 169 ff.; definitions of 10, 93, 216; effect of social change on 227–9; entering the system 195–7; extent of participation in ch. 7 *passim*; 'extra gifts' 99, 101, 120, 129, 147, 155, 183, 184, 241; failure of 175–83; individual partnerships in 115, 158–66, 197–9; initiatory gifts 97, 115, 122, 135, 154, 216; moka chains 47, 60, 115, 121–34, 176, 179, 181, 219–20; money moka 180; pig-moka, categories in 97, 98, 99, 115, 116, 120, 133, 240–1; regional integration in 122 ff., 131, 220; *rok-moka* 195; shell-moka 97, 98, 118, 179; showing of gifts 117–18, 172; speech-making in 116, 118, 120, 240–2

Mokei tribe 7, 17, 29–30, 66–7, 77, 236

Mt Giluwe 236

Mount Hagen, derivation of name 4

Mount Hagen township xii, 7, 110

Mør, K. Kund. 199

Mul Council 232

Mul-Dei constituency 184

Mundika tribe 77, 96, 232

Murli, K. Membo 163

Names, of groups 31

Ndamba, K. Kund. 134, 194, 199, 208

Ndani 53

Ndika tribe 7, 17, 20, 21, 41, 66, 77, 96, 163, 206, 232, 236

Ndip, K. Membo 154, 155, 158, 161

Nditing, T. Kit. 47, 89, 138, 148, 152, 160, 173, 212, 243

Nebilyer Valley 4, 6, 15, 20, 38, 39, 66, 81, 97, 105, 107, 111, 120, 134, 192, 210, 230, 233–4, 235

Nengka tribe 17, 21, 77, 232

Neu Guinea Kompagnie 4

Nɪmb, Ndika, compared to Tom Ellis 77

Nggoimba, K. Membo 155

Noman 77

Nore, T. Kengeke 141

Nothofagus 29

'Nouveaux riches' 207

Nøring, M. Engambo 193

Nuer 53, 54, 64, 72

Nukint, T. Kit. 139, 243

Nunga ceremonial ground 47

Nykint, K. Kur. 48, 154, 158, 161, 163

Ogelbeng 6, 7, 55, 70

Okopuka tribe 20

Oliver D. 2, 224

Omak tally 6, 189, 192, 238, 239

Omens 234

Ongka, K. Nggl. 47–8, 49, 53, 73, 78, 79, 86, 91, 106, 134, 136, 141, 154, 155, 160, 163, 172, 173–5, 177, 181, 182, 183, 201, 226–7, 243

Origin myths 19, 28 ff., 32, 58

Pakl, M. Ruprupkae 91

Palke tribe 71, 123

Pana, K. Membo 155, 158

Pangia 189

Pandanus 94, 101, 238

Parka, T. Elt. 173–5

Peace-making 55, 76 ff., 83, 92

Pena, K. Nggl. 226

Penambe tribe 22, 66, 85

Pengk, K. Membo 240

Peng mumuk 190

Phallic symbolism 190

Index

Pigs (*see also* Death-compensation, Moka, Sacrifice), agistment of 66; behaviour of at moka 48, 118, 119, 120; breeding sows 196; care of 8, 202, 205; cooking of 38, 39, 118, 135, 191–2; destruction in warfare 67; use of as exchange media 102 ff., wild 101

Ploeg A. 53

Poisoning 57 ff., 74, 75, 76, 81, 82, 84–5, 193–5, 207

Pokla mak 40

Poklambo 38–9, 48, 118, 226, 234, 241

Pokløndi ceremonial ground 48

Popokl 77, 79, 80, 83, 226

Population density 17, 27, 53, 231–2

Potlatch 13

Powell J. 29

Pørwa, T. Kit. 139, 141, 163, 164, 184–6, 212, 222

Radcliffe-Brown A. 130

Raiapu Enga 27

Rain, as sign of ancestral displeasure 181, 242

Rangk, M. Yel. 178–83, 235

Rappaport R. 18, 25, 37, 50, 64, 67, 105, 112

Read K. 77, 224, 225

Reay M. 18, 33, 67, 105, 192, 211, 234

Red ochre 101–2, 118, 192, 236, 238

Refugees 56, 58, 59, 62, 66, 67, 69, 72, 78, 154, 178, 189, 194, 206, 232

Revenge 23, 67, 72–3, 77, 79–80, 80 ff., 95, 191, 192, 193

Rituals (*see also* Ghosts, Sacrifice, Spells, Spirit-cults) 38, 82, 190, 233–4

Rokla, T. Okl. 108

Roklaka tribe 72, 107–8, 123, 136

Roklpa, K. Nggl. 49

Rokopa, M. Engambo 194

Roltinga, K. Kund. 35, 79, 197–9, 204, 208

Rop, K. Membo 163

Rope of moka (*moka ka:n*) xvi, 115, 121, 123, 131–2, 133, 135, 136, 229

Ross, Fr. W. 6–7, 104, 109

Rowe W. 1

Røi, M. Yel. 178, 181, 182

Ru, K. Kur. 115, 117

Rubbish-men (*see under* 'Little men')

Ruin, M. Yel. 178

Ruk, T. Elt. 46, 173, 183, 222

Rumba, K. Kur. 225

Rumba, K. Nggl. 158

Rumba, T. Kit. 158

Ruri, M. Yel. 180

Rutaceae *Evodiella* sp. 234

Rying, M. Engambo 193–4

Ryan D. 35

Sacrifice 25, 37, 38, 39, 73, 80, 191, 192, 238

Sahlins M. 2, 4, 36, 214, 216, 223

Salisbury R. 1, 3, 4, 23, 28, 53, 54, 105, 109, 112, 223, 224, 227

Salt 73, 96, 101, 105–6, 112–14, 133

Schäfer, Fr. A. 224

Scheffler H. 36

Schismogenesis 222–3

Self-decoration 119, 240; summary of use of shells in 103

Settlement pattern 8

Shame 168, 172, 175

Shell valuables xii, 94, 107–8; broken over body of dead man 191–2; judgements of quality 237; mounted on boards 234, 238–9; preparation of 237–8; replacement by money 110, 170; scarcity of in past 108, 196, 236; trade routes for 235–6; types of and rates of exchange: bailer 102 ff., 236, 239, conus 102 ff., 108, 111, 112, 239, cowrie 96, 102 ff., 107, 239, green-snail 102 ff., 111, 119, 236, 239–40, nassa 102 ff., 111, 239, pearl 96, 102 ff., 108, 112, 119, 236–9

Siane 23, 28, 53, 54, 113, 236

Sickness (*see also* Maternal kin), resulting from *popokl* (*q.v.*); sent by maternal kin 140, 164

Sinha D. 1

Siuai people 2, 224

'Slaves' 205–8

Snakes 101

Sorcery 80–1

Speech-making, at moka 116, 118, 120, 169, 182, 240–2

Spells 38, 40, 82, 233–4

Spinks, K. 4

Spirit-cults 39, 80, 103, 135, 190

Steadman L. 53

Stick-fighting 25, 87, 91, 168, 171, 173

Stone axes 96, 101–5, 106, 107, 111, 112–14, 133

Stones flint tools 239; magical 38, 81; spirit-cult 39

Stopp K. 105

Stratification, social (*see also* Big-men) 200–13

Straatmans W. 1

Strathern A. J. 9, 25, 27, 36, 80, 93, 97, 114, 119, 131, 134, 137, 211, 225, 226, 233, 234

Strathern A. M. 9, 77, 80, 93, 97, 104, 105, 119, 157, 206

Index

Strauss H. 19, 28, 32, 34, 87, 96, 118, 187, 190, 232–3
Succession 210–12
Suicide 39

Taboos, on women entering cemeteries 73; taboo-sign on path 79
Tairora 53, 224
Tambul 4, 6, 103, 105, 111, 133, 134, 236, 238
Taylor J. xii, 7, 48, 107–8, 235
Tee 54, 114, 121, 131, 133, 134
Temboka (*see also* Nebilyer Valley) 6, 189, 190
Tipuka tribe 42, 56, 57, 60–2, 64–6, 68, 71–2, 87–8, 240; internal moka 138–40, 142, 143, 145, 149, 171–2, 173, 184–5; particular clans (*see also* foregoing sub-entry 'internal moka'): Eltimbo 45–7, 173; Kelmbo 71; Kendike 60, 62, 72, 127, 133, 145, 242–3; Kengeke 46, 60, 65, 72–3, 122, 127, 133, 134, 136, 178, 180; Kitepi 45, 47, 50, 60, 62, 65, 72, 87–8, 123, 127, 132–3, 135, 136, 138, 180, 199, 222, 241, 242, 243; Ndikmbo–Wanyembo pair 60, 62, 142, 145; Oklembo 45, 46, 48, 60, 71, 73–4, 123, 127, 135, 136, 142, 176, 179, 241
Tipuka–Kawelka relations, close alliance 87, 163, 240; in moka-chain 121 ff.; Kitepi and Oklembo to K. Membo and Mandembo 142, 150 ff., 169, 171, 183; marriages between 156; relations [1965–9] 134 ff., 136, chs. 7 and 8 *passim*
Tomba 133
Trade 101–2, 104–6, 106 ff., 111–14, 216–17, 225, 235
Treachery 72, 83
Trees, named in spells 233–4; planted at ceremonial grounds 38–9
Trobriands 115

Ui, T. Okl. 241–2
Ui-mel 91
Ukl, Ulka 39, 40
Ulka tribe 20

Vayda A. 18
Vehicles, purchased by groups 110, 228
Vial L. 105

Vicedom G. 4, 23, 34, 37, 39, 40, 55, 67, 75, 76, 96, 101, 103, 105, 108, 189, 200–8, 232–3, 237, 238, 239

Wabag 114, 132
Waddell E. 27
Waema, K. Membo 155, 161, 163
Wage-labour 196, 204, 208, 228
Wagner R. 234
Wahgi area (*see also* Kuma) 105, 107, 111, 236, 238
Wai, T. Kit. 185, 212
Waimorong ceremonial ground 46
Wakl te kng 93
Walya 133, 236
Wapenamanda 133
Warfare (*see also* Death-compensation, Peace-making, Refugees) 15, 17, 20, 21, 47; and territory 50, 56, 65, 67, 72; *el pukl wuə–kui wuə* relationship 55, 87, 88; escalation of 56, 61–2, 64, 65; fields of 56 ff., 67–71; leadership in 72 ff.; major and minor enemies 55, 59 ff., 67, 72, 85, 87–8, 90–2, 130; poisoning in 87–8; power imbalances in 59, 65, 66; results of ending 51, 54, 121, 207, 224; stress on 53, 54; weapons used in 75
Watson J. 53, 224
West Irian 53
Westermann E. 225
Wəlyi tribe 60, 69–70, 71–2, 122
Widows 25, 84, 191, 194, 196, 202, 206
Williams F. 37, 105, 111, 237
Wiru speakers 189, 234
Witchcraft 192
Women (*see also* Marriage patterns, Widows), as intermediaries 157, 165, 195; care for pigs 202; dance *werl* 119; death-payments for 235; in dispute with husbands 172; jealousy of co-wives 172; position of in warfare 67; suspected of poisoning 74, 82, 86; taboo on entering cemetery 73
Wøya, M. Yel. 178, 181
Wurm S. 4

Yamka tribe 77, 236
Yei, M. Yel. 150, 182